BUILDING PORTSMOUTH

The Neighborhoods & Architecture of New Hampshire's Oldest City

Richard M. Candee

& ....

Contributors	Shantia Anderheggen	SA	Elizabeth Hostutler	EH
	Richard M. Candee	RMC	Anne Masury	AM
	Martha Fuller Clark	MFC	Nancy Muller	NM
	Claire W. Dempsey	CWD	Woodard Openo	WO
	Thomas Denenberg	TD	Jane Porter	JP
	Erica Dodge	ED	Martha Pinello	MEP
	Ellen Fineberg	EF	Diane Rodolitz	DR
	James L. Garvin	JLG	Mark J. Sammons	MS
	Sarah Giffen	SG	Barbara Ward	BW
	Bernard L. Herman	BLH		

Illustrations	Aldrich Associates	Elizabeth Hostutler
	Amy Amidon	Philip Kendrick
	Aring-Schroeder Architects	Gabrielle Lanier
	Richard Candee	Steven McHenry
	Erica Dodge	William Paarlberg
	Dean Doerrfeld	Judy Quinn
	James Garvin	Philip Tambling
	David Hart	Nancy Van Dolsen
	Allen Charles Hill	

| *Cartography* | Robert J. Kozman | William Paarlberg |
| | Eliza McClennen | Barbara Schmidt |

Portsmouth Advocates is a non-profit organization established in 1980 to promote preservation of the unique historic and architectural character of the city of Portsmouth. Our members are all volunteers — citizens dedicated to the preservation of Portsmouth's distinctive heritage.

Portsmouth Advocates provides area residents with a collective voice and a means to influence changes that affect the visual character of our city. Preservation for its own sake is not our goal. We believe that the demolition of older, viable buildings and neighborhoods diminishes and threatens Portmouth's historic assets. The thoughtful re-use and rehabilitation of existing buildings represents conservation at its best, making sense in both economic and cultural terms.

To receive more information on our educational and advocacy programs or to order *Building Portsmouth* please write to:

Portsmouth Advocates, Inc.
P.O. Box 4066
Portsmouth, NH 03802-4066

International Standard Book Number (ISBN):
0-96-34539-0-4

Contents

··

This book is dedicated to Arthur Gerrier,
a colleague and friend, whose love and understanding
of old buildings would have enlightened us all.

PREFACE

The 1992 Vernacular Architecture Forum conference was the catalyst for this guide to the architecture of Portsmouth's neighborhoods. Tours organized by Portsmouth Advocates and Strawbery Banke Museum for that international group of scholars consolidated twenty years of architectural surveys and newly uncovered historical data with the insights of others who have looked closely at Portsmouth's architecture. *Building Portsmouth* attempts to define physical changes to the city over three centuries by looking at how land development shapes the urban landscape and by examining buildings that form neighborhoods. Not only mansions of the rich, but everyday homes, stores, churches, warehouses and factories are part of this rich cultural landscape.

Like many long-settled places, a number of myths have grown up about the nature of this city as historic artifact. Its main claim to fame, according to earlier historians, was as the colonial capital of the New Hampshire. A handful of large elaborate colonial homes, built for members of an economic and political oligarchy, (now preserved as museums) continues to reinforce this view. Architectural historians since John Mead Howells have also noted the fine buildings and streetscapes from the federal period as the apogee of local wealth and building. It is this Portsmouth that is protected by the local historic district. Other historians have pointed to the local brewer, politician, and railroad magnate, Frank Jones, as the city's most important rebuilder during the late 19th century, while maritime historians note the continuing impact of ship building and waterborn trade. Internationalists find significance in the city's momentary reflected glory during the negotiations ending the Russo-Japanese War and the signing of Treaty of Portsmouth in 1905. Each era produced buildings of architectural interest and many are included here.

The text is structured like a catalog with information on the development of many neighborhoods and short entries on individual buildings or special topics. It explores Portsmouth's development in a roughly chronological sequence in three nearly concentric semi-circles. The oldest buildings are found in the compact part of wooden city built along the river during the colonial and federal eras. The next band of growth reflects the expansion and restructuring of Portsmouth during the 19th century: its brick commercial core, the impact of a new industrial economy on the city's western periphery, and the development of new residential streetscapes. An outer ring contains the architecture of late 19th and early 20th century summer people, remnants of the brewing industry and shipbuilding, and housing built for workers. Later suburban development contains such modern building changes as the development of the factory-built home.

The emphasis on the sequence of neighborhood development unfortunately ignores many newer buildings that have been added to the South End and the commercial core as fires, decay, and purposeful demolition provided opportunities for replacement. It also slights the older agricultural community along South Street and at the Portsmouth Plains; the well-documented buildings of one of the city's major employers, the Portsmouth Naval Ship Yard; and early twentieth century homes inserted into the Victorian district. Nor does this book attempt to explore later parts of Portsmouth such as the much-altered housing at Mariner's Village, the post-World War II development of Pease Air Force Base, Elwyn Park or the commercial development along Route 1. These, too, deserve further study. I hope, however, that the neighborhoods and buildings described here spur others to look at the many places not yet been fully documented.

In this study individual buildings are usually named after their first or longest permanent owners. If others made significant changes to the structure, hyphenated last names are used. This occasionally results in building names that differ from those used by earlier writers. I have also used old photographs whenever possible, rather than simply illustrate current appearances. If *Building Portsmouth* is used as a guidebook to explore the city, these images will help the reader understand many later architectural changes.

RMC

ACKNOWLEDGMENTS

The research for *Building Portsmouth* was greatly assisted by volunteers and survey historians from Portsmouth Advocates and by staff members of Strawbery Banke Museum, the Portsmouth Athenaeum, the Society for the Preservation of New England Antiquities, the Portsmouth Naval Shipyard Museum, the Old York Historical Society, the New Hampshire Division of Historical Resources and representatives of many historic house museums. I thank the Trustees of Boston University for a sabbatical, the Boston Foundation for financial support, and the Greater Portsmouth Community Foundation for a grant to Portsmouth Advocates for its West End architectural survey. Carolyn Eastman, Kevin Shupe, and Jane Porter of the Portsmouth Athenaeum staff helped find historic photographs and new original sources. The staff at Strawbery Banke Museum also assisted in this effort: Mark Sammons, Gerald and Barbara Ward, Martha Pinello, Anne Masury, and Greg Colati were important contributors.

Among the many individual contributors, I owe special thanks to Martha Fuller Clark who took time from her busy legislative schedule to promote the architectural survey and add her own research to mine. My Boston University colleague, Claire Dempsey, made invaluable contributions by helping to define the domestic building types of 19th century Portsmouth, rethink the 18th century evidence, and articulate the town's religious diversity. Ellen Fineberg summarized the building history of the downtown churches, shared her own research on the many changes to Temple Israel, and analyzed the work of local architect William Ashe.

James L. Garvin, architectural historian of the New Hampshire Division of Historic Resources, graciously allowed me to paraphrase large chunks of his doctoral dissertation and provided several original measured drawings for the guidebook. Professor Bernard L. Herman of the University of Delaware, with the help of several students, provided many new floor plans of houses recorded for a future book on American cities in the late 18th and early 19th century. Elizabeth Hostutler not only assisted Portsmouth Advocates with the West End survey but helped to proofread my text.

Sarah Giffen and Kevin Murphy kindly allowed me to recycle certain portions of my own and other contributions to their new book, *"A Noble and Dignified Stream" The Piscataqua Region in the*

Colonial Revival, 1860–1930. Woodard Openo took time from his study of Portsmouth tug boats and clubs to revisit the colonial revival homes of summer visitors in Little Harbor and New Castle, the subject of his recent doctoral dissertation.

Steven McHenry of Interface Architects took an early interest, especially in the recording of certain key buildings. Many other architects also donated their work. Philip Kendrick generously shared his personal recording effort and other drawings for this project, while Roomet Aring provided plans of the Wentworth Home and Philip Tambling and Donna Lee Woods made available plans of the Bodge-Chase house. In addition, Judith Quinn of the National Park Service in Boston and Amy Amidon of the Boston University Preservation Studies Program provided many new drawings of historic structures from the measurements of others.

I am especially indebted to the highly skilled architectural renderer William Paarlberg of Kittery for drawing Market Square as it was in 1812, also used as a poster for the Vernacular Architecture Forum's conference, and to Robert Kozman for the graphic design of this entire volume.

Richard M. Candee
July 1992

INTRODUCTION

PORTSMOUTH'S HISTORICAL DEVELOPMENT

The Piscataqua River is a very deep, swift tidal thoroughfare that enabled Portsmouth to develop as a center of colonial and early 19th-century mercantile activity. The river divided the 17th century patents for New Hampshire from those to Maine, just as it separates the two states today. The mouth of the Piscataqua opens between Great Island (later New Castle) on the southwest and a group of ledges and islets extending off Gerrish Island (Kittery, Maine) on the northeast. The state boundary line extends through a treeless archipelago known as the Isle of Shoals 9 miles out, the center of European and later colonial fishing fleets during the early colonial period. Little Harbor, a small shallow bay on the south side of New Castle that is fed by Sagamore Creek, acts as a secondary mouth of the Piscataqua River. A half-mile wide crook in the elbow of the river forms Portsmouth Harbor, the major ice-free, deep-water anchorage between Boston and Portland, Maine. This made Portsmouth colonial New Hampshire's main center of settlement, trade and government.

The landmass of Portsmouth today encompasses 15.2 square miles or 9728 acres, slightly smaller than its colonial boundaries, which included all or part of several neighboring towns. The greater part has always been a rural hinterland, inland and saltwater farms that provided produce and rental income or an outlying estate. The early 17th-century maritime center was on Great Island, until the riverfront mainland known as "Strawberry Banke" was developed after the 1680s. Here the riverfront is penetrated by several tidal ponds and coves separated by three granite knolls: Meeting House Hill in the midst of the South End, Church Hill where an Anglican Church was built in 1732, and another rise largely lost to the building of the Sheraton Portsmouth Hotel but early used for windmills. The South Mill Pond was exploited as a tidal grist mill by the Pickering family from the mid-17th century and its waters once overflowed into the cove that formed Puddle Dock, an early quay and commercial center. The North Mill Pond's fresh water creek was used for water-powered saw milling from the 1660s; its mouth was dammed in 1764 for use as another tidal grist mill.

Seventeenth-century maritime settlement on Great Island and two agricultural clusters on the mainland, at Strawbery Banke (where a small Anglican chapel is thought to have existed by the 1640s) and Sagamore Creek, demanded a central location for a public meeting house once the nascent colony fell under the domination of Puritan Massachusetts in the 1650s. In 1659 this was placed immediately south of the Pickering mill, below the South Mill Pond. It was not until the four major landholders to the north began to subdivide their agricultural lands about 1690 that the riverfront began to take on a the character of a provincial urban

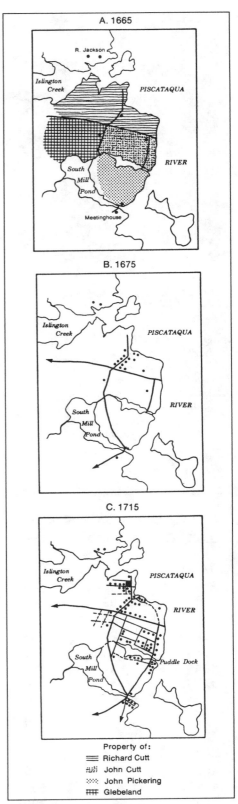

Clark University, for Richard Candee
Portsmouth Development 1665-1715.

town. This created the basic 18th-century urban plan, a linear development along the river extending a few blocks inland intersecting with the leg of a T where in 1705 the town laid out a grid of streets west of present-day Pleasant Street to lease as houselots for ministerial support. Here certain lots were reserved for civic functions, a new north meeting house (still the site of North Church), a prison, almshouse, and a burial ground eventually used for slaves and free blacks.

This maritime port quickly became the center of Royal government under an oligarchy of merchant families clustered around the political dynasty of the Wentworths and the establishment of a Church of England chapel that helped separate the Anglican elite from the Puritan heritage of the north and south congregations. A state house for the colonial legislature was erected in the 1750s opposite the North Meeting House, facing the Parade or public training ground. The governmental structure was later described as "a large building, unornamented, and not in the most frequented part of the Town," testimony to the greater importance given to commercial activity along the wharves that projected into the river. Yet by the Revolution the original land divisions that created the urban core of the town had hardly been expanded. Historically, the colonial population is thought to have been near 5000. After the Revolution the city experienced two peaks of 19th century population increase that greatly affected its form and architectural development. The earliest of these occurred between 1790 and 1810 as the city gained nearly 2500 new residents; the second came during the 1840s when new immigrants and others added more than 1800 to the population in that decade.

The city grew as trade with Europe and the West Indies revived after 1790 and New Hampshire's exports through the Port of Portsmouth quadrupled to $555,055 annually over the decade. Land on the western edges of the colonial core, farms owned by leading pre-Revolutionary families, was sold and subdivided — often by absentee heirs — into new streets and houselots. Besides a number of good local surveyors, Portsmouth also attracted a trained English cartographer who produced in 1812 the first map of the city replete with building footprints differentiated domestic, public and utilitarian uses. Published in a larger format, John G. Hales's 1813 map of the urban core also documents the restructuring of the city plan by two major fires in 1802, 1806, and was reissued to show the area burned by another fire in December 1813. To help prevent future conflagrations, burned-out streets were widened and new buildings were built of brick. In 1814 the town requested that the state mandate all future construction over 12 feet high to be of masonry. Combined with economic impacts of the Embargo and the War of 1812, this slowed the rebuilding and even stopped building beyond the brick zone as artisans found themselves less able to afford new homes.

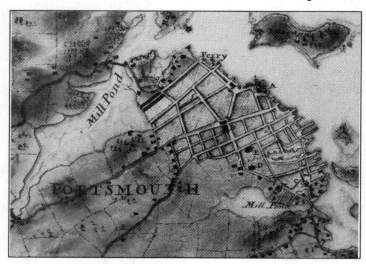

Courtesy NHHS

Detail, A Plan of Piscataqua Harbor, by James Grant, 1774.

Key:
A. Queen's Chapel
B. North Meeting House
C. South Meeting House
D. Sandemanian Meeting House
E. Independent Meeting House
F. State House
G. Spring Market
H. Gov. Wentworth House

Population: Portsmouth		
Year	Population	Gain
1775	4,590	-
1790	4,720	230
1800	5,339*	619
1810	6,934	1,595
1820	7,327	393
1830	8,082	755
1840	7,887	(195)
1850	9,738	1,851
1860	9,335	(403)
1870	9,211	(124)
1880	9,732	531
1890	9,827	95
1900	10,637	610
1910	11,269	632
1920	13,569	2, 300

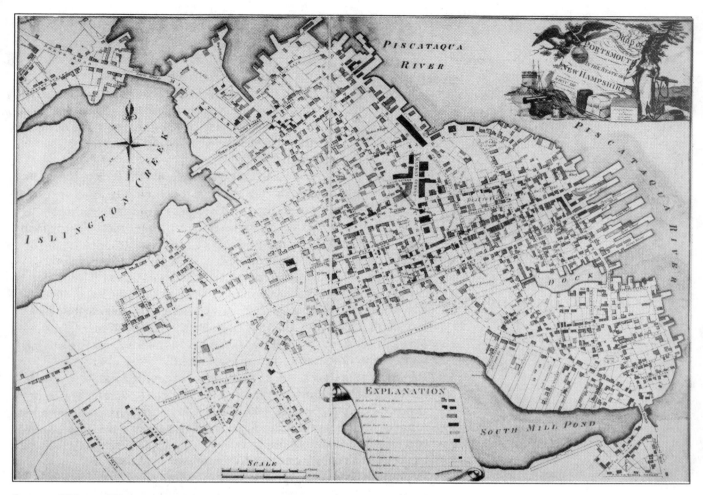

Courtesy of Library of Congress

Map of the Compact part of the Town of Portsmouth, by John G. Hales, 1813.

Industrialization occurred later in Portsmouth than in the water-powered mill towns of the upper Piscataqua founded in the 1820s, but was almost simultaneous with the larger and faster corporate development of Manchester, NH. Except for a small water powered site at the western end of the North Mill Pond, operated in the 1830s as a spinning mill producing woolen yarn for hand weaving of hosiery, the coastal city required the steam engine. This occurred in the mid-1840s when steam fueled a mixed economy of new foundries, machine shops, lumber yards, and textile mills. While shipbuilding revived from 1840 to 1860 in yards along the river, manufacturing was sited either on waterfront wharves or along the southern edge of the North Mill Pond adjacent to railroad tracks that connected the port to Boston and other inland towns after 1840. To accommodate several railroads, the mill pond was partially filled, and an industrial neighborhood evolved around one large cotton textile mill and several other small industries.

By the Civil War, brewing of ale began to supplant the city's textile mill as the city's most successful enterprise. The Frank Jones Brewery, the largest American manufactury of ale, came to

Advertising print, Frank Jones Brewery.

Population: Portsmouth		
Place of Birth	1850	1870
NH	6387	6931
ME	1107	771
MA	525	314
Other New Eng.	98	59
Other US	117	136
Unknown	263	
Total US-born	8380	8211
Foreign		
Canada	208	86
England	330	322
Ireland	580	542
Scotland/Wales	72	18
Germany	22	
Other	29	32
Total Foreign	1241	1006

chart 2.

dominate the western end of the North Mill Pond together with the smaller Eldridge Brewery, which replaced the old hosiery mill. These industries helped pull later speculative development westward from the old core. The Creek area above of the North Mill Pond became a center of Irish settlement, and new streets interlaced those laid out nearly a century before between Middle and Islington Streets.

Increased economic activity and a growing middle class of retailers, businessmen, and professionals in the third quarter of the 19th century helped create a new suburban district on a large tract of hilly land between Middle and South Streets. This land had been held from development during the lifetime of owner James Rundlet, whose large federal home occupied most of the block across Middle Street. When newspaper publisher F.W. Miller and contractor Benjamin Franklin Webster began to develop their portions of Rundlet's Mountain, the first large homes clustered near South Road. Webster's own estate, designed by the local architect Albert C. Fernald, dominated the crest of the hill.

After a half century of near stasis, except for modest growth in the 1870s, the population grew to 13,569 in 1920, an increase of almost 3000 people since 1900. This third major population burst resulted, in part, from European immigration to the United States and a revival of ship building in Portsmouth, Newington and Kittery as the country entered World War I. To solve the shipbuilder's "housing problem," the government initiated special mass transportation and construction programs. North of the city the Atlantic Shipyard Corporation acquired an unused industrial facility and won contracts for 10 steel merchant ships. The federal government also provided financing to build an architect-designed "garden suburb" for the shipyard workers, known as Atlantic Heights, along the bluff overlooking the river. In the heart of Portsmouth, however, worker housing took the form of two- and three-deckers, multi-family blocks, and the continued conversion of older housing into tenements. For middle-class families new streets were laid out between South Street and Islington Road and bungalows and other popular single family house types helped expand the edge of the city. This was made possible by an electric streetcar trolley system; its generators were based at the Morley Button Company, established in 1891, beyond the breweries on Islington Road.

From the 1920s, when a new bridge across the Piscataqua made Middle and State Streets part of U.S. Route 1, the private automobile and national public policy were central to how the city grew. Prohibition killed the breweries, and the Depression hit the city hard. World War II turned the city's waterfront and commercial center into a navy town as the U.S. Naval Shipyard became the region's largest employer. When new worker housing was needed, however, it was no longer necessary to build next to the shipyard.

Pannaway Manor was a government-funded suburb west of the city center and linked to work and services by busses. Post World War II private housing development followed the same suburban pattern based on the expectation that families who could own their own home had a car.

The automobile also altered the traditional character of the old city. Islington Street, where many wealthy merchants and ship captains of the early 19th century built their mansions, was redeveloped to service this new technology. In the 1930s one three-story Federal style mansion was converted to a garage, and others were lost altogether for schools, telephone exchanges, and stores.

Three large government programs dominate the mid-20th century history of the city: the Interstate Highway system, Pease Air Force Base, and Urban Renewal. Highway expansion generated two new bridges to by-pass the city center, and, at the junction with other major roads, sites for malls and industrial parks. The economic engine driving this development was a Strategic Air Command facility, Pease Air Force Base. Begun in 1954, it took some 15% to 20% of the city's land area plus parts of adjoining Newington and Greenland for its more than 1600 acre site. The city's official 1990 population of 25,925 was reduced to 20,856 later that year by the closing of Pease Air Force Base, a victim of the demise of the Cold War and government retrenchment, and the relocation of its 5,069 people.

These products of mid 20th-century national policy initially accelerated the decline of the traditional urban core. Downtown Portsmouth in the 1950s and 1960s was a gritty, blue collar, industrial city. Its neighborhoods were officially declared blighted and poor. Washington's solution was urban renewal through slum clearance. Local action to modify total demolition produced one of the few urban outdoor history sites in the country, Strawbery Banke Museum, but huge tracts of the historic North End working class neighborhood and parts of the commercial core were lost to later projects. The combined effect of these locally administered federal programs was to reinforce depressed real estate values of urban property while providing better highway access to and from the city. It also generated political resistance and private efforts to reinvest in existing buildings. From the late 1960s and accelerating through the 1980s the city experienced a major population shift as some long-time residents and newer middle class buyers began to restore and renovate old buildings throughout the local historic districts.

RMC

HABS, Library of Congress
Captain Samuel Chauncey House, Islington St., converted to gas station 1935.

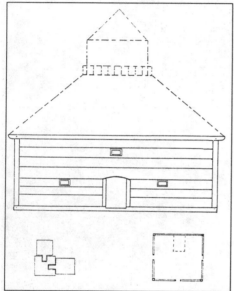

Drawing for Richard Candee, by David Hart
One-Room Plan, Sherburne House, 1695.

drawing by Richard Candee from building contract
1659 Portsmouth Meeting House.

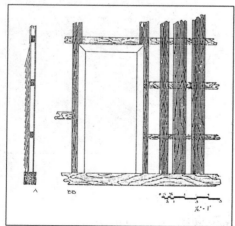

Drawing by Amy Amidon
Framing, Oracle House.

THE LANGUAGE OF PORTSMOUTH ARCHITECTURE

Wood Building Systems: George Washington noted that the houses of Portsmouth were "indifferent, and almost entirely of wood." Piscataqua's settlers brought with them the box frame English timber frame tradition of an independent roof truss atop a cube. Vertical posts sat above sills at each corner as well as at chimney or other structural bays. The posts were joined together with girts at each story of two and three story buildings, and at the plate. Interior support was provided by the summer beam, running longitudinally (parallel to the ridge) on most ground floors and often as a tie beam on the upper floor, which supported smaller floor joists. Normally braces and studs stiffen the frame provide a surface for interior lath and plaster walls.

The 17th- and 18th- century wooden tradition of northern New England included not only Anglo-American timber framing but several local variations. One was what the original builders called "logg" (later "garrison" or "blockhouse") construction. This employed thick planks of wood, usually sawn at one of the area's many water powered sawmills, seven to ten inches in thick. Buildings of logg might be dovetailed at the corners, with second floors overhanging on all four sides, or slotted into corner posts. The earliest documentary evidence for a logg structure in New England is the 1659 Portsmouth meeting house building contract with a Newbury, Massachusetts carpenter, John Hutchins. It called for a typically square plan, 16 feet high to the wall plate, with 12 windows and three doors. Its walls were to be "of Loggs 9 Inches thick, let into side posts wth a rabbet." Only the Gilman garrison (so-called) in Exeter, N.H., probably built in the early 18th century, survives with logg walls into corner posts.

A larger regional building tradition was the use of vertical planks or boards instead of studs between corner posts. Such practices were known in England for cladding of church towers but had a widespread revival in the timber economy of northern New England. As early as the 1660s some buildings used 2" to 3" thick vertical planks as the primary walling material, while others simply sheathed the hewn frame with thin 1" sawn lumber. In all cases the planking replaces the use of studs. Usually interior braces (especially at the second story) are exposed inside the room as there are no studs and lath and plaster is applied directly to the back of the exterior boarding. *[see Richard Jackson House]* Vertically boarded frames were also used for barns, warehouses, and other utilitarian structures from the earliest period. Often boarding is attached to the exterior not only at sill and plate, but stiffened with one or more horizontal rails framed between the posts. *[see Sheafe Warehouse]* Occasionally, as at the Oracle House this early 18th-century utilitarian frame might be enlarged and adapted to domestic use.

No systematic investigation has been made of later 18th and 19th century framing techniques. Depthwise joists appear as early as 1725 (see Fitch House, The Hill) but in the 1760s often return to square sectioned joists. Framing with corner posts behind boxing can be seen as late as the 1850s but most other materials by then were likely commercial sawn lumber.

Masonry Construction: Washington wondered in 1789 why Portsmouth had so few masonry houses, "as the country is full of stone and good clay for bricks." Indeed, until after the Revolution the city — like the Piscataqua region as a whole — displayed a marked reluctance to build in anything but wood. A few wealthy merchants of the first two decades of the eighteenth century had built in brick *[see MacPheadris-Warner House]*, but until Woodbury Langdon erected his house *[see Rockingham Hotel]* in the mid-1780s none of the other large houses were of brick.

Chimneys, of course, were built of brick; timber-framed chimneys of the 1630s are known in the Piscataqua only archaeologically and remain in the documents as late as 1651. The apparently original brick stack (now replaced) of the ca. 1664 Richard Jackson house was laid in clay, a practice sometimes continued into the 1730s. John Jones provided end chimneys with an oval decoration above the roof his own Deer Street home (ca. 1702), and may have also built a pilastered chimney (ca. 1725) on nearby High Street. *[see The Hill]* Most colonial chimney stacks rest on a solid stone foundation and brick arches support fireplaces of the late colonial and federal periods. Brick "beehive" ovens in New England shift from the rear wall of the fireplace to the rear corner or side of the firebox over the 17th-century, and face the room beside the fireplace in the early 19th century.

One 18th-century foreign visitor noted in 1784, "the cold is so continuous that for nine months of the year the inhabitants are forced to maintain fires constantly in their homes." Until the advent of cast iron stoves and central heating, chimneys were a key element of New England domestic planning. Even after open fires ceased to be the primary heat source, stove flues were often located in the traditional chimney locations. Auxiliary fireplaces were revived as part of 20th century neo-colonial decorating.
[see Wendell House]

The Federal rebuilding of Portsmouth's commercial core adopted brick as a fire preventative. These were used a larger New England building vocabulary: the curved row of buildings on Market Square are like Bulfinch's Boston crescent and its English prototypes, while the widespread use of rounded walls to turn the façade of corner lots could be found all over the region's urban centers. While most stores and warehouses adopted a simple commercial vernacular, marble drip courses or horizontal bands were common on their façades. A very general index for dating the common bond walls of New England uses the number of rows of stretchers between rows of headers. Abbott Cummings offers this rule of thumb for Massachusetts: 17th century has a ratio of 1: 1; the early 18th century has 1 row of headers to 3 stretchers. By the mid 18th century the ratio may become 1: 5 and before the end of 18th century 1: 7 is known. The early 19th century shows wide variation but some buildings exhibit even greater ratios than 1: 7.

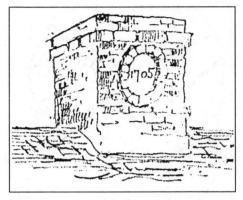

1889 sketchbook, Walter Kolham, architect
Decorated chimney, John Jones house, ca. 1705.

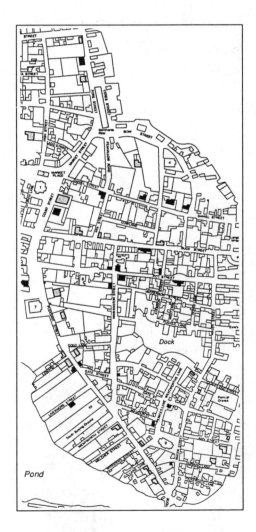

Eliza McClennen after J. G. Hales 1812
Complex roof forms:

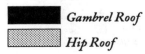

Gambrel Roof

Hip Roof

7

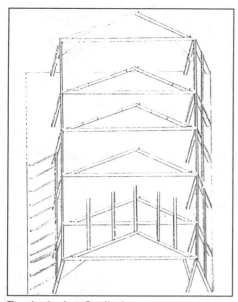

Drawing by Amy Sundback

Roof Frame, Samuel Langdon House ca. 1750.

A test of Portsmouth's federal rebuilding seems to demonstrate the 1: 7 ratio on common buildings and spacing as low as 1: 5 on more elaborate ones *[see 1816 Custom House and Sheafe Street Row]*.

There were also a handful of ruble stone commercial and industrial buildings in the 1820s and 30s, as well as the ashlar South Church of 1824. From the mid-19th century on, Portsmouth occassionally used terra-cotta *[see North Church and Rockingham Hotel]* and brownstone. Later commercial and domestic buildings adopted press brick and other widely available masonry building materials. Yellow brick became popular in the 1890s and early twentieth century.

Roofs: The most common roof after 1660 was a departure from English practice. It was composed of paired principal rafters with common purlins trenched across their face to support vertical roof boarding. Even more complex gambrels and hip roofs adopted the basic elements of the principal rafter and common purlin system. However, the gambrel roof, so common as to become an icon of colonial work among later colonial revival architects, was a popular alternative by the second quarter of the 18th century. The earliest extant gambrel is that of the rebuilding of the Oracle house sometime around 1730. In Portsmouth the gambrel was also occassionally built with a clerestory of sash windows in place of one slope of the roof. Sometimes called a 'running dormer' none survive today in the Piscataqua; the Samuel Langdon house, the last known example, was moved to Old Sturbridge Village. The late Arthur Gerrier suggested that this Portsmouth roof type may have been the ultimate source for several surviving examples of late 18th century date along the coast of Maine.

The other unusual roof feature, also limited to larger homes, is the long use of the high hip roof. This was a common Georgian form, here as elsewhere throughout Anglo-America. Less common is the continuation of the higher hip roof form well into the early 19th century as an alternative to the lower hip roof commonly associated with the federal style. A house with a high hip roof at the corner of Middle and Summer Streets may be as late as 1825; the brick house opposite the parking garage entrance on Hanover Street is even later.

DOMESTIC PLAN TYPES

Colonial domestic plan types in Portsmouth range from the single room plan with chimney bay, as in the first phase of the Sherburne house at Strawbery Banke, to the complex accumulation of rooms that makes up the mid-18th century Benning Wentworth mansion in Little Harbor. The majority of these forms are differentiated by the number of rooms on the ground floor and the position of one or more chimney stacks. As else where throughout the Atlantic coast, the earliest and smallest house types have been destroyed or so altered as to have received little study. The most common surviving form is the two-story house with one room on either side of a central chimney, either constructed at once or added to an earlier one-room core. A one-cell two story house was built as late

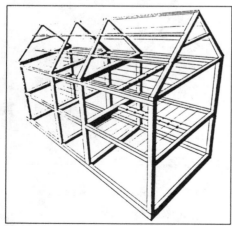

Drawing for Richard Candee, by David Hart

Central Chimney Plan, John Lowe House ca. 1705 (Deer Tavern), destroyed.

as 1814 for a black mariner and enlarged to two room plan perhaps in the 1870s *[see 214 Union Street]*. One variant of the common two-room central chimney plan is that with two rooms and end chimneys. As early as about 1702 such a house, with entries and stairs in front of the chimneys, was built with only a vertical board partition dividing the interior. By the 1730s a two room end-chimney house (210 Gates St. at the corner of Mechanic St.) added a central hallway between its two end chimney rooms.

Survival of one story colonial houses is so rare as to be virtually non-existent throughout the Piscataqua, although there are extant examples from 1814 through the 1850s. In 1798 the U.S. Direct Tax found only 86 one story homes of the 626 dwellings valued over $100 in Portsmouth, although several of the 148 homes worth less than $100 may also have been one story high. The vast majority, 524 higher valued homes, were of two stories. No example of the small center chimney house type without lobby entry has been found in this urban context.

A rear lean-to was often added to center chimney houses. The earliest *[Richard Jackson House]* was an unheated service space. The first documented integral lean-to (for a kitchen) was constructed in 1698. A mid-18th-century lean-to (171 Gates St.) eliminated studs from the first-floor rear wall to combine part of the main block and the lean-to into a single kitchen. L or T-shaped additions were common from the last decade of the 17th century, as a 1705 sketch of Governor Allen's house at New Castle illustrates. The Sherburne house at Strawbery Banke had a rear ell, perhaps of one story and a gabled attic, along Horse Lane by the 1720s. By the 1790s chimneys were erected with fireplaces awaiting a planned later addition *[see Samuel Jackson House, Strawbery Banke]*. In the late 18th and early 19th century gabled ells also provided service space behind the main block; as narrow lots led to siting houses gable end to the street, service ells often extended beyond the rear gable.

The earliest local example of a five-room central-chimney plan carried to both floors of the house (rather than just the ground floor lean-to) was that for Lt. Governor John Wentworth in 1699. This plan type continued to be built into the late 18th and early 19th centuries *[see Benjamin Holmes, Jr. House]* here as throughout New England.

The full two-story Georgian plan of two rooms on either side of the central hallway was known in Portsmouth as a "Double House" during the 18th century. Five-bay, bilaterally symmetrical, center entrance façades faced the street. Their depth required a variety of roof forms: M-shaped, gambrel, and hip. The gable-on-hip is only known in Portsmouth from documentary sources *[see Boyd Estate]*. The earliest known example of the Georgian double house is the MacPheadris-Warner House of 1716, a brick house with end-wall fireplaces and an M-shaped roof later modified to a gambrel.

Reference to many new 1750s Portsmouth houses of three stories can only be accounted for by a dormered gambrel roof over

Courtesy Metropolitan Museum of Art
Five-Room Plan, Center Chimney House. Lt. John Wentworth House, 1699.

Courtesy British Library
L-Plan, Col. Allen House, Newcastle, drawing 1699.

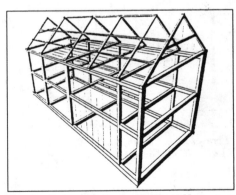

Drawing for Richard Candee, by David Hart
End-Chimney Plan, John Jones House. Moved.

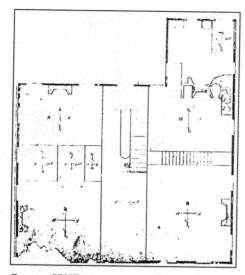

Courtesy SPNEA
*Georgian or "Double House" Plan,
Rundlet-May House, 1807.*

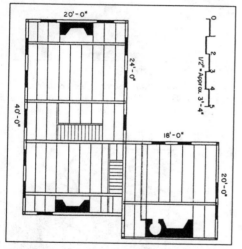

Courtesy Baker Library, Harvard Business School
*Three-Room L Plan, ca. 1800–1820
unidentified Portsmouth framing plan.*

Courtesy Strawbery Banke Museum
*Three-Story Georgian Double House,
ca. 1760 Brewster House, destroyed.*

two story frames, although full three story homes appear at the upper end of the social scale in the 1760s. In 1798 there were only 16 dwellings of three stories, although rapid growth along Court Street and Haymarket Square raised that number to 21 by 1800. Such houses, executed in a wide range of ornament, can be seen as the height of elite architecture from the 1790s to the 1830s.

In the 1750s and 60s a new variant of internal planning is seen in two houses where the common center entry opens into a large reception room occupying an entire quadrant of the square floor plan. *[see Moffatt-Ladd and Mills-Whipple houses]* During the Federal period other ambitious houses sometimes also broke out of the common four room arrangement, employing octagonal rooms *[see Woodbury Langdon House]* or a separate stair alcove off the center passage *[John Peirce and Boardman Houses]*.

The kitchen of the largest double houses was in the main block throughout the colonial period. Second kitchens in the cellar (by the 1760s) or in an ell (by the 1780s) first appear in the homes of the wealthy. By the first decade of the 19th century they are also found in artisan as well as elite homes. A few of the smallest early 19th-century houses *[see Hoit House]* have cooking fireplaces and bake ovens in both ground floor rooms. Occassionally there is evidence that two families occupied such small houses. Elsewhere, two cooking fireplaces seem to merely reflect a potential for multiple or extended family use that did not happened.

In the Federal period many adopted a façade that looked like the most ambitious double house, but reduced the total size through a three room plan with L-shaped footprint that led to the period designation as an "L-house" or "ell house." These appear in both two and three story versions. In fact, for many the ideal was a three room ground floor plan. It often appears in homes where one rear wall chimney heats a front parlor or dining room and a kitchen placed in an ell. It can be seen at many social levels: the Pleasant Street mansion of Joshua Haven house (1801), the two-story South Street home of Isaac Nelson house (ca. 1800) and in artisan housing on Franklin Street like that of Samuel Fernald (ca. 1813). While Haven's ell continued up three stories, Nelson had a two story rear ell of lower stud than his front rooms and Fernald had a lean-to addition behind the two room block. An unidentified plan for an early 19th-century house with two story rear ell, off-set to provide a back hallway, provides another variant on this plan. The largest and most unusual three room plan was the three-story mansion of Daniel Austin (now 43-53 Austin Street). It was originally a single room deep with three major rooms separated by two hallways and stairs.

The most common small house type during the first half of the 19th century has a lobby entrance and staircase but removed the central chimney (sometimes literally, as at the Marden House in Strawbery Banke) to the rear walls of both rooms. The space formerly occupied by a central chimney created a small unheated room, sometimes a bedroom. This plan, resembles what other regions call the "I-house," though no one in New England ever calls them that. They are often sited with their narrow end wall to the street, placing the entrance in the middle of the long wall and away from the street. Some had kitchens in a rear lean-to, a rear gable ell, or where topography permitted, in the cellar. Two room houses of one or two stories, with chimneys centered or some combination of rear and end positions, were built into the 1840s for artisan and tenant houses.

A few 18th- and early 19th-century houses varied in the width across their façade and commonly produced a three bay, side entry façade with side passage plan, known to some as the two-thirds georgian or half house. These are common elsewhere along the east coast, but in Portsmouth this configuration is rare among single family houses before the second quarter of the 19th century. The earliest known existing use of this plan is found in a small number of duplexes built by 1810. In these houses, two living units were arranged side-by-side in mirror image under a common roof. Entries were paired at the center of a six bay façade, each half was seldom wider than a single room and entry hall, and seldom wider than two rooms [see Cottars Lane]. Plan variations of this type were based on the choice of lobby entry or passage, and the location of a kitchen in the main block, rear or side ell, or cellar.

As Portsmouth shifted to an industrial economy in the 1840s, new types of house forms and designs began to be built. This is especially noticeable, perhaps, because of the paucity of buildings surviving from the 1830s [see Haines-Fonda House] and a general continuation of the federal style and its common domestic forms into that decade. The introduction of new heating technologies; the availability of machine planed and dimensioned lumber; and increasing popularity, at least among middle class owner-occupants, of published design ideas from pattern books contributed to the form and detailing of many mid to late 19th-century buildings. The vast majority of the new homes throughout the second half of the century were fairly standard products of local carpenters and contractors. Real estate agents throughout the region call them "New Englanders," a name broadly applied to almost any boxy mid to late 19th century wooden vernacular dwelling. They range from modestly stylish Greek Revival and Italianate homes for prosperous store owners and businessmen, to speculative single- and double-family homes for factory workers. While they share standard manufactured products like brackets for cornices or door hoods, milled ornamental trim, and other mass-produced details, the range of common forms and plan types is relatively small.

While relatively rare in Portsmouth during the early 19th century (although it can be found in rural Massachusetts Federal style houses during the 1810s), this floor plan experienced a rapid rise in popularity beginning in the 1830s. It was an important characteristic of a New England-wide rebuilding of the first half of the century. With the newly popular plan came an important change in the outward appearance of the house. Reorientation toward the street made the gable end the front of the house.

Rear Wall Chimney Plan, Garland House.

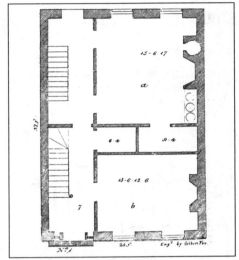
from A Benjamin *American Builder's Companion* (1827)
Ground floor plan for a Town House (kitchen and breakfast room).

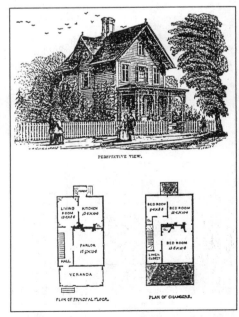
Calvert Vaux Villas and Cottages (1864) Design 1.
A simple Suburban Cottage.

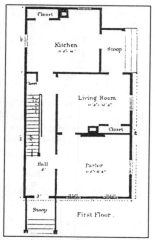

Bicknell's Village Builder and Supplement (1878)
Supplementary Pl. 13

Side entry plans.

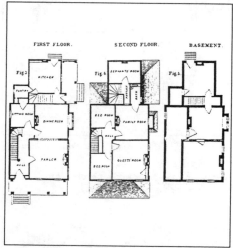

Bicknell's Village Builder and Supplement (1878)
Pl. 15

Side entry plans.

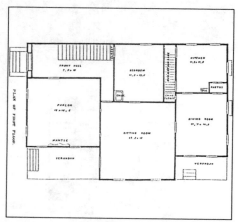

Bicknell's Village Builder and Supplement (1878)
Pl. 13

Side entry plans.

Many names have been postulated for this form and, at least in Massachusetts, their period name was "end house." It became common to employ a narrow three bay façade with a side entry, creating a new treatment for single family homes that remained enormously popular throughout the 19th century. The earliest of these employed the regional tradition of front and side elevations with closely fitted windows. Most early examples are simple blocks, here most commonly of two stories, with the common addition of a lower rear ell. This basic block could be simplified through using fewer windows on the façade and sides, or occasionally be making the whole building exceptionally narrow. It could also be made bigger, taking on characteristics of the picturesque, through the addition of bay windows (one story or two), use of a variety of dormers along the roof, or by projecting bays rising to the same height as the main block.

The side or corner passage and stair plans inside these houses were executed with numerous variation on the number and relationship of rooms on the main floor. Indeed, it may have been the adaptability of these general forms to a wide variety of interior planning needs that made them so enduring within the region. The array of plans in these blocks may ultimately prove as various than their many exterior modifications. Small versions of this house may enclose a side hall, kitchen, and parlor; larger versions include a side hall, two parlors, and a kitchen or a side hall, two parlors (occasionally paired), and a kitchen ell; where the hall does not extend the whole depth of the main block, a small room may be added to these plans. If projecting bays are present, rooms to the rear are larger and a second, set-back entry may be found. Later examples were constructed to deeper dimensions, adding more tiers of rooms from front to rear.

The persistence of traditional floor plans can be seen in Portsmouth as in other regions. While single pile (one room deep) and L-plan houses lost popularity, the center hall georgian plan and the side/corner passage family of plans were the most common in the mid and late 19th century. Georgian floor plan types provided builders with an effective large plan that remains popular even today. Large houses with Italianate trim were popular during the mid 19th century; somewhat later builders might adopt the mansard roof or add porches, ells, and bays to provide a picturesque outline. The side/corner passage plans can be seen, not only in great numbers of single family homes, but in duplexes *[see State, Cabot and Union Streets]* and rows *[see McDonough Street]* that were built in larger numbers as the century progressed. Late 19th-century duplexes in Portsmouth often have larger and more complex plans.

In Portsmouth builders seem to have drawn on books occasionally for ornament and unusual elements of plan, but normally applied these to otherwise familiar houses. When offered houses and plans close enough to popular local types, in other words, some were constructed; other related plans were altered to resemble more popular ones. Published sources are most readily evident for several gothic revival cottages built throughout the western edge of the city near the new steam-powered industries soon after the mid-1840s. A large villa erected for the Congregational minister on Middle Street and a small "laborer's cottage" at the far end of Austin Street clearly derive from designs promulgated in *The Horticuluralist* (1849) and A.J. Downing's books. In the last quarter of the century, several people turned to mail order designs, especially *Palliser's American Cottage Homes* (1878).

With the rise of mail-order house plans, more novel houses were constructed, particularly for those who chose to build large homes. Some, like the exceptionally large duplex at 266 Middle St. appear to be derived from a *Palliser's Model Dwellings ... For Industrial Americans* (1893), but modified to a more local configuration. During the early 20th century, this national trend made itself felt in the region with the introduction of a new group of domestic forms: the small house known as the bungalow and the larger four-square. Examples of the latter can be seen on Islington Street and one of rusticated cement block at the corner of Madison and Austin streets. Bungalows tend to be found in later subdivisions beyond the west end.

Duplexes remained popular, with the two-families divided horizontally as well as vertically. Tenement blocks and large boarding houses, as well as one apartment block, were built in isolated cases. Typical of New England industrial cities and working class suburbs is the three-decker, and the related two-decker. *[see Hancock Street]* These houses are divided into single or paired horizontal flats or, occasionally, expanded to multiples of vertically divided rows. The three decker is a three story building under a nearly flat roof, with a front elevation divided between entry and stair bay to one side and projecting bay windows on the other, and marked by rear (and sometimes front) porches at each floor. The deep interior plans are normally two rooms wide, opening onto a short narrow center corridor and extending to two or three rooms from front to back. Many contain front paired parlors and rear kitchens, with bedrooms located in the center and rear of the plan. This arrangement seems rooted in the deepest side/corner passage plans as well as those published for bungalows and other related popular house types.

Interest in historical revivals manifested itself throughout New England in a preference for local, Colonial models and brought a return to the edicts of symmetry and the construction of some familiar house types. Thus, in new construction, the modern Cape shares with its ancestor small size and single story, the two-story modern Colonial echoes the gable block with revival entry treatments, and the Dutch Colonial subtype masks its second story behind a false gambrel and dormer roof. Only rarely in Portsmouth did builders employ various Tudor elements so popular elsewhere in the 1920s. Good examples of Colonial upper middle class houses of the 1890s and early 20th century can be seen along Middle Street *[see the Hackett house]*.

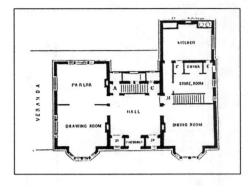

A.J. Downing The Architecture of Rural Cottages (1850)
Timber-Frame Villa, Gervase Wheeler, architect.

Palliser's Model Dwellings ... For Industrial Americans (1893)
Duplex used as model for two family houses.

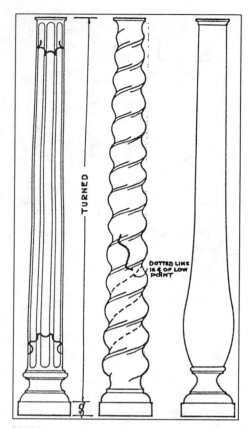

Detail, turned balusters, Joshua Wentworth House, ca. 1770.

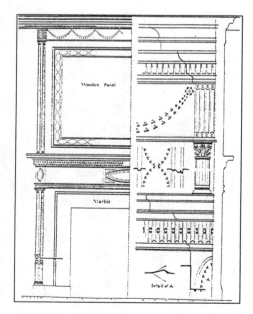

The Georgian Period (1900)

John Haven House mantel and details after F.M. Mann 1895.

STYLE AND ORNAMENT

The few surviving examples of first-period (ca. 1664-1720) construction in the Piscataqua exhibit decorated exposed timber-frames similar to a far larger number in Massachusetts. Indeed, the only known chamfer used to decorate summer beams is the quarter-round, usually ending in lambs-tongue stops. The Jackson house is the sole structure with significant first-period interior finish, not only shadow molded vertical sheathing but alterations of the early 18th century that include bolection moldings applied to batten doors as panels. Similar evidence for a room built before 1703 remains in the Sherburne House at Strawbery Banke and in an attic door of the Oracle house.

Georgian panel walls, carved and turned classical details, and boxing over the frame elements appeared in new homes and in rebuilding of older ones over the first decade of the 18th century. Soon after 1700 several houses had plaster ceilings and boxed summers (at least in upper chambers) as well as interior cornice moldings. At the elite level, the Warner House is the earliest (and likely the first local) fully Georgian plan house. Its exterior ornament is that of mid-18th century changes, but its interior is largely original.

Several ways of handling particular elements may be said to be Piscataqua localisms within the larger regional Georgian mode. While none may be totally unknown outside the area, these features seem to be widespread in Portsmouth and its hinterland over the 18th century. For example, the Piscataqua had a long love affair with the broken scroll pediment over windows as well as doorways. As a door enframement it appears in by the mid-18th century, although that at the Wentworth-Gardner house is a reproduction based in part on that of the Shortridge House on Deer Street. Several houses of the 1760s exhibit this detail, and the Langdon and other high-style houses of the 1780s continued the tradition. The dormers of the Langdon mansion are also heavily modillioned in a manner copied by other house builders of the early Federal era. Two brick houses of the early 19th century on State Street (ca. 1820) and another the Daniel Marden house (ca. 1810) on Cabot Street at the corner of Coffin's Court, employ decorative window caps with broken scroll motifs above third-story windows. Although they may be of later 19th century date, some have suggested they may actually date to the original period of construction.

Other classical window pediments also show a specific local handling. Thus, the triangular or "pitched" pediment is normally composed only of the beveled pair of cornice moldings using the backboard as the only closure at the base of the triangle.

Inside, decorative wall cornices indicate the presence of an original door or window locations by breaking and projecting a few inches from the plane, offering useful (if sometimes confusing) insight into earlier fenestration patterns. Exterior cornices, at least on homes of sufficient height to permit a full cornice, may also break out above upper exterior windows. *[see Mills-Whipple House]*

Specific hands, like the Dearing family of carvers, may also be identified with certain types of ornament. The Dearings most lavish work is the naturalistic rococo carvings found in several houses built or remodeled in the 1760s and in the Langdon Mansion of the late 1780s.

From perhaps as early as 1785, certainly by the late 1790s, ornament drawn from English and American popularizers of the Adamesque style can be found in Portsmouth houses. Fan doorways beneath a triangular pediment come directly from the 1790s published works of William Pain and Asher Benjamin, as does other ornament on the large homes around Haymarket Square. Two early mansions, those for Woodbury Langdon and the John Peirce, seem to have set the pattern for their use of waffle-like banding, delicate elongated colonnettes (often paired or tripled) above or below a mantelpiece, thinly turned balusters for a spiral staircase, and cut-out S or C blocks in the riser ends. Just after 1800 fireplaces commonly adopt contrasting woods inset into the top blocks of the vertical members supporting the mantel shelf.

Staircases with three different turnings (fluted, vase, and spiral) on each step appear in many high-style Portsmouth houses of the mid to late 18th century after the immigrant turner Richard Mills settled in Portsmouth. *[see Moffatt-Ladd and Mills-Whipple houses]* In addition to the dog-leg and straight run stair, spiral and elliptical staircases can be found, not only in large stylish homes of the Federal period but also in quite small ones.

19th and Early 20th Centuries: Just as the central-chimney and center-hall floor plans continued well into the early national period, the Federal style proved quite durable in Portsmouth. This continuing popularity may have contributed to the relatively small proportion of buildings in the Greek Revival style. Except for a handful of lost 1830s temple-front public buildings (an Episcopal chapel on State Street and a court house that gave its name to Court Street) the major monument of the style is the stone South (Unitarian) Church. The old North Meeting House was remodeled to conform to Greek Revival proportions and details. *[see Civic and Religious Buildings]* New brick commercial blocks near the corner of Bow and Market Streets adopted the Boston style of post and lintel shop fronts *[see Commercial Portsmouth]*, but domestic designs employing a colossal or first floor portico were few. Where Greek Revival houses are found, they are often decorated with elements of the Doric entablature, at the door and the cornice and, in the most elaborate examples, boast pilasters at the door and corners of the dwelling. The regional passion for things Grecian was manifested here in the addition of new porticos, probably lifted from pattern books, and the redecoration of interiors. The Federal style Folsom-Salter house, moved across Court Street (now # 95) to make way for elderly housing, contains extensive alterations to fireplaces and other trim with Greek Revival details as well as a typical portico of this period. This may have occurred around 1852, when Captain John Salter installed the Zubar wallpaper *Scenic America* that once decorated an upper chamber.

Frank E. Wallis, *American Architecture, Decoration and Furniture of the 18th Century* (1894)
Nathaniel A. Haven House composition mantelpiece.

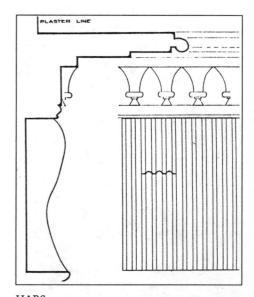

HABS
Cornice Detail, Captain Samuel Chauncey House, 1807.

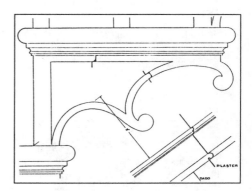

HABS
Stair Scroll Detail, Captain Samuel Chauncey House, 1807.

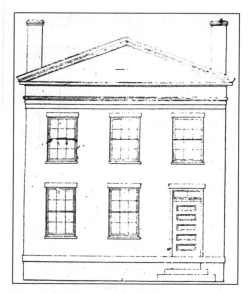

Chester Hills, The Builder's Guide, (1834) Pl. 26.
Greek Revival gable-end house.

A.J. Downing, *The Architecture of Rural Cottages*
(1850), Design 1.
Laborer's Cottage, model for 292 Austin St.

Calvert Vaux, Villas and Cottages (1864) Design 29.
Wooden Villa with curved roof.

Although isolated examples of 1840s and early 1850s gothic cottages were constructed on the edges of the town along Middle, Islington, and streets between, the tenants of the picturesque did not take firm hold here. Several are clearly drawn from pattern books, from those for the literary elite *[see Peabody house, Middle Street]* to the smallest laborer's cottage *[292 Austin Street]*. Only near the turn of the 20th century does the one-story cottage with steep pointed façade gable make a return appearance, especially at The Creek (the northwestern edge of the North Mill Pond) where many Irish families settled.

More popular was the style now known as the Italianate, the clearly related successor to the Greek Revival. Brick Portsmouth was resurfaced with paint or mastic to replicate brownstone, roofs were bracketed, and quoins added to corners. Photographs and other evidence show that the rounded block curing around Market Street next to the Athenæum, Temple Israel on State Street, and many other old buildings were similarly transformed. In new construction the High School on Daniel Street and North Church in Market Square adopted the round-headed style, while the granite Custom House was built to the federally-funded palazzo version of the style.

In New England the Italianate is often an additive style: to an otherwise Greek Revival house a builder would add brackets to the entablature and panels to the pilasters. It became extremely common to purchase an elaborately detailed console to support a hood above the entry. Plans in 1848 proposed adding a bracketed balcony over the fanlight doorway to the Portsmouth Athenæum. By the 1870s commercially available door hoods with brackets in many styles were found on homes throughout the town. More elaborate wooden buildings added round headed and label-treated windows, quoins to the corners, or scored flushboard façades, few towered villas were ever built in this city. The addition of a mansard roof to an otherwise Italianate building, as commonly occurred in the 1860s and 1870s, constitutes the appearance of the Second Empire style in Portsmouth.

Traditional house forms could, and did, sustain a broad range in the amount of exterior ornament applied to them in an effort to achieve the complex massing and textured wall surfaces of the Queen Anne style. The plainest examples maintained the simple block and decorated edges of the first half of the century, adding newly available consoles to support door hoods, brackets to their cornices, and more frequent and larger porches, whose ornamental spindle-work carried much of the weight of the style. Houses were covered with shingles, sometimes shaped and arranged in patterns, as well as more traditional clapboard, and bays and floors were marked with bands of boards.

As the planning and construction modes shifted toward more complex massing, the basic box was modified through the addition of bay windows, dormers, projecting structural bays, as well as porches. The gablefront form proved remarkably adaptable and popular throughout the 19th century, but the center hall plans were also elaborated in this way as well.

The earliest phases of the Colonial Revival in Portsmouth, were often played out in the interior and exterior remodeling of authentic 18th and early 19th century buildings. Sometimes this merely added emphasis to the building's original ornament *[see Abraham Shaw house]*, but others were more fully transformed. By the turn of the century commercially available Colonial ornament entirely changed several houses near Haymarket Square *[see Capt. Richard Shapleigh and the N.K. Walker houses]* into elaborate Adamesque or Georgian creations.

Public buildings, like the Cottage Hospital (1894) that terminates the vista across the South Mill Pond from Market Square, and private residences for the city's leading citizens like the Masonic Temple on Middle Street *[see Hackett House]* — both by Harry Ball of the Boston firm Ball & Dabney — were built in the Colonial and Georgian Revival Styles. Elsewhere in the west end local architect William A. Ashe and other architects occasionally adopted the forms and ornament of shingled Colonial summer homes of the 1880s for new industrial and suburban houses throughout the next two decades.

Early 20th century small house design followed national and regional trends. Bungalows, four-squares, 3-deckers, and popular revival style cottages dot the streets of the western fring. Mail-order, factory-made homes, home-made resticated concrete block forms, and stick-built balloon frames were decorated in many styles. Modern small homes with "American colonial" details remained popular from Atlantic Heights (1918) to Pannaway Manor (1941) and Maplewood Acres (1941-47).

RMC & CWP

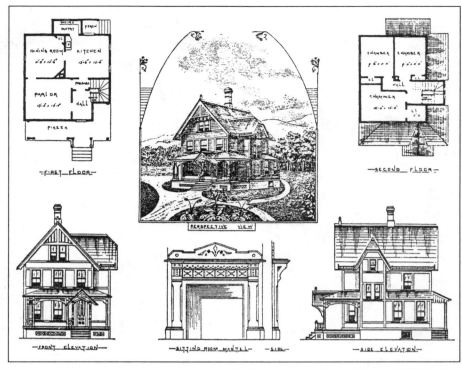

Palliser's American Cottage Homes (1878) Pl. 5

$1400 Home, probable model for house (below) 280 Wibird Street at the corner of Orchard Street.

Courtesy Portsmouth Athenæum
Cottage Hospital.

17

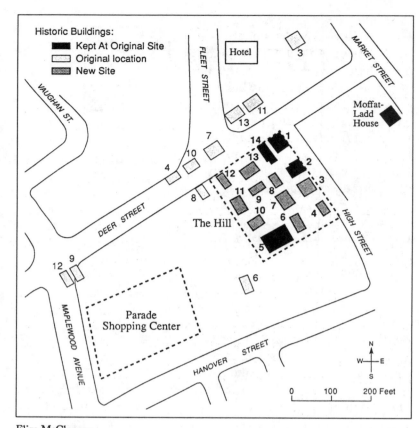

Eliza McClennen.

Map of The Hill and original locations of moved houses.

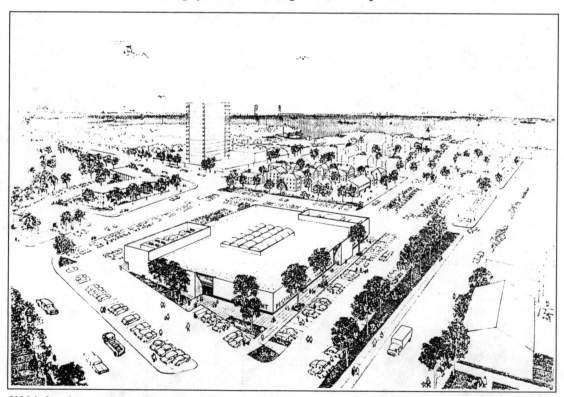

Aldrich Associates.

Architectural drawings of relocated houses in the Hill.

THE NORTH END AND THE HILL

Across from the Sheraton Portsmouth Hotel and Conference Center stands a cluster of old houses reused for commercial and institutional purposes. They are all that is left of a North End neighborhood, a baker's dozen saved from among some 400 structures in the Vaughan Street Urban Renewal Project area. Targeted by the Portsmouth Housing Authority (PHA) in 1963, the area was to be levelled to provide improved shopping and parking, new industrial zoning along the waterfront, and a site for a municipal building. The project was given final approval in 1964, and a federal appropriation was authorized the morning before President Johnson signed the National Historic Preservation Act of 1966, making it ineligible for review.

While neighborhood activists in the South End had resisted both Urban Renewal and Strawbery Banke museum, few residents opposed this second project that promised to be "Portsmouth's Path to Progress." As a product of urban renewal itself, Strawbery Banke felt unable to protest the projected demolition of the North End. But newcomers and others who were drawn to the city by its architecture and the idea of its outdoor museum sought a variety of private non-museum solutions to prevent this demolition. The five year political controversy exposed competing visions for the city as preservation clashed with the twin ideals of clearance and new construction. The New Hampshire Council on the Arts did more than any other state or federal agency to explore new strategies for preservation. Ten years before there was any form of federal tax incentive for historic preservation, Portsmouth Preservation Inc., a for-profit preservation corporation formed in 1968, acquired and stored selected houses while unsuccessfully attempting to gain permission to rehabilitate them.

In the end, the major parcel was sold to the Boston architect Nelson Aldrich, who acted as his own development firm in cooperation with Portsmouth Preservation. An early proponent of International Style design, Aldrich was nearing the end of a successful career when he attempted this disastrous urban renewal commercial development to keep his staff of young architects and planners employed during the Nixon recession. A cynical late-comer to preservation ideals, the Portsmouth Housing Authority acquired new HUD funding to move, "restore" exteriors, and restructure interiors of buildings saved from their own bulldozers. Despite the apparent subsidy, these poorly executed expenditures actually raised the cost of each structure to the new developer, who ultimately failed altogether. The buildings were sold to local property managers at a loss.

Selection of houses to purchase and moth-ball was dictated by phased demolition contracts. Traditional standards of age (pre-1820) and style (colonial or federal), as well as physical condition drove the choice of which buildings Portsmouth Preservation could try to "save." Unswerving commitment to commercial use by the

Drawing by James Garvin
Doorway, Shortridge-Rice House (see #13).

PHA deflected visions of preservation by residential renovation or gentrification. While other buyers salvaged a late first-period frame too damaged for simple relocation, the economics of commercial reuse guided the choices toward larger structures.

The design of The Hill, this enclave of "saved" old buildings (the new shopping mall was called The Parade), was partially determined by the location of five houses to remain *in situ* between the brick house near the corner of Deer and High Streets and the double houses on the former School Street. At best, the clustered site suggests something of the density of 18th- and early 19th-century buildings that once filled the area and provides a buffer between the Parade parking lot and gardens of the Moffatt-Ladd House. A remnant of conflicting community values and the transition between "old" and "new" preservation methods, the houses of The Hill only begin to suggest the diverse North End neighborhood replaced by public policy.

RMC

Archaeology: In preparation for the construction of the Sheraton Portsmouth Hotel, Strawbery Banke Museum's archaeology department contracted with the city and land owner to explore the archaeological resources of the key two acre parcel along Deer and Vaughan Streets. Beginning in 1981 historical archaeologists examined the architectural and land use changes of six house lots between 1700 and 1860, as well as changes in the consumer patterns of their residents. Subsurface foundations, wells, and privies were identified and excavated. They were filled with hundreds of glass and ceramic vessels, household trash, and architectural fragments. Many deposits have since been linked to changes in property ownership through transmission in the female line. This work documents a kin-related neighborhood from the creation of Deer Street in 1700 until the railroad arrived at the far end of Deer Street in 1840. Three generations of the Hart family and their relatives, for example, worked here as blacksmiths, builders, ropemakers, and merchants. They and their enslaved servants lived here from 1702 to 1830.

MEP

Sources:

Richard M. Candee, *Wooden Building in Early Maine and New Hampshire.* Ph.D. diss., University of PA, 1976.

Robert S. Chase, "New Faces for Old Buildings," *NH Profiles* (Mar. 1970):28-32.

Jack Arnold Gold, *The Evolution of Historic Preservation in Portsmouth, N.H.; Strategies for Improved Preservation Planning Services.* M.A. Thesis, Cornell University, 1978.

Martha Elaine Pinello, *Archaeological Formation Processes and Household Boundaries at Four Domestic Lots in the North End of Portsmouth, N.H., 1730-1830.* M.A. Thesis, Univ. of MA, 1989.

Portsmouth Housing Authority. "Urban Renewal in Portsmouth, New Hampshire." August, 1965.

_____. "Portsmouth's Path to Progress." (Portsmouth, nd).

"Portsmouth Parade," *New England Architect* (Sept. 1972.)

"Wanted: Reliable Persons To Rescue 18th Century Houses!" *NH Profiles* (Feb. 1969): 48-53.

Courtesy Strawbery Banke Museum
Deer Street, ca. 1900.

The Houses of THE HILL

The larger urban renewal zone contained a full range of 18th-through 20th-century urban house forms, yet houses selected for retention were variants of georgian layouts and early national house forms. Their plans are fairly representative of domestic forms originally built for lesser merchants, successful artisans, and others during the colonial and early national periods throughout Portsmouth. Those originally located along Deer Street are larger in plan and scale than those once located on back and cross streets. Several wooden homes in this area date between 1814 and 1825, a period during which all new construction in Portsmouth was by law supposed to have been of brick. While merchants such as James Neal continued to erect brick homes even after the statute was moot, most artisans in the North End resented the added cost and many seem to have ignored the law.

1. The Samuel Gerrish House (*in situ*) was built or, perhaps, rebuilt in 1822. In the break-up of merchant Isaac Rindge's estate there were a pair of workshops here in 1806 in a building shown on the 1812 map as a house. The land was sold in two parcels in 1815 to Samuel Gerrish although it is unclear whether the new owner constructed a new house. On Sept. 8, 1822 the building was consumed by a fire that nearly took the adjoining Jabez Fitch house (then lived in by wheelwright Simeon Stiles). Gerrish apparently had James Nutter design and/or rebuild this new house facing both Deer and High Streets, originally an L-plan house with a semi-circular staircase inside the Deer Street door. Late 19th century additions across the back and west side completed the existing plan.

2. The Fitch House, also on its original High Street site, was built ca. 1725. When the North Church agreed to provide its minister, the Rev. Jabez Fitch, with financial support for a home, he acquired the lot south of the corner of High and Deer Streets and built a framed central-chimney hall-parlor house that exhibits several early 18th-century construction techniques. The pilaster chimney corbels out just below the ridge to decorate the stack, a feature common only in the first decades of the 18th century in New England and perhaps the work of John Jones, the brickmason of the "1705" House formerly across Deer Street. This is the earliest surviving house in Portsmouth to use depthwise (7" x 3") joists to support plaster ceilings flush with the tie beam or summers. Later additions to the rear wall have enlarged the house.

3. The Simeon P. Smith House, was built between 1812 and 1823 and moved from Russell St. (the site of the Sheraton Hotel). The Smiths were living in the old Jabez Fitch house in 1822 and on Russell Street in 1823-24. The house may have been built simultaneously with the Gerrish House [# 1] as both houses demonstrate a new scale of artisan-mechanic domestic building but continued use of georgian floor plans and neoclassical detailing in the urban vernacular.

Hill First Floor Plans by Aldrich Associates

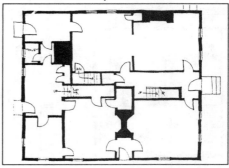

1.

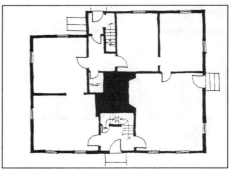

2.

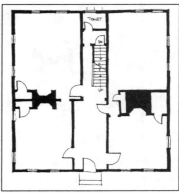

3.

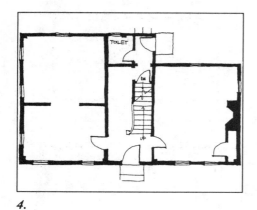

4.

4. The Whidden-Ward House was built by the housewright and joiner Michael Whidden Jr., perhaps as early as the 1720s, and rebuilt and enlarged in the decade after 1773 when Whidden's heirs sold it to Nathum Ward. Michael Whidden was one of a large extended family of joiners related to John Drew, the emigrant master-builder [see MacPheadris Warner House]. It was Drew, as James Garvin has demonstrated, who introduced the new formal Georgian style to Portsmouth after 1715 and, through the Whiddens, extended that tradition to the building of the Gov. John Langdon Mansion (1789) by Michael Whidden III. Ward sold the house in 1783 (presumably enlarged and improved) to blacksmith James Hill, who we know supplied architectural hardware to the New Hampshire Bank of 1804 [see Market Square]. HABS drawings of the 1930s show a typical Portsmouth triangular pediment over the doorway and a fine Georgian staircase inside.

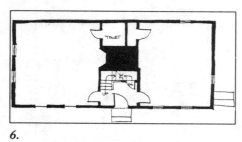

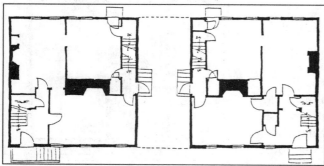

5. First and second floor plans.

5. The Nutter-Rymes Double Houses (*in situ*) could have been built as early as 1808-1809, although they do not appear as houses on the 1812 map. They were built by and for the master-builder/joiner James Nutter (who lived in the western end — "The Codfish" dining rooms and bar); Christopher Rymes, a merchant and land speculator rented out the eastern half. The house is unusual for the carriage drive archway between the two halves, with the second floor property line dividing the keystone. The odd interior plans (mirror images) and the interior detailing are a catalogue of Nutter's joiners work.

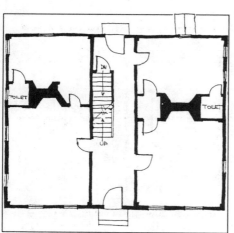

6.

6. A Sugar Warehouse, built ca. 1780 as part of a complex for distilling rum, was moved from School Street and remodeled into a home (c. 1810). It is said that John Goddard, one of the leading merchants along Market Street, moved his shop into this sugar warehouse after the fire of 1802 destroyed his place of business. It suggests the maritime and industrial character of these streets in the late 18th century and is only one of several Portsmouth houses that seem to have utilitarian structures at their rebuilt cores [see *Oracle House and Wentworth-Coolidge Mansion*].

7.

7. The Hart-Rice House (ca. 1756), originally located at 95 Deer Street next to the Shortridge-Rice House (with the broken scroll pediment), was the improvement to the empty lot mentioned in a deed of 1756. A typical larger Georgian house in style and plan, it demonstrates the high quality craftsmanship of its owner,

joiner Samuel Hart, Jr. (1701-1766). He was connected to both the Cutts and Moffatt families through his wife Bridget *[see Moffatt-Ladd House]*. Later owners Daniel Hart (1792) and Capt. William Rice (1804) remodeled very little, but rear kitchen additions of probable early date were removed during the relocation.

8. The Jeremiah Hill House, moved from the south side of Deer Street near the corner of Vaughan Street, was probably built about 1800 for one of the blacksmithing family of Hills.

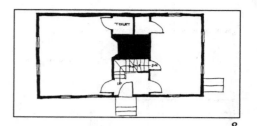

8.

9. Widow Phoebe Hart received the land on the western end of Deer Street when it was divided after her husband's death in 1808. Built sometime after 1812, the house has a circular staircase and a doorway that are usually associated with the pattern books of the English architectural writer, William Pain.

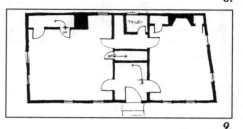

9.

10. Thomas Beck's 1760s five-room plan central chimney house was heavily remodeled ca. 1792. Fragments of the interior cornices were signed Hart, presumably the work of his cousin and neighbor Samuel Hart [see # 7]. The front doorway with a fanlight and pediment may derive from the style books of William Pain or, if after 1797, Asher Benjamin.

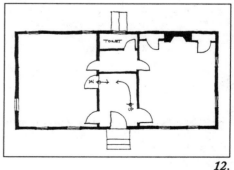

10.

11. The Hart-Shortridge Mansion was built ca. 1760 (perhaps by his cousin Daniel Hart) for John Hart, whose ropewalks were just south of the North Cemetery. When he died in 1790 he left this house to his housekeeper, Sarah Tripe, who became a widow in 1803. She passed it to Lois and Richard Shortridge (blacksmith) under the administration of her executor John Hart Shortridge. Between 1811-13 Shortridge transformed the Georgian two-story house (looking perhaps like #13 next door) into a Federal three-story mansion, paying local joiner Jacob Marston for work totaling $7000. Marston had just finished James Rundlet's house in 1807 *[see Rundlet-May House]* and was, therefore well acquainted with such formal ideas. Inside, the side rooms reflect changes of not only ca. 1812, but later efforts as well. In 1843 Richard Jenness (a future mayor of Portsmouth) acquired the house and may have added the portico, although it may have been built as late as 1877 when this became the "Home for Indigent Women."

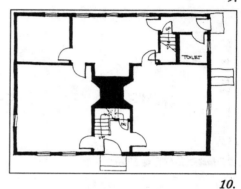

11.

12. Daniel Pinkham, a sea captain, built this three-story house just beyond the Phoebe Hart house about 1815 in contravention of the brick building law. His brother, Isaac, a cabinetmaker, may have been responsible for the interior detailing. Note how the narrow urban lots of western Deer Street (opposite what would later become the RR station) used a one-room deep plan with rear-wall chimneys and sited gable end to the street. The house also had a kitchen ell at the far end (now gone).

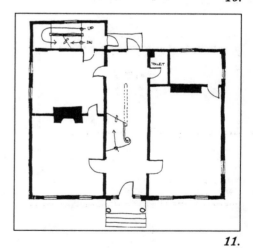

12.

13. Shortridge-Rice House, with a broken scroll pediment doorway (see p. 19) similar to the Moffatt Ladd window caps, was built about 1766 as the home of cabinetmaker Richard Shortridge. He died in 1777 leaving a "mansion house" to his widow. The house held his cabinet shop in one front room, and the front yard

contained a small house of earlier 18th century date. After the Revolution, his widow and her new husband sold the house in 1783 to Samuel and Thomas Rice, merchant brothers. Samuel and his wife (Elizabeth Hart) changed the front yard by finally removing the small house.

14. James Neal, an early 19th century import merchant, with his brother bought an empty lot here between the house of Samuel Gerrish and the Nathaniel Pierce estate in 1830. In 1832 Neal paid city tax on a new brick house (*in situ*), valued at $1700. A variant of the single pile plans of the two decades after the fire of 1813, the house has end chimneys and a service staircase to the kitchen ell. The curving staircase and much interior trim is rendered in the new Greek Revival style.

RMC

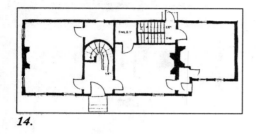

14.

Mofatt-Ladd Site Plan.

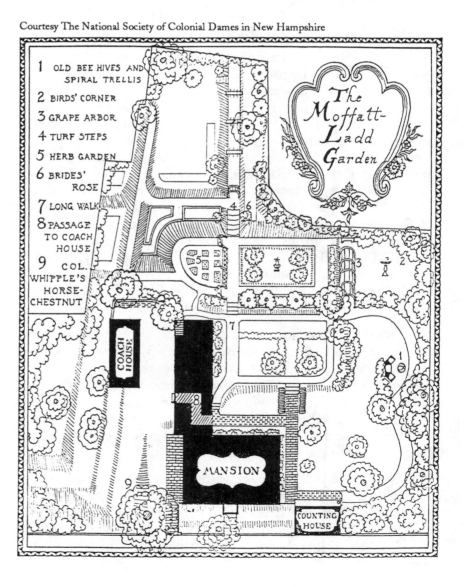

1 OLD BEE HIVES AND SPIRAL TRELLIS
2 BIRDS' CORNER
3 GRAPE ARBOR
4 TURF STEPS
5 HERB GARDEN
6 BRIDES' ROSE
7 LONG WALK
8 PASSAGE TO COACH HOUSE
9 COL. WHIPPLE'S HORSE-CHESTNUT

The Moffatt-Ladd Garden

COACH HOUSE

MANSION

COUNTING HOUSE

Moffatt-Ladd House

Built 1760-64
154 Market Street
Michael Whidden III, chief joiner; Richard Mills, turner;
Ebenezer Dearing, carver.

Of all the elite merchant houses of the 1760s, this built between 1760 and 1764 by Captain John Moffatt for the use of his son, Samuel (1738-80), was the most extraordinary and elaborate. A native of Somersetshire, Moffatt (1691-1786) arrived in the Piscataqua in 1723 as commander of a mast ship. After marrying the daughter of a wealthy Kittery landowner, he began purchasing land in Portsmouth in the 1730s. In the following decades Moffatt became one of the town's most prosperous merchant-ship owners and was a leader among the Masonian Proprietors. He began planning the house for his son as early as 1758 while his son was in England courting Catherine Mason, the daughter of the heir to huge tracts of New Hampshire lands controlled by the local elite. The conspicuous dwelling was apparently completed by their marriage in Portsmouth in January 1764. When Catherine wrote her father that month, she described herself as "now at housekeeping... Our house is Chiefly furnish'd and in a very genteel Maner for so large a one and young beginners."

The Moffatt house exceeded every known house in the Piscataqua in its grand size (nearly 50' x 40'), and few others approached it in conception or equalled it in finish. It used the hip-roofed frame in a new way, dispensing with the common "double-house" Georgian plan by placing chimneys on outer walls, in a way that John Mills, an English immigrant turner from Bristol who arrived in 1725, had just introduced locally *[see Mills-Whipple House]*. In the smaller Mills and larger Moffatt houses, nearly a quarter of the ground floor plan is given over to an impressive and spacious hall, entered directly from the street, in which the corner staircase and intermediate landing form the central focus. The Moffatt stairhall must have served as a summer parlor; a 1768 inventory of Samuel Moffatt's bankruptcy records 16 chairs, a 4 ½ foot mahogany table and a Persian carpet in this space.

Construction: Beginning in 1760, the house was raised by Michael Whidden III and sheathed, shingled, and fully finished by his crew of nine apprentices and two journeymen at a cost of some 14,000 pounds. This included the "Shop & Counting Room @ ye frunt of the house," but not the existing ca. 1830 office. The account was largely paid in credit at Moffatt's store over the next 20 years. The turnings of the stairs are attributed to Richard Mills (1730-1800), son of John Mills, on the basis of the identical plan and turned balusters in his own home (now moved to Middle Street) and charges in the Moffatt accounts from 1763–1766 *[see Mills-Whipple House]*. The Millses probably originated the distinctively ornamented mid-18th century triple balustrades (reeded, vase, and twisted) seen in the homes of the local elite.

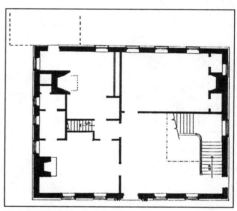

Drawing by Judy Quinn after
Great Georgian Houses of America
First Floor Plan, Moffatt-Ladd House.

While the fine joiner's work is that of Whidden and his crew, the lavish carving of Ebenezer Dearing provides much of the spectacular quality of the house's interior. This carver, then in his early thirties and living in Kittery, Maine, provided Moffatt with the sumptuous moldings and carved capitals, modillions, stair brackets, two chimney pieces, and "18 Roses." As the earliest work documented to a single carver in the area, it is a rosetta stone for attributing other surviving work. Like joiners and carvers in Portsmouth before and since, Dearing also provided a variety of craft work for Moffatt's small fleet of ships during the 1760s.

JLG

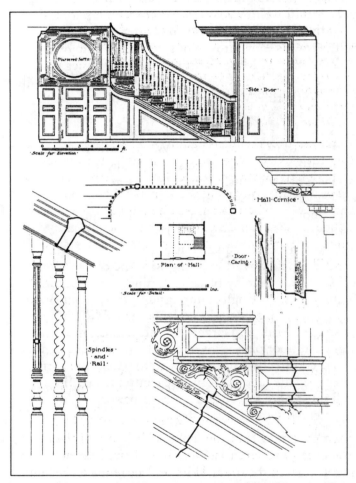

Hall and Stairway (1894) after F.M. Mann, The Georgian Period.

Later Alterations: Several significant changes appear to coincide with transfers of the property between generations into new families. In the great stair hall the imported scenic wallpaper, Vues d' Italie, dates to the 1815-1820 period. At this date a new side door near the foot of the stairs was cut through to provide access to the garden or counting house. The dining room also exhibits alterations of its interior finish from this period, including a new mantle, door moldings, and the introduction of an arched niche for the sideboard. All this work followed the 1814 transfer of the house from the last heir of John Moffatt to John and

Nathaniel A. Haven. Nathaniel's daughter, Maria Haven, and her husband, Alexander Ladd, moved their family into the house in 1819.

In 1861, after a century of modest alterations, Alexander H. Ladd purchased his sisters' interests in the house and embarked on large scale renovations. In November 1862 the local paper commented on:

> the extensive repairs, improvements, and general re-juvination which it has undergone the past season... make it a really new house in which all the rich outlines of a superb mansion of eighty years ago have been carefully preserved. The unique entrance hall of some twenty foot square remains as of old. The ancient paper on the walls of the chambers had passed too far to be retained. We noticed on one chamber the paper had been put on in single sheets, and that a series of copper-plate representations of hunting scenes blended in the figures of the paper, was extended around the wall... The extensive garden reaching to High street, makes this one of the most desirable seats in the centre of the city.

Ladd's alterations also included adding a vertical row of windows lighting the service spaces behind the kitchen chimney, modernizing the original southwest corner kitchen with a cast iron stove, and changes in paint colors and wallpapers throughout. This was removed in the 1960s when the museum restored the space as the original kitchen, discovering the fireplace and the decorative end of the original kitchen shelves like those in the Wentworth-Gardner house (which served as a model for missing elements).

RMC

The National Society of The Colonial Dames of America in the State of New Hampshire: Founded in 1892, the New Hampshire Society of the Colonial Dames is one of the many patriotic groups for women of proven colonial lineage that came into being at the turn of the century. In 1911 the Ladd family offered to long-term lease the house to the organization as a house museum. Mrs. James R. May *[see Rundlet-May house]* chaired the house committee during the 1912 restoration. Alterations of 1815-20 were generally accepted as part of the "colonial" history of the house, but those of later generations were not. Mrs. May generally followed antique scholar and curator Luke V. Lockewood's recommendations that the Colonial Dames remove most later gas chandeliers, paint the woodwork dead white, strip the floors of paint, and beautify the house according to the dictates of other colonial revival restorations. A second round of restoration activity in the 1960s removed the old cast iron stove and opened the kitchen fireplace to show the colonial kitchen. This was part of a movement to match the house to a 1768 room-by-room inventory of Samuel Moffatt's bankruptcy that has guided much of the museum's subsequent activity.

SG

Sources:

Architects Emergency Committee, *Great Georgian Houses of America* (1933):249-251

Garvin, *Academic Architecture* (1983).

_____, "That Little World Portsmouth," *Portsmouth Furniture*, Brock Jobe, ed.

Jane Nylander, "The Moffatt-Ladd House," *"A Noble and Dignified Stream"* (1992).

Philip Dana Orcutt, *The Moffatt-Ladd House, Its Garden and Its Period, 1763*. Portsmouth: NH Society of Colonial Dames of America, 1935.

Courtesy The Lamont Gallery, Phillips Exeter Academy, Exeter, New Hampshire (Gift of Thomas W. Lamont, Class of 1888)
"South West Prospect of the Seat of Colonel George Boyd at Portsmouth, New Hampshire, New England, 1774."

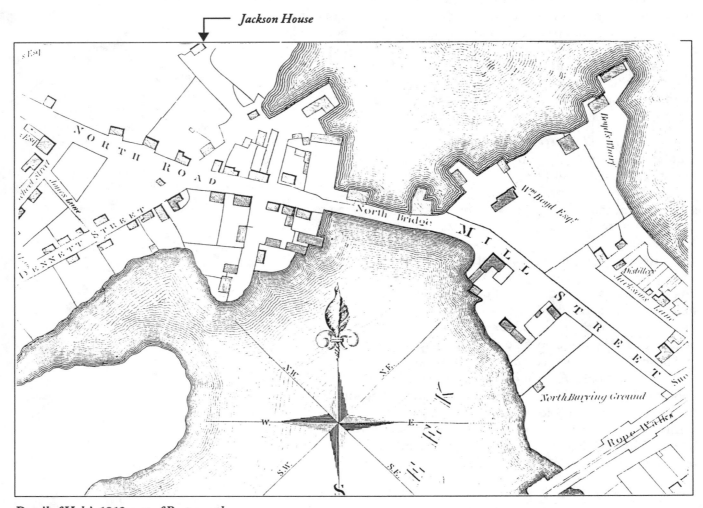

Detail of Hale's 1813 map of Portsmouth.

MAPLEWOOD AVENUE
BETWEEN DEER STREET AND
CHRISTIAN SHORE

Boyd–Raynes House
Built after 1744, enlarged after 1774

This 1774 landscape painting of the Boyd estate along the southern edge Islington Creek documents the successive achievements of several prosperous merchant shipbuilders. It is likely that the house was originally built by Michael Whidden II after 1744 for his cousin Nathaniel Meserve. Meserve (1705-58) was one of the Masonian Proprietors and the builder of the ship *America* for the Royal Navy in 1749. After both he and his eldest son lost their lives to smallpox in the second siege of Louisbourg in 1758, the property was sold in 1764 to the ambitious European immigrant merchant Peter Livius. Livius also acquired the right to dam the creek for power "capable of turning 7 or 8 different kinds of works besides 4 grist mills."

In 1771 the estate, with its mills and profitable shipyard, was purchased by George Boyd for whom this painting was done. The garden was surrounded by a white picket fence "and at intervals ... handsomely carved towering Grenadier's heads were placed on posts." Although Boyd was an opponent of the Wentworth's 'family government', he sought sanctuary in England after Congress banned exports to Britain and the West Indies. While his family remained and avoided confiscation of the estate, Boyd was proscribed and remained in self-imposed exile. When he finally attempted to return in 1787, he died on board ship two days before it reached Portsmouth.

After 1774, the house was dramatically expanded into a huge gambrel that dominated the northern waterfront. The gardens and adjoining lands were sold off for houses, and 19th century shipbuilder George Raynes occupied the mansion at the center of the city's largest shipyard at mid-century. The site is now occupied by the *Portsmouth Herald*, whose support for urban renewal in Portsmouth was consistent, and other commercial properties along the edge of the mill pond.

RMC

Sources:

Garvin, *Academic Architecture*: 157-162

Charles Wetherell, "The Letterbook of George Boyd, Portsmouth, New Hampshire, Merchant-shipbuilder, 1773-1775," *Historical New Hampshire*, 46:1-3 (Spring-Fall 1991).

CHRISTIAN SHORE

Known in the 17th century simply as the Fresh Creek area, the land across the waterway was first laid out after the great division of 1660 *[see Jackson House]*. According to local tradition, in the 18th century "when there were but few families beyond... the North mill bridge," some of these yeomen and artisans were said to be "strict adherents to puritan principles." Others, "more loose in their habits" frequented Foss's Tavern across the creek in the old North End and, after drinking and socializing, would joke, "Well, we must leave for Christian Shore," sarcastic reference to their neighbors.

The bridge over the water course formed a direct connection between the North End and the farms and craft industries of Christian Shore. After 1795 North Road, now Maplewood Avenue, connected the town with the Piscataqua Bridge and the First New Hampshire Turnpike beyond. When 15 house lots in "New or North Portsmouth" were advertised in 1805, their value was enhanced by this highway to Concord. The "largest part of the country produce passes by those lots into town... [and] there are several good stands for stores." Other advertisements show the increasing density of this neighborhood; one suggested "altering the Blacksmith's shop into a Dwelling House."

Houses clustered near the mill bridge extended down Dennett Street and around a new brick school house by 1800 on North School [now Prospect] Street. To the west, beyond Col. Samuel Sherburne's 18th-century farm and orchard, a large tract was subdivided into house lots by local joiner John Miller, "an enterprising, capable architect." Miller built several of the best houses on Islington Street and "on land on Christian Shore, where he laid out Woodbury and Sparhawk Streets." When he died in 1813 Miller had lumber waiting on the southern shore of the mill pond for a bridge to be built to connect his lands to the Rock Pasture.

Among the best documented new houses is that built and finished for Captain John Bowles by John Miller and James Nutter in 1806. A 50 foot square lot, formerly owned by Peter Livius, provided the site near Bowles's wharf and grist mill. Surrounded by smaller central chimney house types (many attributable to Miller) the Bowles house was among the largest of the new homes at Christian Shore; the 1807 tax shows Bowles among the top 20% of Portsmouth's taxpayers [see John Bowles House].

In 1817 the state legislature exempted Capt. John Bowles's new grist mill from brick construction required by Portsmouth's fire laws because it "can not be erected of brick or stone without great inconvenience & additional expence." This was, in fact, a wind mill placed atop the knoll on the southern shore approximately where the Sheraton Hotel stands today. He also had a mill along the north mill dam which, like Gideon Walker's, ground grains for local use and possibly for export as meal or as ship's biscuits. When he died in 1837, Bowles also owned a "Glue House" containing an iron boiler behind his home. In fact, Bowles's 1806 contract with Miller and Nutter, like that with Thomas Leigh, was to be paid in "merchantable sole leather."

A plan of the site and its neighborhood shows where Bowles acquired the hides of tanned leather used to pay for his house and why he invested in a glue house. The waterfront east of Bowles's house was occupied by Jackson's slaughter house, bark house, and tan yard. Nathaniel Jackson III, one of five master tanners to join the local Mechanic's Society at its 1803 inception, died in 1810. His old tannery was later run by Gilman Dearborn and, from the mid-1830s, by Moses Horoe Goodrich. When Goodrich retired in 1895 at age 80, he was the last tanner and currier in Portsmouth and the Goodrich Tannery the sole survivor of this once-flourishing trade.

When Richard Shortridge advertised nine acres along the North Mill Pond for sale in 1805, he described it as having "Clay sufficient to make bricks for a century." Across the street from John Bowles's new house, along the edge of the mill pond, was the Dodge Pottery. By 1821 the pottery at this wharf was operated by Joseph Dodge and his son and was listed in 1832 as employing three men at $1 a day and making $1200 worth of wares each year for local distribution in Maine and New Hampshire. As late as the 1850 census, a Jabez Dodge had his house and potters shop at 13 North Road, although he was the only potter and only part-time. In 1839 Nathaniel Jackson IV sold two and a half acres east of his farm on Northwest Street [see Richard Jackson House] to George Rogers, of Eliot, Maine, with "the privilege of building a brick yard on the flat." Rogers is listed in the city Directory as a "brick manufacturer" from 1839 until 1860. The brick trade was revived in 1873 when Jenness and Lamprey, using brick molding machinery that could turn out 10,000 bricks a day, erected kilns and a drying floor large enough for 40,000 at once.

Christian Shore was also home to half a dozen joiners in 1821, about equal to the number of tanners and cordwainers working at Jackson's tannery. By 1850 the number of joiners had risen to 15, many of whom helped construct the Franklin School in 1847. By 1850 the number of "carpenters" exploded to 29, including 13 from as far south as Massachusetts and north as the Canadian maritimes who lived together at Mary Dixon's boarding house. Undoubtedly, they all worked as ships carpenters at one of the four large ship yards in Portsmouth. The George Raynes ship yard was just across the creek, while the Tobey & Littlefield yard, established in 1853 during the peak of a second ship building boom, was located nearby on Nobles Island. Between 1840 and 1859 the District of Portsmouth built 169 vessels, including 115 three-masted sailing ships and 28 clipper ships. The Raynes yard alone built 10 clippers, five of them more than 1000 tons.

RMC

Sources:

Garvin, *Historic Portsmouth*.

Pickett, *Portsmouth's Heyday in Shipbuilding*.

John Miller in *Portsmouth Morning Chronicle*, 12 May 1876.

1850 U.S. Census enumeration and manufacturing schedules.

Bowles Collection, Portsmouth Athenæum.

Portsmouth Oracle and *New Hampshire Gazette*, 1805-1810.

John Bowles House

Built 1806
259 Maplewood Ave.
John Miller and James Nutter, joiners

Crossing over the bridge into Christian Shore, the first house on the right is a large house covered with gray siding and recognizable by the two protruding window bays on the first story. This much-altered 1806 house is one of the few Christian Shore houses for which several building documents survive. While it is not available to tour, its construction history is a valuable illustration of the methods by which this and other neighborhoods were built in the early 19th century.

John Bowles House.

In December 1805 Bowles hired Thomas Leigh of Berwick, Maine, to provide a 40 by 32 foot house frame and timbers "for a hipt roof agreeable to a plan." Sills, plates, and posts of pine were to be stiffened with hardwood braces; the remaining studs, joists, and other materials to be of hemlock according to a schedule of timbers. Leigh promised to deliver the framing members, pine and hemlock boards, and shingles by water to Bowles's wharf by the next May. On February 9, 1806 Bowles agreed with Miller and Nutter to raise this frame over a cellar near his wharf, to frame and build a two story scullery addition, 15 feet long and 10 feet wide, across the back of Leigh's frame (taking care that the ridge pole of the rear ell's hipped roof fall well below the dentilled "Double Cornice" of the main block).

The Bowles contract is a virtual catalog of Portsmouth building ideas and ornament for this era. The six-paneled front door, identical to many found throughout the city, was capped by a "pitched pediment and fan light." The rear 9 over 6 windows had but "single architraves," the six-panel back door was capped with a flat entablature and transom lights, and the addition had a simple four-panel door and four windows of smaller six over six sash. The roof had "board spouts" or gutters all round with "a Conduction to Lead the water into the Cellar near the Scullary." On the roof was a glazed scuttle or "ski light" and there was lead flashing used around the chimney. Window frames were to be installed "agreeable to the plan." Those on the front and ends, for 10" x 14" sash (below) and 10'x 13" (above), were surrounded by "Double Architraves" with three inch plain sills.

Inside only the western half and the rear ell were completely finished, the eastern rooms were left unfinished although flooring was laid throughout. This was not uncommon, although such detailed evidence of partial completion is rare. The two western rooms and the entry hall on both floors were lathed and plastered, the back and cellar stairs finished, but the "fore Stairs" or main staircase was only "to be rough stept." Doors to the completed western side were finished, those from the hall to the eastern rooms and addition were not. The sitting room contained three six-panel doors and three windows with sliding shutters in two parts, all with "double architrave" surrounding them. Two doors led to closets on either side of the chimney and its "handsome chimney pease" containing ovals with inlaid exotic woods. Walls were plastered to the boxing of the corner posts and a single cornice above. The kitchen and the upstairs rooms had more simple finishes: six doors of only four panels in the kitchen, "common" chimney or mantel-pieces upstairs, and "as many Closets as Can be made Convenient." The ell contained a nine foot-wide scullery with a sink, closets, and shelves, as well as a six foot wide pantry and a small flight of stairs to an unfinished scullery chamber and a six foot long "meal room" that had a door leading back to the upper rear hall.

RMC

Richard Jackson House

Built ca. 1664 with additions
Northwest Street
Owner: Society for the Preservation of New England Antiquities

The earliest extant timber-framed building in either Maine or New Hampshire, the ca. 1664 Jackson House is noteworthy for its use of sawn lumber, for its cumulative plan development, and for the relatively unobtrusive 1930-32 restoration by SPNEA founder, William Sumner Appleton. Sited on a hillside overlooking the North Mill Pond, its added lean-to roof slopes nearly into the earth. An important early example of the impact of the region's commercial lumbering on traditional English timber-framed building practices, it is located at the opposite end of the mill pond from John Cutt's 1660 saw mill. The vast export trade in sawn lumber from the Piscataqua would have made these building materials readily available even without this local source. Occupied by Jackson descendents until purchased for the SPNEA, the house was already a well-known antiquarian landmark evoking romantic images because it had not suffered massive changes during the 19th century.

Ownership: The agricultural site was laid out to Richard Jackson, a cooper by trade. In 1664 he was one of several living "on the other side of Strawbery bank Creek" who petitioned their grants in the great land division of 1660 be laid out along the northern edge of the creek. His initial 25 acres adjoined the lands of his wife's father and brother, shipbuilders whom Jackson is said to have assisted in their trade.

Richard Jackson died in 1718, having outlived two sons, John and Nathaniel (names repeated in most succeeding generations). It was not until 1727, however, that the house and lands were divided between Nathaniel's widow and her other children. In that year, the farm lands and animals for which Margaret Elkins Jackson was taxed included 12 polls, the largest single number of adult males over 16 under a single roof in town. The additions and interior alterations of the late 17th and early 18th centuries reflect this complex family history that kept the dwelling in multiple family ownership over several generations.

Courtesy Strawbery Banke Museum
Richard Jackson House before restoration.

Plan: The original ca. 1664 house is the two-story, central chimney, lobby entrance hall and parlor core. Half of the house was deeded to John Jackson in 1690/91, described as "all ye chambers & halfe of ye Garrett, ye use of ye Lower Westward Room [kitchen], not hindering me sd Richard for my necessary occassion [i.e. cooking] as also ye seller under ye Westward end." John died in 1691 and his brother, Nathaniel, in 1713.

The first addition, a partial lean-to called "the butry" in Nathaniel's 1715 probate inventory, was cut into the bank behind the west kitchen and later extended across the whole rear wall. This third ground-floor room was an unheated service space, like that originally added to the ca. 1637 Fairbanks house in Dedham, Massachusetts, a pattern now thought typical of New England central chimney houses well into the 18th century. That this lean-to was completed across the whole rear wall by 1727 is suggested by the division of the old kitchen and "the Western end of the lean-to" to Nathaniel's widow. At this time her son Nathaniel was granted the other ground floor room, "the Eastern ground room in the Lento" and "one half the Western Chamber."

His brother John, who had been "Delerious above one year," was granted only "one half of ye Western Chamber." The divided western chamber still survives and appears to be part of a substantial interior renovation of the early 18th century that also saw the staircase rebuilt, altered the partition wall to the west chamber, and remodeled the doors with applied bolection moldings in imitation of panels.

At some unidentified mid-18th century date, a one story addition to the east end extended beyond the façade of the old house; its garret was called a "Shop Chamber" in the 1810 inventory of tanner Nathaniel Jackson III. It is not clear whether the division of the east ell is original or whether the stair to the garret that divides the structure into two lower rooms is a later alteration. If so, it must date no later than the chalk graffiti dates of 1769 on boarding in its front room.

The fourth Nathaniel Jackson willed the western half of the house to his brother Benjamin in 1824, which may be near the date of a shed-roof lean-to at the western end of the house, which brought the plan to its present configuration.

Construction: The frame of the original core is composed of an exposed sill, massive corner and chimney posts jowled and braced at the second story, a ceiling frame of longitudinal summers at both stories, and a purlin roof of principal rafters over the four pairs of major posts.

There were no original wall studs, except those holding the window frames. The exterior walling is entirely composed of 1" thick vertical cladding or boards running from sill to plate. These were battened on the inside with waney strips, still evidenced in the rear west chamber, and elsewhere covered with lath and plaster. The unclapboarded exterior of the vertical board walls can be seen from within the rear lean-to; the west wall, which may have been reboarded before the early 19th-century lean-to addition, can be seen from a small door in the west front chamber.

As with all vertical plank houses in the Piscataqua, the second floor wall braces — like the window studs — are "exposed," as the lath and plaster is applied directly to the inside battens and vertical boarding. In the rear western chamber (divided by 1727 for the insane John) there is no evidence that portions of the rear wall were ever plastered (at least, after the rear lean-to was constructed).

Drawings by David Hart for Richard Candee
Framing of 1664 Jackson House.

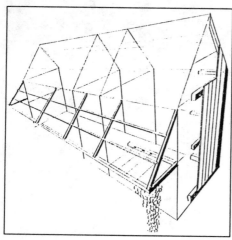

D. Hart
Vertical board walling, Jackson House.

The principal and purlin roof frame is ubiquitous in Piscataqua first-period buildings, perhaps reflecting the substantial settlement from the British west-country (as Cummings asserts) but certainly a function of the widespread availability of sawn lumber as the sub-surface for shingles. The Jackson house roof uses four pairs of principal rafters framed above the major posts, collar beams, two purlins, and a ridgepole at the apex to support vertical roof boards.

The floor/ceiling framing is composed of longitudinal summer beams at both stories, atypical in Massachusetts and later Piscataqua buildings. Cummings has suggested this feature may have once been common in houses of less expensive construction, which might include the Jackson house with its simple three-bay roof frame.

The exposed ceiling frame, cleaned of later paint evidence by Appleton during restoration, is decorated with quarter-round chamfers with a collar and lambs tongue termination. Floor joists are tusk tenoned into the summer beams, but rest on the front and rear girts. The joists, which may have been waterpower-sawn like the floor boarding, have been planed and neatly chamfered at their bottom edges.

Other significant interior finish includes the shadow-molded overlapping wall sheathing between the staircase and east parlor (like that at Gedney House, 1665, Salem, Massachusetts) and several batten doors. The door from the hall-kitchen to the lean-to has shadow molded decoration as does that from the entry to the parlor chamber. Doors to the east chamber lean-to and the parlor door to the entry show applied bolection moldings dating from the 1700-1720 alterations. Window casements are restored to the clear measurements of the window-stud locations and notching in the exterior boarding for window sill and header. Casement design was based on a Nantucket partial frame and the window frame Appleton had discovered *in situ* at the Browne house in Watertown, Massachusetts.

Courtesy SPNEA
West Chamber during restoration, 1920s.

Courtesy SPNEA
Principal rafter/common purlin roof frame.

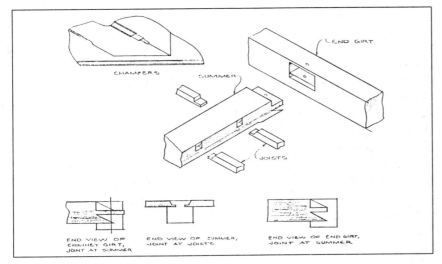

Hart drawing
Floor Framing.

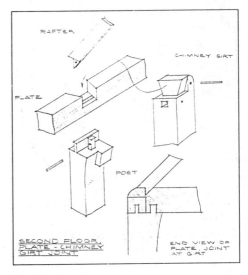

Hart drawing
Plate, Post, and Tie-Beam.

Masonry: The central chimney stack as well as the majority of the cellar foundation and first-floor framing were all replaced in 1949 by a restoration contractor working for the Society's curator of properties, Felicia Doughty Kingsbury. She and the contractor claim to have followed the evidence of what they thought was a replacement (18th century) stack, although Appleton's earlier assessment was that because of its clay mortar the stack was original but altered. Pre-restoration photographs show the outward appearance to be nearly identical to the much altered chimney. This includes the rounded west or rear end that protrudes into the lean-to space at the ground story. Appleton interpreted this as a rebuilding; we will never know now.

Restoration Philosophy:
Letter from William Sumner Appleton to John P. Brown, 1932:

You ask why we kept the empty little bedroom with the corner fireplace. There were many who advised its removal and we consulted local sentiment in the matter and were informed that it was overwhelming in favor of keeping the additions at each end of the house. These two extensions with the lean-to are the three additions that make the building so picturesque... The house is... one of those best left showing the course of its evolution. I wouldn't have even changed the windows, excepting that the evidence was so overwhelming; also the window frames that were found would have to have been scrapped anyway, and the building lent itself admirably to a restoration of the five old ones on its front. I was strongly urged by some to remove the partition in the west chamber, making that again one large chamber like the other. This seems to me a most unwise proceeding for... I would have to destroy much interesting old work and should have substituted for it a new wall on the staircase and entry. Even were this new wall built of old stock, it would still remain mine, and I much prefer the interesting alteration made by some long dead generation of Jacksons.

RMC

Sources:

Candee, *Wooden Building in Early Maine & NH* (1976).

Cummings, *The Framed Houses of Massachusetts Bay, 1625-1725.*

SPNEA Archives

Franklin School

Built 1847
348 Maplewood Ave.
attributed to William Tucker after Henry Barnard

Constructed in 1847, as can be seen from the cast iron date in the south gable, the Franklin School replaced an early 19th century brick Christian Shore school house on Prospect Street afterward remodeled as a dwelling. The new structure was perhaps the first large school in New Hampshire that incorporated ideas about the proper environment for education promoted by Henry Barnard's *School-House Architecture* (Hartford: 1842) and followed his plans for the Public High School in Middletown, Connecticut.

This school preceded the efforts of the Commissioner for Common Schools in New Hampshire between 1847 and 1850 to promote Barnard's ideas and designs. One small school in nearby Greenland, N.H. (published in Barnard's 1850 edition of *School Architecture*) and several one story brick schools erected in Portsmouth's rural districts between 1842 and 1853, were the most common expression of this public effort at educational reform during a flurry of school building in the 1840s and 1850s.

A response to a doubling of the school age population, from 305 in 1841 to 610 ten years later, Christian Shore's new District 1 school was one product of growth spurred by the revival of ship-building and the introduction of a substantial textile industry. Indeed it is probably not accidental that stylistically the Franklin School resembles a Greek Revival high school at Lowell, Massachusetts, published in Barnard's book. In 1847 it clearly echoed the brick and granite design of the new Portsmouth Steam Factory directly across the North Mill Pond.

While its local designer has not been identified, it is tentatively assigned to William Tucker, a local carpenter-builder, who was reimbursed in 1849 for travel to Roxbury "to obtain school plans" for another school project, and who sketched a balcony proposed for the Athenæum (see p. 93). The itemized construction costs in the 1848 Town Report are a catalog of the city's and the neighborhood's building trades. Bricks came from George Rogers' brick yard and were laid up by several masons living on Dennett Street. Neighborhood joiners provided interior finish and others at Christian Shore provided materials as well as stone cutting, blacksmithing, and other services. Boards and other lumber were run through the steam powered saw and planing mill across the mill pond. Used as a grammar school from 1847 to 1919, Franklin School served as a carpenter's millwork shop (1921-23), a furniture warehouse (1923-43), and apartments thereafter until rehabilitated as condominiums in the mid-1980s by its current owners.

WO & RMC

Courtesy Portsmouth Athenæum
Franklin School.

Source:
Research by Woodard Openo

Courtesy Portsmouth Athenæum
61 Bow St. (center) remodelled after 1870 for Eldridge Brewery office.

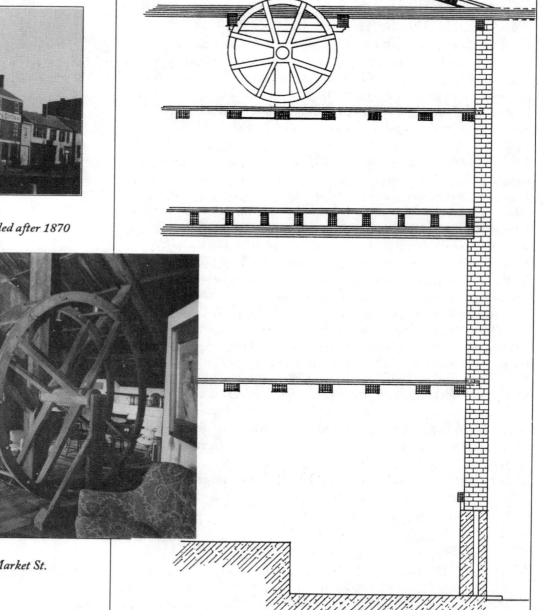

Courtesy M.S. Carter
Hoist and attic frame, 175 Market St.

Measured by Robert Buerglener, Tom Denenberg, drawing by Amy Amidon
Section, warehouse with hoist, 61 Bow St.

PORTSMOUTH HARBOR AND WATERFRONT

The mouth of the Piscataqua opens between New Castle Island on the southwest and the ledges and islets off Gerrish Island on the northeast. A mile up the Piscataqua, a half-mile crook forms Portsmouth Harbor, the major ice-free, deep-water anchorage between Boston, Massachusetts and Portland, Maine. About two miles from the mouth, islands constrict the main channel and produce a very rapid tidal flow. Seven miles from the mouth, the river branches at Dover Point, flowing in and out of Little and Great Bays and tributaries leading to the head-of-tide towns of Exeter, Newmarket, Durham, Dover, and Somersworth in New Hampshire and South Berwick in Maine. A changing stream of cargoes arrived at the wharves of Portsmouth, some for local consumption and others re-loaded in gundalows (shallow draft, lateen rigged cargo boats with masts that could be lowered for passage under bridges) to upriver towns and thence into the hinterlands. European and West Indies goods, salt for the fisheries, cotton for the textile mills begun in the 1820s, and iron for railroad construction and coal for industrial and residential use. Forest depletion brought an end to the milling and export of wood by the 19th century; by the end of the century, upriver brick yards produced the only significant export cargo.

Courtesy Portsmouth Athenæum
Bow Street Waterfront and Church Hill, Davis Bros. 1886.

Today the principal cargoes entering the harbor, aside from seafood brought in by the local fishing fleet, are coal and oil for the electric generating station and Sprague Energy Company's tank farm in Newington, gypsum for a wallboard plant at Freeman's Point, and mountains of salt unloaded at the pier opposite the Sheraton Portsmouth Hotel. Scrap metal stored on the State Pier on Noble's Island and huge reels of transoceanic cable produced at the Simplex plant in Newington are the major outgoing cargoes.

JP

MARKET AND BOW STREETS

From the Sheraton Hotel or Moffatt-Ladd House to the South End of Portsmouth, Market, Ceres and Bow streets follow the river's edge. The large brick buildings with four story façades and exposed basements on the waterside were built as shops and warehouses after the fires of 1802 and 1806. Most street façades have been remodeled over the years, but many buildings still retain large wooden hoists in their top floors. Two hoists still survive *in situ*; that at 61 Bow Street (built 1807) has "1825" gouged into the large wheel. A wheel from the adjoining warehouse can be seen, reused as a ceiling decoration, in the basement of Poco Diablo restaurant (47 Bow Street).

RMC

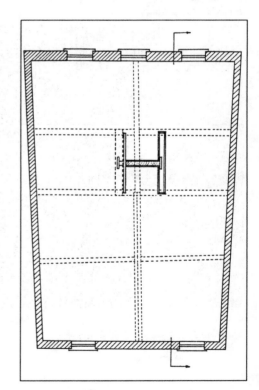

Measured by Robert Buerglener, Tom Denenberg, drawing by Amy Amidon
Plan, 61 Bow St.

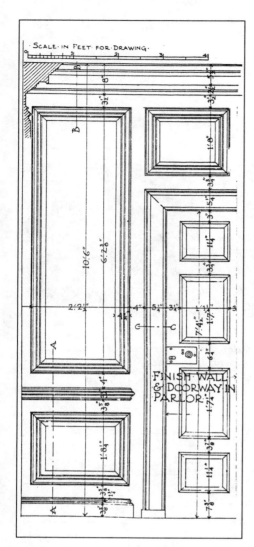

Drawing, Frank Chouteau Brown 1932.
Courtesy SPNEA

Raised panel wall and door, parlor.

Courtesy Warner House Association

*John Drew's bill to Archibald MacPheadris
1716.*

*A Coppy from Mr. J^{no} Drew Acc^o for work done to Capt Arch^d
Macpheadris Brick House at Piscataqua*

To 94 1/2 Squars of framing in the floor	
&c Roofs at 15 ^{d}	70..10..—
42 Sash windows & frame	84.. —..—
8 Lutherns with Ornaments	24.. —..—
to the front door wth Ornaments	10.. —..—
2 back Doors	8.. —..—
2 Celler Doors plaine	3.. —..—
to 100 foot of mod.^{l} on Cornist	20.. —..—
to 250 foot of trunks & Gutter at 2^d/	25.. —..—
to 26 Square of double boarding of roof at 8/	10..12..—
to 33 Sqs of partition at 5/	8.. 5..—
to 80 foot of Cants at 18^d	6.. —..—
to 8 Mantletrees and tassles	1.. 4..—
to 50 3/4 Sq: of flooring at 12/	30.. 9..—
to 3 1/2 Sq: of Ditto at 30/	5.. 5..—
to 63 Steps of back Stairs, Cellar & Cupilo @ 5/	15..15..—
to 26 foot of rails and bannisters	6..10..—
to 24 Steps of the great Stairs	12.. —..—
to 24 foot of raile and bannisters, ramp^d. And twisted	12.. —..—
to 96 foot of Cornist to y^e	4..16..—
to 13 Strait Arches	6..10..—
to 7 Celler windows framed	3..10..—
to 24 foot of posts in the Celler	—..12..—
to 30 Sq: of roof flooring at 4/	6.. —..—
to Dressing 15..0..0 Sheet lead at 9/4	6..15..—
to Casting 700 of Sash leads	2..18.. 4
to ye Cupilow with Ornaments	30.. —..—
to 96 foot rail & Bannisters @ 3/	14.. —..—
to An Arch.^{d} Ceiling & 2 double arches	15.. —..—
from 1.st Decemb.^{r} 1716 to ye 1.st May	
23 weeks lost time	46.. —..—
to Attend ye Bricklay^{er} 23 weeks and	
Giving them directions in their work	23.. —..—
to 874 yd^s of wainscott at 6/	23.. —..—
to 1050 yd^s plaistering @ 12^d	52..10..—
to a Beaufet in the little parlor	3.. —..—
to a Ditto in the Dining room	10.. —..—
to 1230 yds painting at 3/	184..19..—
to 42 window frames at 8/	6.. 6..—
to 776 Sq: of Sashes at @ 3	9..14..—
	£ 1040..12.. 4

MacPheadris-Warner House

Built 1716-18
150 Daniel St., corner Chapel St.
Designer/builder: John Drew

A unique survival in coastal New England, the MacPheadris-Warner House has been described as the finest example of an early 18th-century urban brick residence in the region. It is an early example of the transfer of provincial classical brick design to America, of which there are only fragmentary remains and documents of similar work in Boston. Even more unusual is the survival of original painted murals on the walls of the staircase, evidence of an "M"-shaped roof beneath the later gambrel alterations, and the quality and quantity of high-style interior finish throughout the well-documented house.

The brick house was built for Archibald MacPheadris, a Scots emigrant who established himself in Portsmouth as owner of a nearby ill-fated iron works up the Piscataqua River in 1715. A merchant-ship owner with six vessels by 1717, he attempted to lure Irish tenants to work his large New Hampshire landholdings. By then he could write to England, "I am now settled and married in this place to Col. Wintworth's daughter." Sarah, daughter of Lt. Governor John Wentworth, was then 15 years old. This alliance was successful; MacPheadris entered a business partnership with his brother-in-law Benning Wentworth and in 1722 joined the Royal Governor's council. His two houses, one slave, and stock in trade placed him just in the top 10% of the town's 1727 provincial tax payers. Like most of Portsmouth's elite, he also accumulated extensive lands in rural townships. When he died in 1729, his estate was valued at 6330 pounds and contained (beside his house, ships, and land) two black slaves he acquired in 1726.

Construction: In December 1715/16 MacPheadris bought two large lots on Daniel Street and work commenced immediately. Construction was supervised by John Drew, a London-trained joiner with extensive experience in the newest brick domestic architecture, who seems to have worked in Boston before arriving in the Piscataqua with two other English joiners. As James Garvin has demonstrated, Drew's daughter Ann married into the Whidden family of local housewrights and joiners, establishing a dynasty of builders throughout the 18th century. He is now known to have had access to, and perhaps owned, a copy of Palladio (the first published English translation) between 1716 and 1719, placing him among the first known builders in New England to do so.

Building accounts for this Flemish bond brick house and a similar wooden version across the street have long been known. Our knowledge of Drew's English background and the context for the house design is greatly increased by the discovery of an account book of his 1706-1709 joiner's work in Deptford, a London suburb important for its Royal Dockyards. There, as he would in America, Drew acted as a general contractor overseeing carpentry, brick laying, plastering, tile work, painting and glazing, as well as

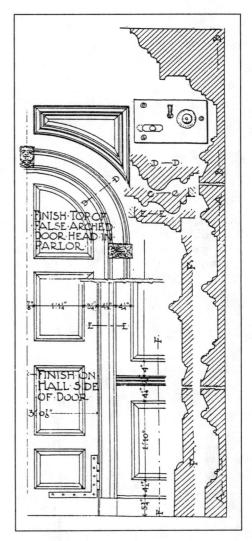

Drawing, Frank Chouteau Brown 1932.
Courtesy SPNEA

Details, arched doorhead, parlor, entry hall door, and profiles.

domestic and ships joinery. One of his English building accounts is for work on a house built by the mason-contractor Thomas Lucas on Union (now Albury) Street. A row of these houses survive to show that Lucas brought Deptford the newest building styles from the center of London. While somewhat smaller than this fully-realized Georgian plan, the Aubury Street row contains elements of spatial organization that can be seen in the MacPheadris house. It may, thus, owe as much to recent London domestic planning of urban terraces as to models like the Clarke-Franklin house in Boston, to which it is often compared.

Drew's bill for erecting and finishing the MacPheadris house noted extensive interior painting, including 'arabesques' on the wainscoting (surviving in the southwest front room), but not the elaborate staircase murals. The murals were discovered about 1850 under layers of later wallpaper. Those flanking the arched window of the stair landing depict two life-size American Indians figures, Mohawk sachems of the Iroquois nation. These are two of the four sachems, or "Indian Kings," taken to London to meet Queen Anne in 1710 by Peter Schuyler of Albany. The four posed for English painters, from which prints were made that circulated to the elite of the colonies. It is believed that either Nehemiah Partridge or a related Piscataqua painter used these prints as the source of the 1718-20 murals. The vignettes on the side walls, including the obscure iconography of the west wall, were apparently done at the same time by this local school of artists.

Later Alterations: After MacPheadris died in 1729, his wife remarried and in 1740 moved to Boston. The house was rented from 1742 to 1759 to her older brother, the royal governor Benning Wentworth. It may be that the house was refitted for the governor's mansion, but the date of the new frontispiece with segmental pediment and the alternating pediments of the roof dormers is uncertain. While it has long been assumed that the roof was almost immediately turned from a pair of pitched roofs in M-shape to a gambrel (by framing over the V), physical evidence suggests that this, too, occurred several years later. The present cupola has also been rebuilt, but it stands upon early supports, probably those for the original cupola described in Drew's accounts.

In the 1750s Benning Wentworth relocated to a rural estate in Little Harbor *[see Wentworth-Coolidge Mansion]* while unsuccessfully asking the provincial legislature to purchase the brick house from his sister as a permanent governor's mansion. Bills in 1759 for the repairs to the windows suggest that he retained the house until that date. In 1760 Jonathan Warner, a Portsmouth merchant and member of the King's Council,

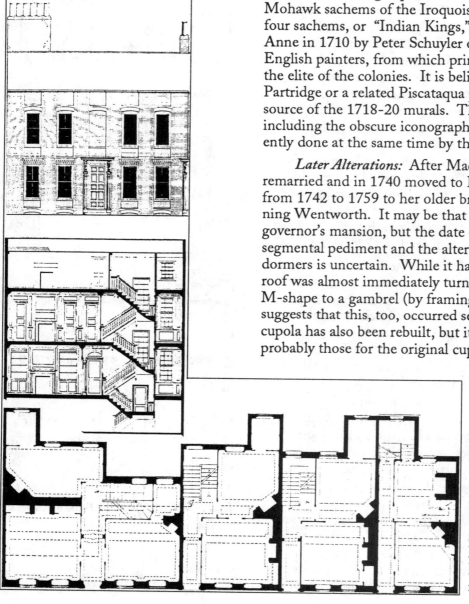

Elevation and section 24 Albury St. Ground floor plans 18-24 Albury St., Deptford, England. Thomas Lucas, mason.
Courtesy English Heritage

married MacPheadris's daughter Mary, a childless widow of John Osborne of Boston. He inherited the house from her and lived there until his death in 1814. Whether the 1750s tiles surrounding the fireplaces, the iron firebacks inside, and the polychrome turned balusters of the main staircase were added during Wentworth's or Warner's occupancy is difficult to determine. Nor is it certain when during the 19th century the door between the front and rear parlors was closed.

Hales's 1812 map shows two rear additions to the house that are no longer extant: a small ell off the small rear parlor or office, and a larger service wing offset from the northwest corner of the kitchen that preceded the present 19th century ell. After Warner's death the wooden kitchen wing was moved to its own site at the corner of Sheafe and Chapel Streets where antiquarians say it became a home for black families. The shadow line of half its two story pitched roof can still be seen on the upper floor of the rear brick wall, as can evidence of an earlier dormer or luthern window that originally cut through the cornice to light the rear service staircase. Until 1963 the east brick wall was covered by clapboarding of apparent 18th century materials, over an earlier rusticated stucco finish. Unwise removal has created serious water damage, possibly the reason these finishes were applied over the brick originally.

After 1814 the house passed to Warner's niece Elizabeth Sherburne (who briefly rented it to a local doctor) and then to her son John N. Sherburne. As early as the 1890s, the Sherburne family seems to have occasionally opened the house to appropriately genteel visitors. New Jersey architect Joy Wheeler Dow visited Portsmouth just to "make the acquaintance of such a raving, tearing beauty as the house built by Capt. McPhaedris." He saw Portsmouth as deserving of special recognition (after Annapolis) as a source city for the American Renaissance he advocated, the use or adaptation of elite domestic architecture from colonial and federal America for contemporary design.

> Here is a wonderful old house intensely affecting to stand and contemplate. It seems to be sinking into the earth, as many old houses in England have the appearance of doing, and possesses a tone like a Stradivarius violin, which cannot be counterfeited. The day in the summer of 1896, when I spent a delightful hour in its company, was a sort of reception day, I remember. There were many summer visitors calling, and they "de-ared" it and gushed over it as society people gush over a Chopin etude, because they think it proper to do so, without appreciating the subtle sentiment of the thing at all.

A number of myths about the house were already current: that it was erected in 1723, that the bricks were imported from England (or Holland), and that it cost the owner "something like the equivalent of $30,000." The house passed from the family to the Warner House Association, formed in 1931, to prevent the house from being sold as a gasoline station site.

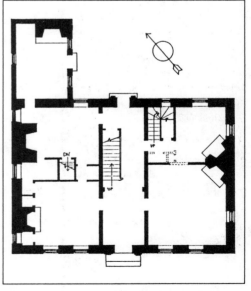

Drawing by Judy Quinn after *Great Georgian Houses of America (1933)*

First floor plan, MacPheadris-Warner House.

Sources:

Malvina Bolus, "Four Kings Came to Dinner With Their Honours," *The Beaver* Autumn 1973): 4-11.

[Charles W. Brewster], "Walks About Portsmouth," *Portsmouth Journal*, June 16, 1853, p. 2.

Richard M. Candee, *Early Wooden Building* (1976): 349-351.

Abbott Lowell Cummings, "The Beginnings of Provincial Renaissance Architecture in Boston, 1690-1725," *Journal of the Society of Architectural Historians*, 42 (March 1983): 43-53.

Joy Wheeler Dow, *American Renaissance* (NY: Wm. Comstock, 1904): 65-67.

James L. Garvin, *Academic Architecture* (1983): 26-74.

_____, "That Little World Portsmouth,"

Charles B. Hosmer, Jr. *Preservation Comes of Age.* Charlottesville, VA: Preservation Press, 1981. 1:134.

Rick Kennedy, "Thomas Brattle, Mathematician-Architect in the Transition of the New England Mind," *Winterthur Portfolio* 24 (Winter 1989): 231-246.

Nina Fletcher Little, *American Decorative Wall Painting, 1700-1850.* Sturbridge, MA: Studio Publications, 1952.

Anthony Quiney, "Thomas Lucas, Bricklayer, 1662 - 1736," *The Archaeological Journal*, 136 (1979): 269-280.

William G. Wendell, *The MacPheadris-Warner House, 1716, Portsmouth, N.H.* Portsmouth: 1966.

With help from Roger Bowdler, historian London Division, English Heritage.

Architectural drawings in:

Architects Emergency Committee, *Great Georgian Houses of America* (1933): 253-5.

Howells, *Architectural Heritage of the Piscataqua* (1937).

Benjamin Graham, "Some New England Staircases — 1670-1770," *The Monograph Series.* XIX: 5.

"Early Interior Doorways in New England," *The [White Pine] Monograph Series.* XVIII:5.

Restoration Philosophy: The leading force in the preservation of the MacPheadris-Warner house was Elizabeth Greenough Wendell, wife of Harvard professor Barrett Wendell [*see Jacob Wendell House*] who led the association throughout the Great Depression. While well connected with various architectural and antiquarian experts of the day, to William Sumner Appleton she was unable *"to appreciate anything that isn't spic and span, neat and clean, and lovely and beautiful according to her ideas of what she would like to live with."*

Restoration was designed to take the house "back" to ca. 1762, the date Franklin installed its lightning rods, which required the least reconstruction of missing or altered features. Later Federal wallpapers and subsequent Victorian alterations were removed from the main rooms in the tradition of contemporary private rehabilitation and, perhaps, under the influence of Colonial Williamsburg's newly recreated Governor's Palace. The formal rooms, paneled in wood from floor to ceiling, still act as a foil to a collection of fine antique furnishings with greater emphasis on the upper parlor chamber's use as a "Council Chamber" than as the best bed chamber it served in the inventories. The service staircase is seldom shown and access to the attic and cupola is restricted.

RMC

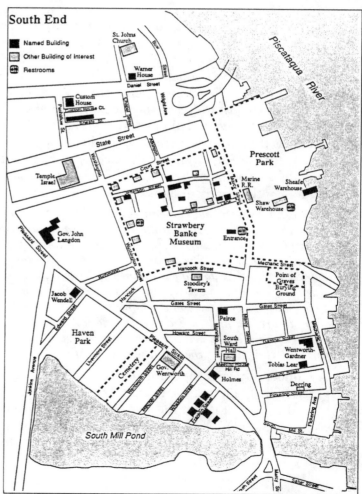

Map, Eliza McClennen

PRESCOTT PARK
AND UPPER MARCY STREET

The Prescott Family: Both of the white wooden buildings on the corners of Court and Marcy Streets were moved here from other parts of the city during the creation of Prescott Park. They actually occupy the traditional site of the first English house erected on the Portsmouth mainland. This was the 1634 Great House, a large timber-framed building with two chimney stacks and four façade gables, which first housed the colony established by John Mason and later the Puritan merchant John Cutt. [See the plaque along the Strawbery Banke Museum fence for a 1660 sketch of the house.]

Two centuries later this site was covered with brick stores and apartments. Across the way, many old riverfront wharves, behind brick houses that lined the street, were turned into coal pockets or filled with gas storage tanks. What was known as Water Street until the early 20th-century became the home of grog shops and the city's red-light district, including Madam Mary Baker's "Gloucester House" at the corner of State Street. The change of name from Water to Marcy Street in 1912 was a part of the city's effort to clean up the area where in one month four bodies were found dead of "Water Street violence."

Before the neighborhood gained its rough reputation, Charles Prescott opened a provisions store here in 1858 and rented an apartment for his young family above another store. Prescott did not prosper. The family moved again, and his son Charles went off to Boston to work at Jordan Marsh. Two sisters, Mary E. and Josie F., remained in Portsmouth with their parents. By the 1870s young Charles followed another Portsmouth merchant to Erie, Pennsylvania, and become a partner in his dry goods store. Over the next 50 years he made a fortune in manufacturing and other investments, leaving more than $2.5 million when he died in 1932. Due to the intercession of a Portsmouth lawyer, Prescott's two unmarried sisters won his contested estate.

They then purchased several sites along Marcy Street to begin a program of demolition and improvement along the waterfront where the Prescott family had first lived and worked. Mary died in 1939 and her sister Josie deeded the core of Prescott Park to the city in 1940. A trust was established when she died in 1949 and its Trustees have continued to expand public ownership of the waterfront, maintain the parks, and support an active summer arts program.

The quiet Prescott sisters were active in middle class religious and social improvement organizations including the Women's City Club, the Family Welfare Association, the Portsmouth District Nurse Association and the Wentworth Home for Chronic Invalids. But their idea for a waterfront park seems related to a proposal made during the Depression to the National Park Service and WPA by architect John Mead Howells and a committee of local historians. This historic plan envisioned the removal of families from the area to a modern housing project to be constructed below South Street. From the waterfront west to Washington Street and

Sources:

C.G. Gurney, *Portsmouth Historic and Picturesque* (1902).

Ray Brighton. *The Prescott Story.* (Portsmouth, NH: Portsmouth Marine Society, 1982).

Richard E. Winslow, III. *The Portsmouth Gundalow: Workhorse for a Tidal Basin Empire.* (Portsmouth: Portsmouth Marine Society, 1983).

_____. *"Wealth and Honour" Portsmouth During the Golden Age of Privateering, 1775-1815.* (Portsmouth: Portsmouth Marine Society, 1988)

HABS, NH-7, Sheafe Warehouse, (Library of Congress).

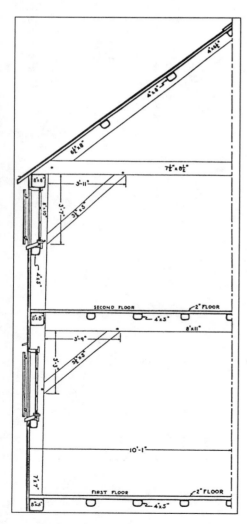

HABS NH-7, Library of Congress
Section, Sheafe Warehouse.

south to Gates Street historic houses would be restored as museums and sustained through tourism. The boundaries of this planned district and those established for expenditures by the Prescott trust are nearly identical. Both plans responded to perceived social and physical decay of an historic neighborhood in different but related ways. The Marcy-Washington Street Urban Renewal Project *[see Strawbery Banke Museum]* in the 1950s was the public manifestation of the same thinking.

Oracle House (ca. 1709? and 1730, moved and remodeled ca. 1800, and relocated to corner Marcy and Court Streets ca. 1935).

This small two story gambrel with T-plan has been moved at least two times. The earliest known location, after 1709, was directly behind the North Meeting House on Market Square. About 1800 it was moved to Haymarket Square, and in the 1930s moved to its present site as part of the Prescott sisters' project. It is known as the Oracle house after the *Portsmouth Oracle* newspaper, which began publication in 1793 within this structure.

Its recent rehabilitation shows it to have originally been a frame of three bays with posts and rails that held vertical boarding. This utilitarian frame, perhaps for a barn, was extended one bay to its present northern end while it still had a pitched roof. At some date, perhaps as part of Richard Wibird's 1730 lease of the Market Square lot, the gambrel roof over the main block and the gambrel rear ell were added. Beside these external features the closed-string three-run staircase and at least one door in the attic survive from this period.

Shaw Wharf and Warehouse: The headquarters of Prescott Park, on what came to be known as Union Wharf, is the last remaining of the large wharves and warehouses that historically defined the southern riverfront. The Shaw warehouse, built perhaps as early as the 1790s, is the only building of its kind still *in situ*. A trap door in its ground floor suggests that small craft or gundalows could off-load directly beneath the wharf of cribbed timbers. It now contains offices, a maintenance shop, and public restrooms.

Abraham and Thomas Shaw were privateers in the War of 1812 and before that time owned the long wharf closest to the mouth of the Puddle Dock inlet. (Captain Thomas M. Shaw's house was moved in the 1930s from the south side of Liberty Bridge to fill the gap left by the demolition of the Gloucester House and other buildings on Marcy Street between Court and State streets.) Shaw's warehouse was the early 20th century home and storehouse of antique dealer and brothel owner "Cappy" Stewart. He later bought the old Sheafe warehouse (below) as a second antiques storage building. Stewart often dealt in architectural materials, selling, for example, the Wentworth House (1699) to the American Wing of the Metropolitan Museum in New York City (Winterthur Museum eventually got the leftovers).

Sheafe Warehouse: The building at the end of Shaw's wharf was originally located at the modern abutment of the Prescott Memorial Bridge to Peirce Island, originally the foot of "Gravesend Street" opposite the Point of Graves. It was here that the *Ranger,* one of two frigates built in Portsmouth for the Continental Navy during the Revolutionary War, is said to have been fitted out. This 18th-century warehouse of uncertain date is the last survivor of this once-widespread Piscataqua mercantile building form.

Measured and photographed in 1935 by the Historic American Building Survey, the vertical plank structure sat on a crib of logs with its overhanging upper story projecting above the river. It continued an older Piscataqua tradition of board walls, but with a frame of posts, studs, and horizontal rails. Its posts have angled braces (except on the ground floor where they have been replaced by modern ships knees) which support tie beams that carry the floor joists. The purlin roof has principal rafters with struts from the tie beams. Evidence survives on the second story for a privy overhanging the water.

Portsmouth Marine Railway: The multi-unit brick building along Marcy Street at the end of the Shaw Wharf was built as head house and office for the Portsmouth Marine Railway, established in 1833. Using animal power (at least through the 1840s) to haul vessels out of the water on a railed ramp, the business failed in 1857. The structure was later used as tenements and now houses exhibits in the summer.

Point of Graves: In 1671 John Pickering Jr. agreed that the town might "enclose about half an acre... where the people have wont to be buried," and the Point of Graves has been a burial ground ever since. Perhaps because of damage from cattle or the use of wooden grave markers, no stone earlier than 1682 survives. A wide range of 17th- and 18th-century headstones can be found through the turnstile entrance, which helped keep roving cows from the burial ground. Gravestone cutting was New England's first fully-developed graphic art. There must have been few local stonecutters, however, for the oldest stones in this cemetery were made in the vicinity of Boston. These stone cutters can be identified from occasional signatures and by stylistic characteristics, including the way they cut the death's heads that form the dominant motif on most stones before 1750. A plaque provides identification of the work of the two John Fosters, the Lamsons, and anonymous artisans known as the "stonecutter of Boston" and the "Essex County Maker" for the locus of their designs in those locations. The street now leading to Peirce Island was formerly Gravesend Street, which provided access to several warehouses (including Sheafe's) along the southern edge of the cove that became Puddle Dock.

RMC

HABS, Library of Congress
Sheafe Warehouse on its original site, 1935.

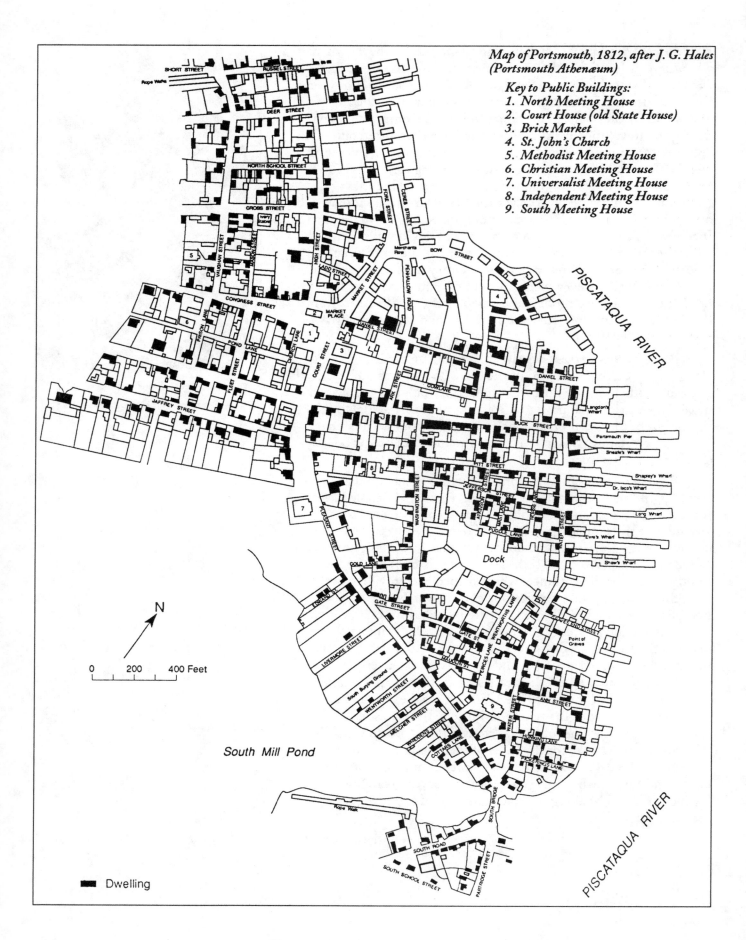

Map of Portsmouth, 1812, after J. G. Hales
(Portsmouth Athenæum)

Key to Public Buildings:
1. North Meeting House
2. Court House (old State House)
3. Brick Market
4. St. John's Church
5. Methodist Meeting House
6. Christian Meeting House
7. Universalist Meeting House
8. Independent Meeting House
9. South Meeting House

PISCATAQUA RIVER

PISCATAQUA RIVER

South Mill Pond

N

0   200   400 Feet

■ Dwelling

STRAWBERY BANKE MUSEUM

Strawbery Banke Museum preserves and interprets more than 300 years of architectural, material, and social change through a combination of restored and furnished houses, formal exhibits, archaeological exploration, and reconstruction of landscape features. Adopting ideas from the new social history in the 1970s, the museum replaced the idea of a one-period outdoor museum with interpretation of many pasts. This work is ongoing; 15 of its 40 buildings are restored to various periods, including the early and mid 20th century, and open to the public as furnished houses or interpretive exhibits.

For those less familiar with the structural practices of New England's timber-framed building or the decorative vocabulary of the post-Revolutionary rebuilding of the urban landscape in the region's coastal cities, it may be useful to explore the architectural exhibits in the Sherburne and Winn houses early in your visit.

Settlement and Evolution: The part of the larger South End now occupied by the museum was first developed in the 1690s when a large farm, containing the Great House of the initial settlement period, was subdivided into house lots. These extended from the riverfront, now encompassed by Prescott Park, westward along the north bank of the tidal creek Puddle Dock. A right of way along this now-vanished cove determined the orientation of Puddle Lane and the buildings that lined it. While the area was rapidly sold and developed between 1690 and 1720, few of these first-period structures remain. *[see Sherburne and Marden Houses]* The street plan, lot lines, and placement of many buildings in the east end of the museum site, however, often preserve these late 17th- and early 18th-century patterns.

The heart of the city's most densely populated neighborhood, this part of Portsmouth was a classic example of the mixed land-use that characterized 18th-century coastal cities. Wharves, warehouses, dwellings of all sizes (many with a small front-room shop),

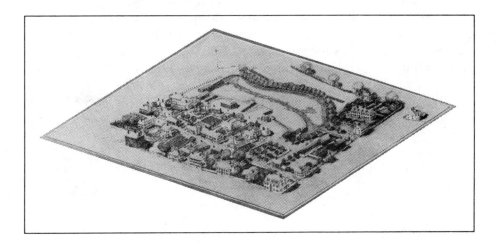

Courtesy Strawbery Banke Museum
Perry, Shaw, and Hepburn, proposed restoration master plan.

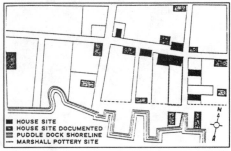

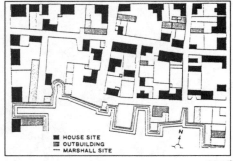

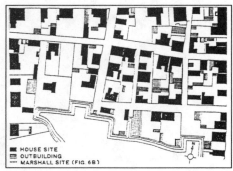

Courtesy Dublin Seminar

Puddle Dock Neighborhood Development, from Pendery (1978).

a tavern, brickyard, pottery, mast yard, and tannery were all crowded into these ten acres. Many of these activities were replaced in the post-Revolutionary rebuilding of the city, either through extensive renovation or new construction. With the emergence of Market Square as the commercial center of the city and the rebuilding of State and Court Streets after the fire of 1813, this older commercial core was reconfigured into a residential neighborhood.

By the second decade of the 19th century, the area around Puddle Dock became increasingly one of rented houses behind an industrial rather than commercial waterfront. After the Civil War the area became a haven for Portsmouth's relatively small immigrant populations as old houses were converted to less expensive multi-family apartments *[see Drisco House]*. Puddle Dock — befouled and useless in a changed economy — was filled and built-over at the turn of the 20th century. A new street through the former waterway eventually became the site for junk yards amidst a neighborhood that reflected Portsmouth's modest increase of European immigration. For the next 50 years this part of the South End attracted a variety of civic visions that would ultimately alter its present and reinterpret its past.

Strawbery Banke Museum occupies a 10-acre tract between Prescott Park and Washington Street taken by eminent domain under urban renewal for a proposed housing project that proved to be economically impractical. In the late 1950s, rental rates were insufficient to justify projected mortgage payments. This, combined with continued private demolition of old houses throughout the city, provoked public librarian Dorothy Vaughan to call for a change of plan that would preserve Portsmouth's history. Miss Vaughan had been active in historical and genealogical activities since the Depression, and was part of the local committee that had proposed preserving the waterfront in the 1930s.

Reviving Portsmouth's original name (used until 1653), Strawbery Banke Museum created its first master plan with the help of Boston architect William Perry, of Perry, Shaw & Hepburn, architects of Colonial Williamsburg. Besides the preservation of extant "colonial" houses, it included sites on which to relocate several historic buildings of patriotic and civic association at the southwest corner of the museum. Here urban renewal demolished "later" houses, garages and fences to provide new sites for a few otherwise unprotected historic structures along the southern edge of the old Puddle Dock. North of this waterway surviving homes and other buildings remain *in situ.*

MS & RMC

ARCHAEOLOGY AND LANDSCAPE AT STRAWBERY BANKE MUSEUM

Sixteen archaeological sites have been excavated within the museum over the past thirty years, pioneering a community-based public archaeology program. Craft production, like the Marshall Pottery [see maps], has been explored, as have landscape features of six specific sites. From this research the museum has recreated representative landscapes ranging in date from the 1720s to the 1940s. A utilitarian garden behind the Sherburne House offers a dramatic comparison with the Victorian flower display at the Goodwin House or the 1908 colonial revival garden beside the Thomas Bailey Aldrich Memorial. With the future installation of the 1940s memory garden of resident Leslie Clough *[see Marden House]*, five of the projected eight period landscape reconstructions will have been completed. Each garden interprets a localized landscape, with an emphasis on fence design, plant materials, garden design, arbors and trellises, and most recently, the physical presence of outbuildings. The new privy building on the Rider-Wood site is the first of several planned reconstructions. The abundance of open space throughout the neighborhood today is a mis-representation of pre-20th-century history, although much had already been removed through decay and changing land use before urban renewal. Absent today at most house sites is a barn, wood-shed or privy that once filled some portion of the small yard space.

AM & MEP

ARCHITECTURE OF THE PUDDLE DOCK NEIGHBORHOOD

While all the museum's exhibit buildings are open, the following sites are particularly recommended for their visible evidence of structural carpentry, variety in domestic planning, and survival of alterations reflecting typical patterns of changing economic and social uses. For this reason this book *excludes* several high-style buildings along Court Street: the L-plan Jones and Lowd houses, the first museum house in New Hampshire (the 1907 refurnishing of the 1797 Thomas Bailey Aldrich Memorial), and the 1762 Chase House with carvings by Ebenezer Dearing and federal period alterations attributed to James Nutter. Nor are the furnished homes along Washington Street (the Capt. Keyran Walsh house) and Hancock Street (the 1811 Governor Goodwin mansion) described here, although VAF members may want to visit them today or later. The Ichabod Goodwin mansion is especially interesting for that later owner was among the leaders who developed the industries that shaped the west-end neighborhood. More information about the other structures is available on the museum's map and official guidebook.

RMC & MS

Sources:

John W. Durel, *From Strawbery Banke to Puddle Dock: The Evolution of a Neighborhood, 1630 - 1850.* Ph.D. diss., Univ. of NH, 1984.

Daniel W. Ingersoll, Jr. *Settlement Archaeology at Puddle Dock.* Ph.D. diss. Harvard Univ., 1971.

Steven Pendery, "Urban Process in Portsmouth, New Hampshire: An Archaeological Perspective," *New England Historical Archeology,* Peter Benes, ed. 1977 Proceedings of the Dublin Seminar for New England Folklife (Boston: Boston University, 1978).

Strawbery Banke, *A Historic Waterfront Neighborhood in Portsmouth, New Hampshire: Official Guidebook* (Portsmouth: 1982).

G. Ward & J. Schnitzler, "The Buildings," Strawbery Banke Museum, *Antiques* (July 1992): 66-75.

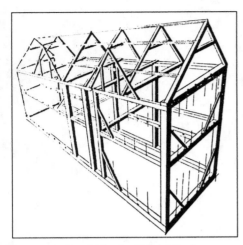

Drawing by David Hart for Richard Candee
Sherburn House Frame after 1703 addition.

Drawing by James Garvin
Conjectural 18th century elevation of Sherburn House remodelling.

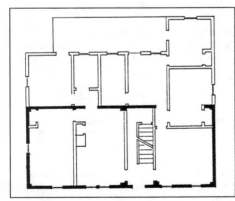

Drawing by Claire Dempsey after James Garvin
Plan, Sherburn House, 1966 before restoration.

Joshua Drisco House

Built 1794
Puddle Lane

Typical of Portsmouth's late 18th-century merchant and sea captain's homes, the Drisco house has a familiar georgian plan with a narrow central hall and two interior chimneys heating eight rooms on its two floors. The second house on its site, replacing one of the 1690s, it once faced its own small wharf and warehouse across Puddle Lane. Built in 1794 by merchant John Shapley, it was sold in 1800 to another merchant, Joshua Drisco, who's heirs retained the house throughout the 19th century. It was converted to a duplex about 1900. In 1957 it was vacated for urban renewal.

Exhibit Rationale: This innovative 1980s restoration of the Drisco House illustrates the museum's interest in tracing change over time by showing three different eras of the building's history. The exterior retains the appearance of its ca. 1900 conversion; the center hall and two rooms to the east (right) are restored to the 1790s; and two west (left) rooms suggest the appearance of interiors during the last generation of occupation in the 1950s.

Center Hall and East Rooms (1790s): The two exterior doors added for duplex conversion opened into separate vestibules, created by dividing the old center hall lengthwise and adding a second staircase beside the original. This division destroyed most of the detailing on the older staircase. Reconstruction is based on shadow evidence of scalloping on the stairends and on surviving fragments of the panelling below the stairs. Balusters and newel post are copied from Portsmouth examples in the museum's architectural fragments collection.

John Shapley's shop-room has been restored from surviving elements and evidence of vanished features. The arrangement of shelving was clearly visible on painted sheathing under later wallpaper. The original shop doors survived intact under later lath and plaster (added when the room was domesticated in the early 19th century). Patches in the sheathing show that the room's narrow front windows replaced wider shop windows. The back sitting room was heavily altered, but original trim fragments survived as models. The fireplace mantel had entirely vanished; the present one copies an original one in an upstairs chamber.

West Rooms (1950s): The lefthand rooms recreate the cumulative appearance of many neighborhood homes during the last decades of occupancy; the effort is generic rather than biographical although former residents have assisted the project. The kitchen was heavily remodeled during the turn of the century conversion with few subsequent changes except the introduction of new technologies. The living room retained much of its late 18th-century woodwork (mantel, floorboards, trim and doors). This provided a framework for a furnishing scheme based on oral history interviews and analysis of upper layers of wall paper and paint. The furniture in the room was marketed as "colonial" when it was made.

RMC & MS

John & Mary Sherburne House

ca. 1695, extended before 1703
Puddle Lane, corner Horse Lane

The only domestic structure to survive from the initial subdivision of house lots in the 1690s, the Sherburne house was originally one of several timber-framed houses of the local maritime elite that circled the inlet and its new wharves. It underwent several campaigns of building, structural alteration and redecoration, of which only the first two building phases are now extant. Its use was clearly domestic, but is typical of many colonial buildings in its combined domestic and commercial functions. In addition to the two main rooms, several ells (since removed) were added along the rear. Later in the 18th century the original chimney block was replaced for rear corner fireplaces and a central hallway and a fashionable remodelling is suggested by reused fragments. This included the removal of the façade gables, substitution of double-hung sash, and new surrounds to windows and doors. Late in the 19th century the house was completely renovated again to convert it to two apartments of nine small rooms on each floor. In 1966 and 1967 the restoration of the house began. The latest rear ell was removed, as was most interior finish, to expose the original frame.

Exhibit Rationale: This somewhat tired exhibit of the frame and its building elements, based on Richard Candee's 1960s research and re-installed with NEH support in the mid-1970s, was originally designed to prevent over-restoration by an outside contractor. The first 'teaching' exhibit (as opposed to furnished period rooms) at Strawbery Banke Museum, it paralleled a similar approach at the SPNEA's Gedney House in Salem, Massachusetts, in trying to explicate the construction evidence of the exposed first-period frame. The first floor lays out the morphology of urban development, especially the houses around Puddle Dock, the growth and alteration of the Sherburne House, and the architectural evidence for its exterior restoration. Fragments found reused during the ill-fated partial restoration are used to show structural carpentry and architectural finish in the 1690s 'Great Hall' and chamber, as well as more progressive features in the ca. 1700 addition.

Structural carpentry and decorative finish: The Sherburn house is the oldest stud-framed house in the Piscataqua, and contrasts in several ways with the older plank-frame of the Richard Jackson House at Christian Shore. The west (left) rooms and part of the chimney bay were constructed between 1695 and 1698; the east rooms (right) were added before 1703. The older frame orients its summers in the common Massachusetts manner of longitudinal below and transverse above, and continues the regional preference for (or survival of) quarter-round chamfers. The three-bay purlin roof-frame of principal rafters with collar ties also retains evidence of its façade gables. Transitions in structural carpentry practices can be seen in the use of tusk-tenon floor joist joints in the ground floor ceiling and butt-cogged joists in the chamber above. In the

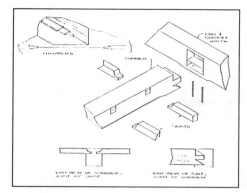

First floor girt and summer joint, ca. 1695.

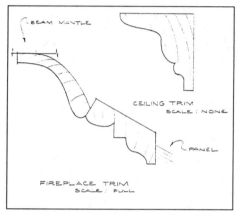

Profiles fireplace and ceiling moldings first floor, ca. 1703 addition.

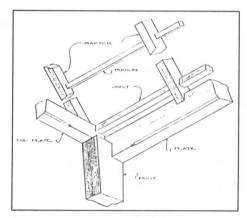

Drawings by David Hart
Detail second floor plate, rafter, post joints ca. 1695.

Sources:

Richard M. Candee. *Early Wooden Building in Maine and New Hampshire.* 1976.

Faith Harrington. "The Emergent Elite in 18th Century Portsmouth Society: The Archaeology of the Joseph Sherburne Houselot, *Historical Archaeology,* 23: 1 (1989):2-18.

east addition, the frame system is similar but fragmentary evidence for the ground floor fireplace wall shows the use of applied moldings to create 'proto-classical' panels on first floor vertical sheathing with paint scar evidence and fragments of cornice moldings. Upstairs was evidence of an original plaster ceilings (removed by the contractor) in the chamber.

Problems of Interpretation: The mistaken belief in a 1660s construction date led the contractor to create exposed sills like the Jackson House, so the ground floor ceiling height appears greater than it was originally. The modern chimney stack was modeled after that in the SPNEA's 1690s Boardman House (with its external brick pilaster ornament), but clearly *not* modified to fit the upper story west room chamfer evidence for location of the original fireplace opening and stack. Only one window opening and part of its ca. 1700 casing (upper east wall) was discovered; the paired casements are a likely but conjectural reconstruction.

RMC & CWD

Samuel Jackson House [formerly "Joshua Jackson" House]

Built ca. 1795 - 1800
Horse Lane near Jefferson Street
builder: Samuel Jackson ?

History: This property stayed in the Jackson family from 1695 to 1800, with only the sale of small strips of land to neighbors north and south before the Revolution. The 1766 estate of Joshua Jackson was divided among several heirs, with Nathaniel Jackson receiving the west half of a house along Horse Lane and Samuel Jackson the east. Except for mortgages and the taking of a strip of land to the north to extend Jefferson Street toward the river in 1797, the property remained undivided and in common until 1800 when Nathaniel sold his portion of this estate to Samuel for $330. Samuel Jackson, a joiner, immediately sold off the whole site for $1600 to William Dennett, a spar maker from Kittery, from whom it passed to several new owners between 1805 to 1815. This house is at least the second house to occupy the site. Its complicated family ownership, combined with physical evidence, suggests a date of 1790-1800, prior to sale out of the extended family. It is sited with its gable end to Horse Lane, providing a southern exposure to the windows along its front façade and allowing the use of a lot that was three feet narrower than the 30' length of the house.

Exhibit Rationale: This small center-chimney house is preserved without restoration to teach visitors about the nature of architectural and documentary evidence. The first-floor rooms have been studied to determine the sequence of alteration and redecoration, then "frozen" for visitors to decode for themselves.

Exhibit panels throughout the building provide documentary, genealogical, and oral history data about the residents and their neighborhood throughout the occupancy of this house.

Domestic Planning: The most unexpected architectural

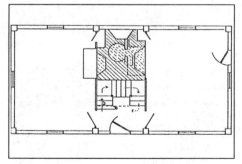

Drawing by Judy Quinn after Strawbery Banke Museum

First floor plan, Samuel Jackson House.

evidence found in this house is best seen along its north exterior wall. Exposed when the museum began sill repairs, an unused rear firebox in the original chimney stack and structural framing for a doorway from the front parlor to a never-constructed rear addition survived under the original sheathing. It is clear that this small two-room house was planned for a rear lean-to or ell whose construction was, for some unknown reason, forestalled — perhaps because by 1814, when two lots next to Jefferson Street were sold, a small house had been built on the corner behind the Jackson house. This evidence suggests that similar fireplace configurations in other New England houses (where the masonry appears to be of a single-build but the rear room is clearly an addition) may have been the result of similar forethought in domestic planning.

Comparative evidence of small houses throughout the city suggests that the original plan of the house is among the rarest small house type to survive. The eastern (right) room was used as the kitchen throughout its history, with a series of alterations to the bakeoven, fireplace, and interior finish of the walls. The three-run staircase along the front of the chimney shares elements of detailing with post-Revolutionary examples throughout the city, while the west parlor was altered in the early 19th century by the addition of a mantel over the original raised panels above the fireplace. Windows throughout the house had their sash replaced in the early 20th century. Above, later subdivision of the kitchen chamber into two rooms and a hallway suggests the early date at which this became a tenant house. A later service ell off the kitchen, now seen in the scar evidence of the exterior wall, was removed.

MS & RMC

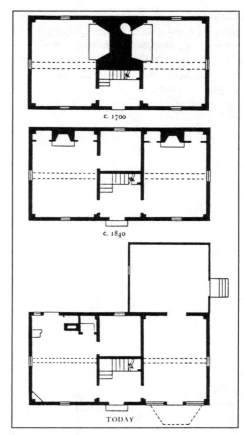

Drawing by James L. Garvin.
Evolution of James Marden House. First floor plans, 1700–1950.

Marden House and Abbott Store

Built ca. 1720, alterations ca. 1840 and 1900
Jefferson Street, corner Mast Lane

History: James Marden purchased the property, including a house, in 1722. Subsequent generations of the Marden family lived in the house and operated the Marden mast yard at the foot of Mast Lane. Heirs of the next James Marden (d. 1821) sold the house to Norad Grover, a mariner, in 1827. The building then passed through many owners until Melvin Gould's widow, Georgia, sold the house and an apartment block on the adjoining property to her sister and brother-in-law, Bertha and Walter Abbott, in 1918.

Exhibit Rationale: Marden House retains almost no remnants of its 18th- century appearance. However, good evidence does remain to tell us what it looked like during the years 1919 to 1950 when it was a store. Old shelving remains in the shed addition, and evidence for all shelf placement is visible in the front room of the store. The display windows are intact and there is evidence in the floor for the depth of display areas. The installation of the Abbott store and family kitchen as an interpretation of the social life of this neighborhood institution during World War II is scheduled to open in the summer of 1993.

Marden House, ca. 1965.

Walter Abbott in the front room of the Little Corner Store, ca. 1937.

Sources:

James L. Garvin, *Strawbery Banke in Portsmouth, New Hampshire: Official Guidebook* (Portsmouth: Strawbery Banke, 1974): 13-15.

John W. Durel, *From Strawbery Banke to Puddle Dock:* 166-167.

Evidence of plan and construction: The house originally had a central chimney and, like the nearby Sherburne House, is of timber frame construction. The central chimney stack was removed in the first half of the 19th century and replaced with two smaller chimneys along the rear wall. This change created a small room behind the staircase on each floor and brought the plan into conformity with several newer homes. The interior was remodeled throughout the century and the rear chimneys removed sometime before the Abbotts acquired the house.

When the house was acquired by the museum, all the windows had 19th-century two over two sash. First-floor windows were replaced in the early 1960s, as were ceilings in the ground story rooms which were used as a craft shop and gallery until 1990.

Abbott Home and Store: When the Abbotts decided to convert the west half of the house into a store, they added the store front windows and a rear shed. The room behind the main stairs was opened to become the "Candy Room," which housed the main check-out counter, and the east room became the family kitchen. The chamber above the kitchen became the master bedroom; the room behind the stairs was another small bedroom. The west chamber served as the living room, enlarged by the addition of a bay window overhanging the street, and a bathroom occupied the southwest corner. A garage was built directly behind the kitchen.

BW

Timothy Winn III and Thales G. Yeaton Connected Houses

Built ca. 1795
Jefferson Street between Mast Lane and Atkinson Street

In 1794 trader Thales Yeaton, later to become a tobacconist and major real estate speculator, purchased a large lot on the corner of Jefferson Street and Mast Lane. Two weeks later he sold the eastern half to his 30-year-old brother-in-law, Timothy Winn III, who moved to Portsmouth from Woburn, Massachusetts, after the war. Together they erected houses sharing a common party wall. A trader or minor merchant, his shop sign TIMOTHY WINN 3ᴰ earned its owner the nickname Three-penny Winn. He lived here only until 1798, during which time he had a liquor license. The next owners of the eastern house, widow Elizabeth Durrel and her new husband Nathaniel Hancock, lived here until Hancock's death in 1813. They took in boarders and in 1809-1810 advertised a shoe shop here.

"To Build a House" Exhibit: This exhibition in the Winn house explores the step-by-step process for constructing a house in the Federal period. The exhibit starts upstairs in the rear room behind the staircase and continues to the right throughout the house. It combines exposed elements of the house frame with tools and elements from the museum's architectural fragments collection to illustrate the materials and methods of building.

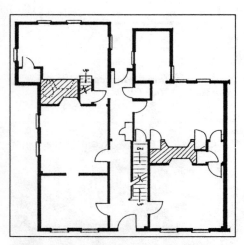

Drawings by Judy Quinn after Strawbery Banke Museum.

First floor plan, Timothy Winn House.

Plan: The façades of the two houses were originally mirror images, with matching main doorways and wide shop windows and doors at opposite ends. The interior plans are, however, very different. Winn adopted the central hall plan, with one chimney pushed toward the back of the house leaving an unheated front shop-room. The two-chimney plan of this house with two kitchen fireplaces might suggest it was used by two families living on either side of a common stair hall, but there is no evidence of this.

The Yeaton House employs an unorthodox variant on the center-chimney five-room plan that also provided an unheated front shop room. The "setting room" behind the small shop was further shortened by partitions, creating a six-foot wide pantry and small bedroom along the rear wall. When later owner Joseph Amazeen, a trader, died in 1824 the Yeaton house was inventoried with a separate list of property belonging to his wife, Lydia, before the marriage. A real estate division provided her dower, naming the rooms of her third portion. In addition to the shop, sitting room, and rear bedroom, she owned the chambers directly above the western half, a quarter of the cellar, and shared common use of the entries, stairs, back yard, privy, well and cistern. Unrestored, except for modern paints used as background colors for former museum exhibits, the house also offers glimpses into the modest level of alterations and insertions for earlier 20th-century living. The bathroom was inserted at the top of the back stairs and one must go through it to reach the attic.

MS

Small house variants along Atkinson Street

Built ca. 1800- 1840

Immediately across from and adjacent to the Yeaton House, along both sides of Atkinson Street, four small houses were purpose-built as rental properties over the first third of the 19th century. Together with the Samuel Jackson House these buildings suggest the common types of speculative building for working families who lived around the docks.

Yeaton built the small house behind his own in a former mast yard between Mast Lane and Atkinson Street by 1803. The small center-chimney house passed quickly through several hands before merchant Joseph Low acquired it in 1811. He bought additional land for a garden in front at auction in 1813. When he died ten years later, the property was sketched as part of the probate settlement. While widow Elizabeth Low received the house and a third of the garden as her dower right, she continued to live in her Water (now Marcy) Street home, and this house served as an income-property. After she moved to Boston in 1848 she sold the tenant house to Leonard Cotton, the city's largest rental property owner.

Cotton had already built two tenements across Atkinson Street about 1834. Both have two main rooms with chimneys along the rear wall, a center entry with small room behind, plus a variety of added service rooms. One is sited gable end to the street with a

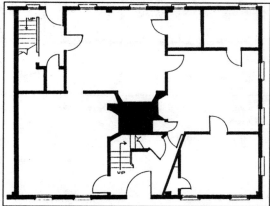

Drawings by Judy Quinn after Strawbery Banke Museum.

First floor plan, Thales G. Yeaton House.

Widow's dower plat, Joseph Low Estate.

57

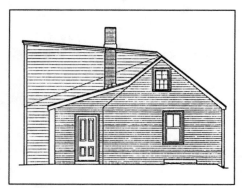

Drawings by Judy Quinn after Strawbery Banke Museum
Side Elevation, Peacock House.

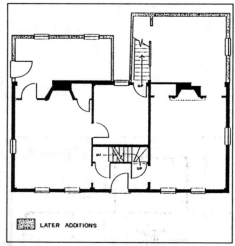

LATER ADDITIONS

Drawings by Judy Quinn after Strawbery Banke Museum
First floor plan, Peacock House.

lobby entry along the side and later extensions to the back gable end; the other is of identical plan-type but faces Atkinson Street and has an added rear lean-to along its rear wall. Their framing is of dimensioned stock and the roof rafters are without purlins. A cooper who made money in the West Indies trade, Cotton bought — especially at auction — all the inexpensive real estate he could. While rental housing did not pay well, by his death in 1872 he owned more than 40 properties in the neighborhood. Portraits of Cotton and his wife are in the Wentworth-Gardner Mansion and their home (purported date 1747) stands on Washington Street, between (new) Hancock Street and Richmond Lane.

Peacock House (ca. 1821), directly opposite the Winn-Yeaton houses at the northeast corner of Atkinson and Jefferson streets, shares the same ground floor plan of lobby entry and rear wall chimneys but in a single-story form. After the 1813 fire wooden building was regulated throughout this area and only houses of under 12 foot stud were supposed to be erected in wood; this example is one of the few surviving one-story houses erected during this period. The house was later enlarged with rear additions now interpreted in the rooflines of the gable end. It was occupied by tenants of Reuben Shapley, who owned much of this block.

MS

Rider-Wood House

Built ca. 1800, shop addition, ca. 1811
builder: Samuel Jackson ?,
Jefferson Street

This small post-Revolutionary dwelling was perhaps built by joiner Samuel Jackson, as it shares the same floor-plan and stylistic vocabulary of Jackson's own house on Horse Lane. This house was purchased from Henry Jackson in 1809 by John and Mary Rider, who immigrated to the United States from Devonshire, England, in 1790. They may have added the shop at the west end, perhaps in 1811, the only year when a joiner named Tate and a cabinet-maker named Morrison were taxed as living in the Rider house.

When Mary Rider was widowed in 1818 she operated the shop as a grocery (for which she was licensed to sell rum and molasses) into the 1830s. Until her death in 1861, her ownership of rental real estate, stock dividends, and interest on money allowed her live without shopkeeping. From an estate of $13,000 she left a bequest to St. John's Church and the house to her nephew James Wood, who lived here until 1900. The house was subsequently modified for a kosher butcher serving the neighborhood's growing eastern European Jewish community; later it was divided into apartments before being vacated for urban renewal.

Exhibit Rationale: The restoration of the house focuses on part of the 90-year Rider-Wood occupancy and Mary Rider's room-by-room probate inventory provided the basis for its furnishing. Shown as it may have looked in the 1830s, after she had given up shopkeeping, household objects have been selected to suggest the accumulation of goods since their arrival in Portsmouth, with "new" additions of the 1830s.

Physical Evidence: The frame, chimney, pedimented doorway, panelled door, doorstep, and many clapboards and ground-story window caps are original. Deteriorated original sash and frames have been reproduced in kind. The shop addition was altered by later windows also replaced in the restoration.

The high rate of surviving interior finishes made possible detailed paint analysis of woodwork, plaster fireplace interiors, floors, and kitchen plaster walls. In the vestibule fragments of the 1830s stone colored wallpaper survive behind the door. The original staircase and fielded paneling is generally typical of local building at the turn of the 19th century. However, at the upper story no evidence could be found of balusters or a railing, but physical evidence guided the conjectural recreation of a removable board partition that would have facilitated lifting large pieces of furniture onto the upper landing instead of weaving up the narrow stairs.

The kitchen was much changed. Reconstructed built-in shelves are based on shadow evidence of molding profiles and shelf location on the paint layers of the corner post, baseboard, and wall plaster. The original plaster walls were painted until wallpapered about 1840. A narrow closet to the left of the fireplace was enlarged in the early 20th century, cutting the original bake oven in half. The fireplace, wall, and closet door way have been restored. A shed addition contains a rear vestibule and storage area.

The original parlor fireplace interior was plastered and later fitted with a Franklin fireframe. (Portsmouth had several stove stores and manufactories in the 1830s.) The shallow cupboard beside the fireplace is the likely location of the dishes listed in the probate inventory; the door in the rear wall leads to the shed connecting this room to the kitchen. The reconstructed interior window shutters are known only from the physical evidence of hinges on the frames. On the gable end wall a single original window was altered for a door to the ca. 1811 shop room.

Both upper chambers show the characteristic second floor use of a recessed chimney breast. This is partly the function of placing the stairwell between the chimney girts for structural support and the step-back of the chimney at the second floor for reasons of economy. Along the front face of the chimney stack the attic stairway splits in two, providing direct access to each half of the attic. [Please, do not go beyond the first attic stair landing.]

The shop wing was the most heavily altered part of this house. Mary Rider's inventory shows that, by her death at age 92, it had become her ground floor bedroom. When it was again reused as a shop in the 20th-century, the street door was moved and a large display window punched into the wall. Virtually nothing of the original interior arrangement or finish survived except the decorated ceiling joists found above a later ceiling. Exposed joists or, more commonly, flat-chamfered closely spaced beams are found in utilitarian structures in early 19th-century Portsmouth. The depthwise placement and narrow size of the joists now recreated in

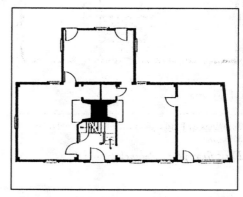

Drawing by Judy Quinn after Strawbery Banke Museum

First floor plan, Rider House.

Source:
Family research by Ed McCarron.

the ceiling frame of the Rider shop are, however, unusual but duplicate the original evidence.

MS

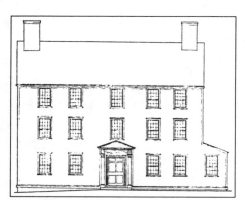

Drawing by James Garvin
Front Elevation, Pitt Tavern.

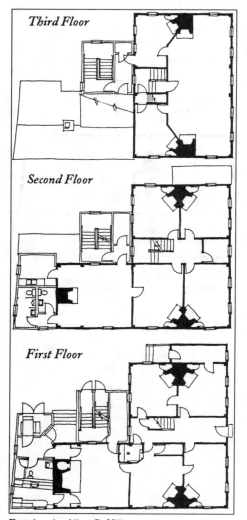

Drawings by Allen C. Hill
Pitt Tavern Floor Plans as Reconstructed.

William Pitt Tavern

originally Earl of Halifax Tavern

Built ca. 1766
Court Street, corner of Atkinson St.
restoration architect Alan C. Hill;
restoration contractors: Dodge, Adams & Roy

History: The Earl of Halifax tavern was built for John Stavers. It was the third tavern he ran since 1755, about five years after the mariner's arrival from England and his marriage to Margaret Clark at Queens Chapel. The new tavern coincided with the last of his six children by second wife Catherine Walker. A mason since 1755, Stavers's new tavern included an assembly hall on the top floor for Masonic meetings, concerts and other gatherings. John's brother, Bartholomew Stavers, operated a stage coach line from here to Boston and a 1772 almanac lists the tavern as one of the three most popular in town.

It was assumed during the early part of the Revolution that Stavers was a loyalist. He lost the patronage of the Masons, suffered mob damage to the tavern, was arrested and released, and renamed the tavern after the more popular William Pitt. After the war Stavers enjoyed renewed patronage of the Masons, who in 1789 organized the state's scattered lodges under a Grand Lodge in this building.

After his death in the 1790s, the building was divided between his daughters Mary and Sussanna. Until 1810 Mary's husband continued the tavern, but with decreasing success, owing — by his own account — to the shift of the town's commercial center from the adjacent waterfront to Market Square. By the 1850s the divided structure housed seven residents and it continued as a multi-family home until vacated for urban renewal a century later.

Structure: Much of the unusual framing evidence can be attributed to the third floor hall that runs the length of the building. Typical of the Portsmouth double house, the tavern was framed to receive a pair of chimneys centered between the front and rear rooms. During construction, however, the frame was modified for corner chimney stacks instead. The upper hall was soundproofed with chaff in the walls and fireproofed with sand beneath the floor; the stairway was also sited to the rear of the building to allow extra depth for the meeting room.

Substantial 19th-century alterations saw the extension of the rear ell, removal of the chimneys, rearrangement of doors and windows, and loss of trim. The museum's restored tavern is a model of 1980s historical reconstruction based on building fragments, scar evidence, and recovered paint layers. The bar, staircase and other interior finish is based on this carefully study and that of original paint colors of both woodwork and plaster. Missing are a long run of stables in the rear, seen in the 1813 map of Portsmouth, whose archaeological record was destroyed by a later 19th century dwelling on the site.

MS

THE SOUTH END

Prescott Park, The Point of Graves, Puddle Dock and Strawbery Banke Museum are today only the most public part of a larger neighborhood, known as the South End. Defined at its northern edge by brick buildings that replace those burned in 1813, wandering along the riverfront wharves to the east and the South Mill Pond to the west, it stretches along the mill pond, South Street, and the short streets leading to the river below the old mill dam. Since the end of urban renewal, this neighborhood retains the bulk of the city's extant colonial building stock although its buildings more often date from the post-Revolutionary rebuilding of Portsmouth.

The land between the former site of Puddle Dock [see *Strawbery Banke Museum*] and the junction of Pleasant and Marcy Streets at the mill dam was originally called Pickering's Neck for the family of millers who controlled the mill pond and its surrounding land in the 17th century. Along the south edge of Puddle Dock stood the 1699 Wentworth house, remnants of which are now in the Metropolitan Museum's American Wing and Winterthur. In 1731, after a bridge connected this neck with the rest of the waterfront, a new meeting house was erected on its central knoll to replace the old 'logg' structure south of the mill pond. This South Meeting House formed a focal point for new houses then being erected, like that of merchant Joshua Peirce.

After the Revolution the South End experienced the same residential rebuilding and subdivision of lots for new housing that can be seen at Strawbery Banke Museum. As larger lots were divided and old houses removed or rebuilt, the neighborhood became a mixture of central chimney, georgian, L-house and a variety of narrow two room plans with rear-wall and/or end chimneys. To the south and southwest, lands near the South Mill Pond were opened for new development between 1800 and 1810. Franklin Street [see *Cottar's Lane*] reflects one set of housing forms for the Federal seaport. To the south of the mill pond, the triangle between South Street, Marcy Street, and South School Street contain houses built on lots sold by the town between 1785 and 1800. These single-family artisan homes were built by individual owners about the same time as those on Franklin Street.

Even the streets surrounding Meeting House Hill contain only remnants of the colonial streetscape. The houses at the corner of Manning and Howard streets are good examples of the changes made to the earliest structures during the post-Revolutionary period. The large gambrel roof of the Captain Daniel Fernald house is an alteration enclosing a late first-period frame on the north end and a large new addition of the 1780s to the south of the present center entrance. The older building shows evidence of once having a pitched roof with a ridge line parallel to Manning St. Across Howard street is a small two story house facing Manning Street with rear-wall chimneys. It was originally a central chimney

Courtesy Erica and George Dodge III
Fernald House, Manning Street, pre-1867.

61

Extant and documented buildings erected 1780-1812. Fire zones derived from Hales published map 1813-1814.

Key:
1. No. Meeting House
2. Court House (old State House)
3. Brick Market
4. St. John's Church
5. Assembly House
6. Christian Meeting House
7. Universalist Meeting House
8. Independent Meeting House
9. South Meeting House

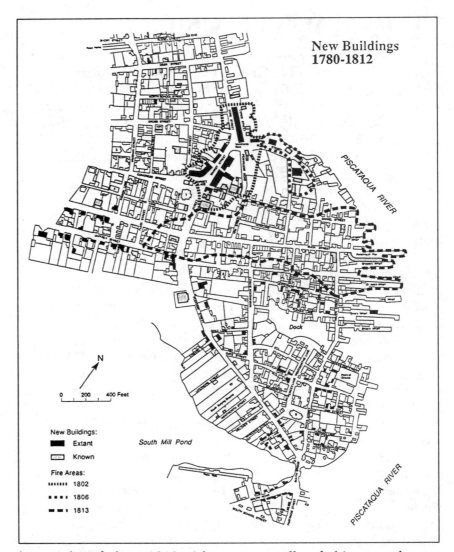

New Buildings
1780-1812

PISCATAQUA RIVER

N

0   200   400 Feet

New Buildings:
■ Extant
▢ Known

Fire Areas:
••••••• 1802
■ ■ ■ ■ 1806
■ — ■ — 1813

Dock

South Mill Pond

PISCATAQUA RIVER

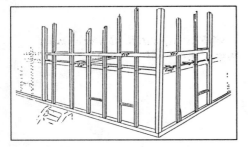

Drawing by Erica Dodge

Framing system, house ca. 1810, Manning St.

Curtesy Portsmouth Athenæum

Drake's Foundry, Mechanic St., rebuilt after 1859 fire.

house, altered about 1810 with a new rear ell and chimneys. A timber-framing variant is found in a small ca. 1810 house at 51 Manning Street. One-and-a-half story studs are spiked to the exterior side of beams that are framed into the main posts. The narrow 2" x 7 1/4" gable end beam holds first floor ceiling joists much like earlier bearer construction methods. The studs continue above this level and are framed into a thin 3" by 8" plate below the window sills of the second story. Is this merely aberrant or a precursor to later balloon contruction?

By the 1830s the waterfront between the Point of Graves and the South Mill Pond began to industrialize with small factories like Drake's foundry, rebuilt after a fire in 1859. The foundry and a planing mill along the waterfront operated among older maritime trades like Laighton's blockmaking and Fernald's ship yard. During the mid- and late-19th century the South End neighborhood also underwent religious and ethnic change as Jews, Catholics, and Yankees rented and bought homes here. Substantial infill housing replaced older barns or dwellings and modest additions or alterations to old homes provided a variety of small commercial spaces like those, for example, along Gates and Washington streets.

South End map detail. Center chimney houses before 1812.

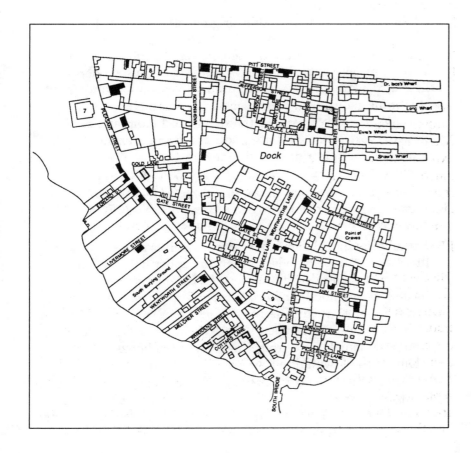

South End map detail. Center hall plan houses before 1812.

■ *"Double House"*

▨ *One room deep and L-houses*

Two elaborate houses on either side of Pickering's Neck, both associated with the Wentworth family, suggest in their internal ornament that their builders were familiar with specific English architectural publications. Together with the Moffatt-Ladd House and the Mills-Whipple house, they form part of a group of large, hip roofed, georgian homes for the colonial elite dating from the 1760s . Both were gifts of Mark Hunking Wentworth, mast merchant and Masonian Proprietor, to his children. While their gardens have been lost to later subdivision and building, mid-19th century surveys record something of the landscape once surrounding them. The first is the Wentworth-Gardner House; the other is the Pleasant Street Home of Gov. John Wentworth.

RMC

Wentworth – Gardner House

Built ca. 1760,
ca. 1915 restoration by Wallace Nutting
177 Mechanic Street, corner Gardner Street

A larger version of the Portsmouth hipped roof double house, built around 1760 as a wedding gift for Thomas Wentworth (1740-68) from his mother, Madam Mark Hunking Wentworth, this building preserves much original interior finish despite substantial restoration to the exterior. Sited facing the riverfront opposite Peirce's Island, the Wentworth-Gardner house has been photographed many times.

While the front door itself is original, photographs before Wallace Nutting's restoration show a Victorian portico that destroyed the door surround; the broken scroll pediment with gold pineapple was copied from a Salem, Massachusetts doorway in the Essex Institute. Its original imitation ashlar masonry façade, and the front quoins have been recently reconstructed.

Inside, the carved work of the stairs, modillions and door casings are those of the Moffatt-Ladd house and identified as the work of Ebenezer Dearing. Nutting wrote:

> *The interior required no restoration except to return to their proper places the stair spindles, newel, and the under mantel carving of the parlor, which had been removed in 1871 to another house.*

Nearly all the original paneled wainscot survives and every principal fireplace is framed by pilasters. In the upper hall, six Ionic pilasters along each side wall support the entablature with pulvinated frieze, modillioned cornice, and coved ceiling. Garvin has identified the structure as one of a group of similar houses, now lost, that may have shared such a pre-Revolutionary application of classical ornament derived from English pattern books.

During the Revolution it was occupied by the Nichols family and it may be they who commissioned the rose carved panel above the Southeast parlor fireplace. Such rococo carvings, attributed to Ebenezer Dearing, appear in other colonial houses remodeled after

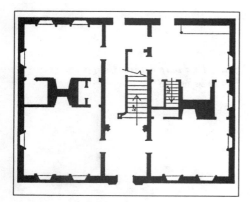

Drawing by Judy Quinn after HABS.
Floor Plan, Wentworth-Gardner House.

Drawing by Edwin J. Hipkiss
Elevation, Wentworth-Gardner House.

the Revolution, like the Stephen Chase house at Strawbery Banke, and in such new houses of the late 1780s as the Jacob Wendell and Gov. John Langdon mansion (both 1789).

In the 1790s this Wentworth house became the home of William Gardner (1751-1833), commissioner of loans and pension agent appointed during the Washington and Jefferson administrations. At the upper end of the garden he built an arch over Gardner street that contained a room for his United States loan office until his death. While no full illustration is known, it can be seen in plan in the later landscape survey in the rear hallway.

RMC & WO

Sources:

James Garvin, *Academic Architecture.*

Thomas B. Johnson, "Wentworth-Gardner House" in Giffen and Murphy, eds., *"A Noble and Dignified Stream"*

Wallace Nutting, *The Wentworth-Gardner House,* [promotional brochure, ca. 1915].

Edwin J. Hipkiss, "Early American Domestic Architecture: Wentworth-Gardner House, Portsmouth, NH, *The Architectural Forum* 32 (Feb. 1920):101-108.

Tobias Lear House

Built ca. 1740
Hunking Street near Mechanic Street

This typical Georgian plan house with high hip roof is said to date from about 1740 and according to family history was built by the third Tobias Lear. It was the birthplace and later home of the fifth Tobias Lear, secretary to President George Washington. Because of its association with Washington (who actually did visit the Lear's mother here) and its proximity to the larger mansion, it was later acquired by the Wentworth-Gardner Association and is now open to the public. A 1930s partial restoration added interior panelling from elsewhere, but the house has othewise been little altered since.

WO

Sources:

Stephen Decatur, "The Lear House and its Furnishings," *American Collector* 6 (Oct. 1940): 10-15

Joshua and Elizabeth Peirce house

Built ca. 1730
130 Gates Street, corner Manning St.

History and context: Captain Joshua Peirce (1670 -1743) was born in Newbury, Massachusetts and apparently trained as a joiner. He came to town about 1700, married and had a merchant's shop in his gambrel house opposite the North Church *[see Market Square].* By the 1720s he was one of Portsmouth's most successful fishing masters. In 1723 he had six schooners plying the Grand Banks fishing grounds. Each went out four times in the February– through–September fishing season, catching the most merchant- able fish in the earliest two. He made substantial profits selling dried fish to other merchant traders or by sending his own ships to Portugal or the West Indies.

Fishing for Peirce was but a stepping stone to an even more profitable career as an "inveterate illegal trader" transporting proscribed goods between the French colonies at Louisbourg, the West Indies, and New Hampshire. Such smuggling was the basis of many maritime fortunes including that of Archibald MacPheadris, Benning Wentworth, and George Jaffrey — all members of the Wentworth political faction whose cargos were overlooked when Theodore Atkinson was Collector of the Port of

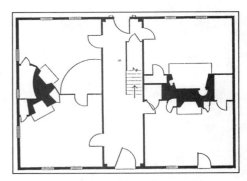

Measured by: Bernard Herman, R. Candee, Erica Dodge, and Claire Dempsey. Drawing by Judy Quinn.

First floor plan. Joshua and Elizabeth Peirce House.

Photo Robert S. Chase
South façade, Joshua Peirce House.

Portsmouth. In time, Peirce served as town clerk, parish clerk, selectman, a representative to the Assembly, and recorder of deeds. The last position was 'inherited' by his Harvard-trained son Daniel.

In 1720 Peirce began to acquire lot in this area and, as he increased his land, holdings he eventually owned almost the entire block. He was probably living in this gambrel-roofed house as early as 1727 when he had Portsmouth's second highest tax assessment (based primarily on the value of his trade). Pierce owned two dwellings while his second son and namesake (listed next to his father on the tax) owned none. Both merchants owned one slave and the father, mother, adult son, and their slaves were likely living here together.

In 1731 this large house on the corner of Gates Street was specified as "Joshua Peirce Esq. his new house" in the deed for a nearby lot given the minister of the South congregation. John Pickering gave land at the top of the knoll for a meeting house in 1721, and Peirce's house originally faced the meeting house (see South Meeting House) in 1732 which formed a new civic and visual focal point for the neighborhood.

In 1742 Joshua Peirce sold most of his land and buildings on Pickering's Neck to his son, Joshua Jr., (although the house was also willed to him the next year in recognition of services he rendered his father in 1721). When Joshua Jr. died unmarried in 1754, the house passed to his brother Nathaniel whose room-by-room inventory of 1762 was valued at more than 13,000 pounds which, according to Daniels' inventory analysis, placed him among the highest 20% of colonial merchant-mariners to die in that difficult decade. Nathaniel's widow married Judge Leaverett Hubbard of Boston (appointed customs officer for Portsmouth), and they occupied the house into the 1790s. Shipmaster Nathaniel Peirce Jr. inherited the house and five mariner sons lived on here until 1850, by which time it was owned by others as a two-family rental property. It remained as such until renovated in 1970.

Physical Evidence: One of the few substantial Georgian houses of the ca. 1730 period left in Portsmouth, Joshua and Elizabeth Peirce's house demonstrates several interesting advances on the first example of elite building for his contemporary, Archibald MacPheadris. Its gambrel roof form, Georgian "double house" floor plan, and fireplace walls of fielded panels define a type that remained the Portsmouth norm for large merchant homes over the rest of the colonial period. Throughout the house the cornices do not yet break out as projections over each door and window as is common in most Piscataqua houses of the 18th century.

Its interior finish, while less elaborated than John Drew's work for Archibald MacPheadris, has one very unusual feature: a swinging paneled wall that opens two rooms into what may be (as described in the 1762 inventory) a single "Lower West Room." Like the front and rear parlors at the MacPheadris house, the two west rooms share a corner chimney stack. This one, however, contains small cupboards built into each fireplace corner and larger closets behind the stack that are lit by a window in the gable wall.

Sources:

Research by James Garvin, George and Erica Dodge, Martha Fuller Clark, Richard Candee.

Bruce C. Daniels, "Defining Economic Classes in Colonial New Hampshire, 1700-1770," *Historical New Hampshire*, 28:1 (Spring 1973): 53-62.

James L. Garvin, *Academic Architecture*: 86-89.

Elizabeth A. Rhodes, "The Furnishing of Portsmouth Houses, 1750-1775," *Historical New Hampshire*, 28:1 (Spring 1973): 1-20.

The eastern side of the kitchen fireplace was partially destroyed by later changes, although part of the bake oven survived. All interior trim in the kitchen was removed at some later date. The entire center stairway has been reconstructed to replace twin stairs that turned the house into a duplex; the arched window at the landing is restored off center, but the evidence of the landing and stairs were clear. The upper hall (that in the 1760s held a" broken couch," pine chest, and six chairs) is largely original with evidence of doors into rooms in the landing when the old stair was removed. Framing for the upper ceiling and floors (and, perhaps, throughout the house) are double framed with separate joists supporting the ceiling and others for the floor above as discovered when changes to the attic were being made.

The most elaborate chamber is in the southwest corner and has a fireplace flanked by two fluted pilasters with Corinthian capitals that Garvin attributes to the local carver Moses Paul (1676-1730). After 1719 Paul owned a house two lots away on Gates Street near the corner of Water (Marcy) Street. Their vertically proportioned carvings with strongly articulated leaves and a flower in the center of the abacus, so different from the later work of the Dearing family of carvers [see the Mills-Whipple and Moffatt-Ladd houses], as Garvin notes, are similar in style to those of the Jaffrey house cupboard removed from Portsmouth to the Museum of Fine Arts, Boston, in the 1920s.

RMC

South or Third Ward Hall and School

1866
Meeting House Hill,
architect: Isaiah Wilson
original site of the South Meeting House (1731)
current use: Portsmouth Children's Museum

In 1863 the city purchased the unused 1731 South Meeting House and "as a matter of safety" had it taken down from its granite knoll in the midst of Pickerings Neck. Residents of Ward 3 petitioned for a building combining a school room, ward hall, and tower in 1864. Plans by local carpenter-architect Isaiah Wilson were adopted that spring. Work was delayed by the war until 1866 when the city Aldermen decided to build it using local labor hired by the day. Building accounts document 44 individuals carpenters, joiners, cabinetmakers, masons, painters, teamsters and laborers as well as purchases from 33 other local suppliers. An eagle weathervane, ordered from John A. Winn & Co. of Boston, was mounted above the cupola that rises over the clock dials.

Beside using the first floor as a school, the auditorium on the second story served a wide range of public functions. When the Rev. Daniel Austin died in 1880 he left the city $250 to enable black residents to celebrate Emancipation Day. The first of these annual events occurred here in the South ward room in January 1882 with orations, dancing, and "a supper, consisting of oysters, meats, salads, cakes, preserves and fruit."

RMC

Sources:

South Meeting House Re-use Feasibility Study, Prepared for Portsmouth Advocates by The Thoresen Group (April 1981).

Receipts and Expenditures of the City of Portsmouth, 1864-1866.

PLEASANT STREET, WEST OF MEETING HOUSE HILL

Benjamin Holmes, Jr. House

Built ca. 1795
395 Pleasant St., corner Manning St.
builder: Benjamin Holmes, Jr.

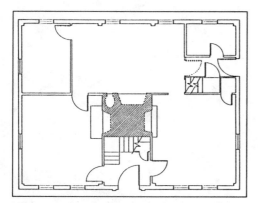

Measured by Bernard Herman, R. Candee.
Drawn by Gabrielle Lanier.

First floor plan, Benjamin Holmes, Jr. House.

This two-story, center chimney house was built during the course of the general redevelopment and expansion of the South End in the 1790s. Its owner and the presumed builder, Benjamin Holmes, Jr., was a master joiner or house carpenter who was among the founders of the local mechanic's society in 1803. In 1794 he combined two small lots at the corner of Pleasant and Manning Streets that backed onto the old South Meeting House. With five ground floor rooms and lobby entry, matched by a nearly identical second floor plan, this house type had been built in Portsmouth and the surrounding New England countryside for nearly a century. While the oldest examples were built for the local elite from 1695 to 1715, Holmes's dwelling represents the upper end of late 18th-century artisan housing. A room-by-room inventory taken after Holmes' death in 1837 lists a parlor, sitting room, kitchen, "little room" and scullery on the first floor. By then he also owned three tenanted houses on the other side of the south mill pond dam, but still owned his joiners tools. The house remains relatively unaltered, although the opening and door to a smoke oven in the central stack, located between floors beside the front staircase, has recently been plastered over.

BLH & RMC

Corner of Pleasant and Franklin Street

Across the street, at the entrance to Franklin Street or Cottars Lane, several large dwellings dominate the corner. On the northwest side, a later tenement now replaces an old house and bakery of Nathaniel Souther who continued the colonial pattern of combining home and craft shop. A dower division made after his death in 1825 gives a sense of the building's appearance. The widow Mehitable Souther received "the corner room on Pleasant Street and Cotters Lane, with the chamber and garret over and celler under." She was also granted an adjoining chamber "over the bake-house" and a piece of land between the bake-house and the house lot to the west. Like other widows she was guaranteed access to her share of the house "with the privilege of passing and repassing through the front door and the front stairs from the lower floor to the garret, also...through the front gate and the yard to the back of the house."

On the southwest corner, a new three-story, L-shaped, center passage plan house was sold by joiner William Marshall to mariner James Hill in 1812. It is shown in an 1814 plat by the English emigre surveyor John G. Hales illustrating the dower widow Mary

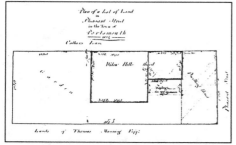

Rockingham County Probate

Plat of James Hill Estate and widow's dower, J.G. Hales, surveyor, 1814.

Hill received. Like Mehitable Souther's dower a decade later, Mary's share of the house — the rear ell and a garden behind — overlooked the lane. It is unclear how long she enjoyed this location; by 1817 the property was transferred to Captain Thomas Shaw [see Shaws Wharf, Prescott Park] and became a rental property like the house facing Pleasant Street next door. That second three-story L-house, built between 1806-1809 for another mariner, was leased to a physician among other early 19th-century tenants. Another three-story L-shaped hip roofed mansion, the now-demolished home of sea captain and distiller Michael Hooker, completed this group along Pleasant Street. All three are clearly visible in a turn-of-the-century photograph taken from across the South Mill Pond.

BLH

Cottars Lane and Pleasant Street from South Mill Pond.

Cottars Lane (Franklin Street)

Cottars Lane, now Franklin Street, is the southernmost of several parallel cul de sacs extending from Pleasant Street to the South Mill Pond that were subdivided during the early 1800s. The architectural development of this street represents a microcosm of one type of speculative housing erected in the city during the early 19th century, both in terms of land division and the types of dwellings constructed. All the land on the south side of this street was acquired by Langley Boardman in 1800; that on the north side was purchased by Thales G. Yeaton [see Strawbery Banke Museum], George Ham and various partners by 1810. From 1804 Boardman sold empty lots to several lesser speculators and builders, including bricklayers Samuel Barnard and Seth Pratt and housewright John Locke. Yeaton and Ham conveyed house lots to hatter Samuel Fernald, chairmaker Henry Beck, chaisemaker Nathaniel Frost, and joiner William Marshall. These second land purchasers, all part of an emerging and increasingly affluent class of urban artisans, either resold their properties or improved them with two-story wooden dwellings. A few artisans-owners adopted the earliest examples of purpose-built two-family urban plans that survive in the Portsmouth. Such houses draw upon similar and older urban forms common in other Atlantic ports, and presage Portsmouth's first limited experiment with row houses [see Sheafe Street] in the next decade. By 1815 the architectural development of Cottars Lane was complete. It remains nearly complete today, missing but one known house along the east side of a short secondary lane running south from Cottars Lane.

By the 1820s residents of Cottars Lane walked to work across Meeting House Hill to the waterfront, up Pleasant Street to the commercial heart of the city, or in at least one case across the South Mill Pond bridge to a nearby ropewalk. The occupational profile of owners and tenants shows that the fully developed Cottars Lane was still home to a variety of artisans: three joiners, a mason, carpenter, shoemaker, blockmaker and boatbuilder. Their neighbors now included at least two individuals in commerce: a trader in lime and wood and a ship master. Seven of the street's 15 residents were renters in 1821. In a town tied to the dangers of sea, widows represented one of the largest single group of householders throughout the city. On Cottars Lane Hannah Nelson, widow of a sailmaker, and Mehitable Barnes, a mariner's widow, each owned half of a duplex; one, at least, took in boarders.

Floor plans of these houses suggest new ideals and requirements of domestic organization common to many surviving homes erected during the city's 1790 to 1815 building boom. While they vary in form, each has either two or three heated rooms on each floor. The kitchen with a cooking fireplace and an oven, either on the ground floor or in the cellar, varied from 169 to 258 square feet. Single family houses had a separate dining room either adjacent to kitchen or directly above a cellar kitchen. The best room was always on the first floor and, even in these very small homes, at a point farthest from the domestic workspace. Only in the duplexes was there less than three ground floor rooms. Separation of male employment from the home also meant that commercial use of a streetfront first floor room or any artisan workshop is conspicuously missing from these modest urban homes.

Two-Family Houses: The duplex at the foot of Cottars Lane overlooking the South Mill Pond was commissioned by shoemakers Samuel and Joshua Rand sometime between 1804 and 1806. The floor plans and interior finish of the two units were nearly identical when first built. Each consisted of a roughly 20 by 30 foot unit laid out on a side-passage plan. Access into the house from the street was gained through an entry hall located on either side of the central party wall and extending a little more than half the depth of the building. Each entry contained a straight run stairway to the second floor, a door opening opposite the foot of the stair into the front room, a doorway at the end of the passage to the kitchen, and a shallow alcove was formed by the end of a centrally-placed chimney. The 12' x 14' front room apparently served as sitting room or parlor and was finished with a simple Federal-period mantel. The back room served as kitchen and domestic workroom. Both kitchens were 11 feet deep by 16 feet

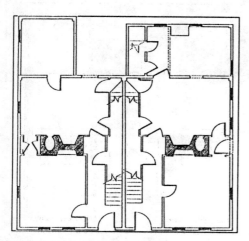

Measured by B. Herman, with R. Candee and Johanna McBrien; drawn by Nancy Van Dolsen.
Samuel and Joshua Rand Houses.

wide and originally had a back door along the rear wall. The cooking fireplace was built with an ash drop to the cellar and an elliptical shaped bake oven built into the chimney jamb. A winder stair in the back corner and a closet beneath the stair on each side of the party wall further separated the kitchens.

The second floor plan consists of a side-passage and front chamber consistent with the first floor. The back of the house was divided into two small (8' x 12') chambers, each with a shallow corner fireplace. The back chamber abutting the party wall was also a passageway; it could be entered from the front stair hallway or the rear winder stair and the entrance to the attic was from this room. The adjacent back chamber had greater privacy, although it could be entered from either of the two adjoining chambers.

While the two units were nearly mirror images on the main floors, their cellars differ significantly. The one adjacent to the mill pond contains a cellar finished with a fireplace, sash windows, and a doorway opening directly on the gable- end dooryard. The front cellar on this side, like the entire cellar beneath the eastern unit, was left as a roughly finished workspace; the chimney base on this side contains a walk-in smoke oven.

If the Rands occupied these houses, rather than rented them, they did so for only a few years. Samuel sold his half in 1817 to Dudley Chase, a joiner turned confectioner; his brother conveyed his house the next year to Elisha Plaisted, a trader in wood and lime. Until 1819 the houses occupied nearly the whole depth of the site. That year Chase and Plaisted purchased the lot behind the house and provided a common six foot common passage along the rear of the enlarged lot, which allowed construction of rear ells probably containing a woodshed and privy.

The mirror image side passage arrangement with front parlor and back kitchen/dining room, common to other Atlantic seaport towns, was new to Portsmouth before the 1813 fire. In fact, these earliest examples were structured almost exactly as a traditional Portsmouth "double house" (four room and central hall plan) with the frame modified by the insertion of the party wall and the particulars of interior finish.

The Rand houses were not the only examples of this form on Cottars Lane. After Nathaniel Frost and Henry Beck purchased a lot across Cottars Lane in 1810, they shared the cost of erecting a similar pair of houses built on speculation. In 1812 Nathaniel sold his half of the new house to joiner Samuel J. Frost, who may have actually been the builder. On the same day Frost and Beck deeded their respective halves to one another and Beck sold his western unit to mariner William Tullock who lived here until 1828. A few days later Shepherd J. Frost sold his half to stage driver Chester Shattuck who occupied the house until his death in 1834.

Both halves are laid out with a side-passage and room plan in a 20' x 30' core like the Rand houses. The major difference is in the configuration of the rooms in the back. Both the Frost and Beck kitchens were shortened by running the entry passage through the entire depth of the house, reducing the kitchens to 169

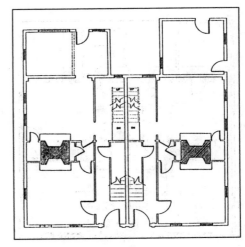

Measured by B. Herman, with R. Candee and Erica Dodge; drawn by Nancy Van Dolsen.

Frost and Beck Houses.

square feet (compared to the 181 square feet in the Rand houses). The builders compensated in at least one of these units with a 10' square back pantry with full cellar beneath. Along the party wall near the back entry were once a pair of straight-run stairs to the second floor and cellar very much like those in the brick rowhouses of Sheafe Street built soon after the 1813 fire. Like those later houses and those of the Rand brothers, the interior finish incorporated Federal period trim including mantels, door and window surrounds, and sometimes elaborate ceiling cornices.

Single-Family Houses: On either side of the Frost-Beck duplex and on lots behind the Rands houses other builders constructed two-story single-family homes. Two appear on an 1813 map and the third was likely built soon thereafter. Each is a different variant on the many single-room deep or L-plan houses with rear-wall chimneys that can be seen in other early 19th-century houses throughout the city. *[see Strawbery Banke Museum]* Both the Laighton House on the mill pond and the Barnard-Lord house immediately behind the Rand houses were designed to incorporate cellar kitchens. This practice is unknown locally before about 1800, but, where sloping land formations allowed, it became nearly ubiquitous. The Portsmouth aqueduct was established in the 1790s and soon brought water directly into the cellars of most new homes. Taking advantage of sloping sites, new houses built around the mill pond allowed the aqueduct to feed directly into cellar kitchens.

The Barnard-Lord House was built in the course of a series of back-and-forth land transactions between the cabinetmaker and land developer Langley Boardman and bricklayer Samuel Barnard. By 1806 Barnard had erected the basic structure, but when he advertised the house for sale in 1813 he cautioned it was "partially finished." The 18 x 36 foot house "with excellent lower kitchen" was completed while a second flurry of mortgages and sales between 1814 and 1824 brought it into the hands of Sampson B. Lord, a boat builder and blockmaker. The kitchen occupies the lower end of the cellar, while the other end was a roughly finished storage area.

The first floor illustrates the most common period plan: two rooms separated by a lobby entry with an open winding staircase (often semi-circular) configured like central chimney houses *[see Benjamin Holmes and Samuel Jackson plans]*. The relocation of chimneys to the rear walls freed up the interior for additional living space. Identified in plats and inventories of other similar houses, the unheated 8' x 9' room behind the lobby entry was often a" chamber" or downstairs bedroom. The interior finish of the main rooms, like most small houses of Portsmouth's federal rebuilding, include modest but fashionable mantels, dados, cornices, window casings and door surrounds.

The Laighton house, the last house built in the development

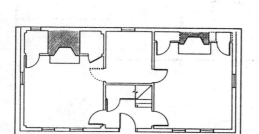

Measured by B. Herman and R. Candee; drawn by Dean Doerrfeld and Gabrielle Lanier
Barnard-Lord House.

of Cottars Lane, is consistent with all the other surviving dwellings in terms of plan, construction, and finish. While the history of ownership is somewhat unclear, it appears that joiner William Marshall bought the land and mortgaged it to blockmaker Luke Laighton by 1810; court action appears to have left the land in Laighton's hands and he may have built the house as a rental shortly after 1813 despite the controversial 1814 law requiring new buildings over 12' high to be of brick. His son John, also a blockmaker, lived here in 1821 although it reverted to tenancy by 1823. This original 18' x 36' center-hall plan house fronted the north side of Cottars Lane near the mill pond. The entry hall contained a straight-run open string staircase like those of its neighboring duplexes. A second stair to the cellar kitchen beneath the main stair was entered through a low doorway at the back of the hall. The rooms on either side of the hall were of nearly equal size, but the room over the kitchen was fitted with closets on either side of the chimney with its Federal style mantel. The cellar kitchen proved to be inconvenient for the occupants and was replaced by the mid-19th century with a one-story rear ell.

The Fernald-Tyler House sits at the head Cottars Lane, behind the site of the Souther home bakery on the corner. Samuel Fernald bought his lot from Yeaton and Ham in 1810 and built the house by 1813 when an auction notice advertised "a new 2 story house for one or two families." It became the home of Benjamin Floyd until the local bookbinder was lost at sea and his wife Betsy was attached for his debts. One creditor received an execution that gave him ownership of the west front room and the privilege of using the front entry and in 1816 Fernald again advertised half the house for sale. In 1823 Betsy Floyd sold whatever remaining rights she had in the property to Phineas Tyler, a carpenter who already occupied the house as a tenant and lived in the house until 1850. The house was later converted to a two family dwelling by the addition of a second rear ell and wing.

The 18' x 36' front block echoes the size and plan of the other rear-wall chimney houses on Cottars Lane, including the lobby entrance, curved staircase, small room behind the stair and the two main rooms. The 1813 map shows the house with a rear ell behind the both rooms, but the house only retains evidence of an original one-story western lean-to with a cooking fireplace and bake oven in a chimney stack that also heated the dining room and its upstairs chamber. Construction of the later wing destroyed the chimney stack and shortened the room's depth by three feet to build a new back staircase from the side entrance. The old stack was replaced by a brick flue for a parlor stove and the room redecorated with new cornices and a chair rail. No evidence survives to indicate whether there could have been a rear kitchen to accommodate a second family to occupy the house as the newspaper advertisements suggest.

BLH

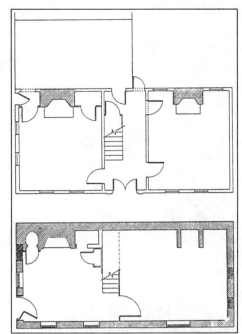

Measured by B. Herman and Claire Dempsey; drawn by Gabrielle Lanier.

Laighton House.

Sources:

Bernard L. Herman, "The Architectural and Social Topography of Portsmouth, NH, 1820-1825. VAF conference paper, 1991, Lexington, KY.

Additional research by Bernard Herman, Johanna McBrien, and Richard Candee.

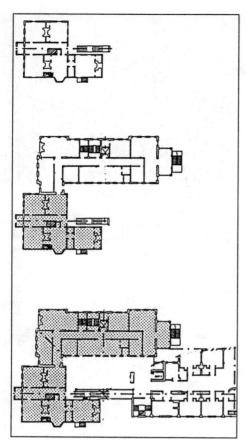

Aring-Schroeder, Architects.

Developmental sequence 1763 to 1987, Gov. John Wentworth House [Mark Wentworth Home for the Aged].

Source:

James Garvin, *Academic Architecture*

Governor John Wentworth House

now The Mark Hunking Wentworth Home for the Aged

Built 1763
346 Pleasant Street

Built in 1763 for Henry Appleton, the house was sold the next year to Mark Hunking Wentworth for his daughter Ann and her husband John Fisher, custom collector of Salem. Three years later Fisher rented it to the province for his brother-in-law, the newly appointed Royal Governor, John Wentworth. The relative isolation of this house is suggested by the governor's own description of it.

> *a Small Hut with little comfortable apartments. On the one Side (we have too much modesty to call it Front) We look over the Town and down the River on to the boundless Atlantic Ocean [,] on the other we overlook a place for a garden... separated from the Fields by a large Sea Water pond which enlivens the usual scene that is our only entertainment here in the morning.*

The façade, articulated by original quoined corners, has been altered by a portico and doorway of early 19th century date. James Garvin has identified some of the interior details, like the opposed fish motif in the frieze of the SE parlor mantel, as having derived from William Kent's Designs of Inigo Jones (1727) or, perhaps, from Edward Hoppus's 1738 plagiarization of Kent's work, *The Gentleman's and Builder's Repository*. He suggests that this may be one of a number of alterations to the house made by Wentworth before 1770. Eighteenth-century flocked wallpaper survives in one room. The staircase departs from the local norm in the use of fluted colonettes for both the balusters and newel post, while the treads do not have the boxed ends seen in larger homes of the 1760s. They do, however, share the carved brackets.

The house is now the Mark H. Wentworth Home for the Aged, which built georgian revival rear additions in 1912 and 1927, and finished a major new addition (1984-86) designed by Aring-Schroeder, a local architectural office.

JLG & RMC

PLEASANT STREET BETWEEN COURT AND LIVERMORE STREETS

The Pickerings gave land for Pleasant Street to the town in 1673 and over the next century it came to be lined with many large gambrel houses for the local elite. The houses on the western side had large gardens stretching to the South Mill Pond. After the Revolution, old lots on the east side were reconfigured, existing houses moved and used as rentals, as Governor John Langdon and others built new homes.

Opposite the Langdon House was a Universalist Church designed in 1807 by John Locke. In 1818 the town voted to establish a Lancastrian School in its basement story; it continued here until the creation of a public high school depleted it of older "monitors" to teach younger students. As late as 1835 the cellar school was said to be "very unhealthy and inconvenient" and "when the wind blows" off the mill pond "school is dismissed until the wind may change."

After the 1813 fire and brick building law, new masonry houses were built for Ann Treadwell (corner of Court and Pleasant), Abraham Wendell (corner Gates and Pleasant), Nathan Parker (end of Livermore Street), and an 1828 Congregational church (corner Livermore and Pleasant). This was later the home of the Christian Church, founded by Elias Smith in 1803, before being converted to houses in 1858. The Colcord House, at the northern juncture of Washington and Pleasant, replaced Governor John Wentworth's stable after it was torn down in 1871.

Courtesy Portsmouth Athenæum

Universalist Church (1807), Samuel Langdon house (ca. 1750), No. Church Parsonage (1791). Photograph ca. 1890.

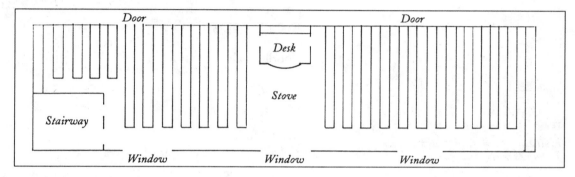

Redrawn by Amy Amidon after original pew plan.

Proposed Plan, Pleasant Street meeting house, 1826.

Haven Park

Created 1900

Pleasant Street, between Edwards and Livermore Streets

Across Edwards Street from the Jacob Wendell House is a small public park that once contained three 18th century houses. All three had gardens that ran down to the South Mill Pond, the most interesting of which was that of Edward Parry. Built by 1798, it terminated in a castellated "Fort Anglesea" along the pond, from which the Market Square English import merchant was wont to fire a cannon. The middle house in this block, a ca. 1760 two-story hip-roof 'double house,' was built for the Reverend Dr. Samuel Haven, minister for the South Church. Soon after 1800 a third story was added and capped by low hip roof in the Federal style. When the last Haven heir died, the house was taken down and the property bequeathed to the City of Portsmouth with sufficient funds to buy and remove the houses on both sides for a public park.

The southernmost gambrel house built in the mid 18th century for lawyer Michael Livermore, is said to have once faced Pleasant Street. By 1813 it was sited gable-end to the street facing Livermore Street. It was later moved across the street and turned to face the new park. Its three-story brick neighbor was erected for The Reverend Nathan Parker, Dr. Haven's successor and a leading Unitarian minister. The cost of its erection, sometime after 1813, was apparently born by several wealthy merchant sons of Samuel Haven.

RMC

Courtesy Portsmouth Athenæum

Samuel Haven House (left), Edward Parry House (center), Jacob Wendell House (right). Photograph ca. 1865.

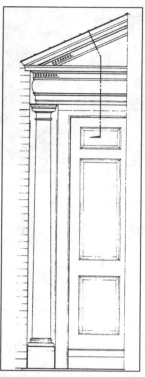

Drawn by Philip Kendrick.

Half Elevation, front entrance,
Joshua Haven House.

Joseph Haven House

Built ca. 1800-01
corner Pleasant and Richmond streets

One of the Rev. Samuel Haven's sons was Joseph Haven, whose three story house is located directly across from Haven Park is a large version of the L-plan rear-wall chimney house. The kitchen was located on the first floor of the three story ell, together with a pantry, back staircase, and rear entry (the projecting side entry was added). A dining room clearly occupied the south front room and contained, until the house was rehabilitated into condominiums, its own china closet with built in sideboard located behind the false window at the south east corner. The north front parlor, with a broken scroll pediment and plaster bust over the fireplace, has greater height and depth than other first floor room and, like the Langdon house, the chamber above is a step higher than the second floor stairhall. This parlor chamber has more composition ornament (on its mantelpiece, cornice frieze, and on elliptical wooden valances above the windows) than any other in the city.

RMC

Wendell House

Built 1789
214 Pleasant St. corner of Edwards St.

Built for Jeremiah Hill in 1789, the house is known by the name of the merchant who bought and redecorated the house in 1815. As constructed it has been called a miniature version of the Gov. Langdon House. Of the original rococo decoration, one major element remains. The rose carved fireplace frieze in the second floor chamber, like that inserted about this same time on the Wentworth-Gardner parlor fireplace, echoes the Dearings work on the Langdon parlors.

Much of the original finish was lost when Jacob Wendell remodeled the house in preparation for his marriage. Because it stayed in the family for several generations, the house gained a reputation for having remained untouched since the early 19th century. Actually, while many of the Jacob Wendell family furnishings were preserved in the house a great deal of later alteration modified the 1816 renovations. After the Civil War the house was redecorated at least twice with new wallpapers, floor coverings, and other finishes as well as the installation of modern technologies.

After Harvard professor, literary critic, and noted nativist Barrett Wendell acquired the house at the turn of this century, he and his wife, Edith Greenough Wendell, embarked on a series of improvements that include a colonial revival mantelpiece to replace a Victorian replacement of the Federal replacement to the original in the front dining room. In addition to a "Chinese puzzle" garden behind the house, the couple added a large two-story space for informal entertainment and study. This loosely "colonial style" summer living room, opening onto a screen porch on one end and an enclosed flower garden through French doors, looks across to a pedimented doorway enframing the back door to the outbuildings. The Wendell House was purchased a few years ago by a local antiques dealer and auctioneer who has begun another round of period style improvements to preserve the house and make it his own.

RMC

Governor Langdon Mansion

Built 1783–86
143 Pleasant St.
master-joiners: Daniel Hart and Michael Whidden III
with Ebenezer Clifford
carvings: Ebenezer and William Dearing
owner: Society for the Preservation of New England Antiquities

Governor John Langdon was a ship captain and Revolutionary leader who profited by the war. During the 1790s he represented New Hampshire in Congress and became the most important Jeffersonian Republican leader in the state upon his return to Portsmouth. He served several terms as governor and established the Jeffersonian majority that kept Portsmouth politics republican throughout most of the 19th century. Republican party leaders were members of a new generation of wealthy merchants and lawyers whose homes included some of the finest federal houses in the town.

Langdon's 1789 mansion was among the first of the large post-Revolutionary new homes that came to dominate and define the residential character of Pleasant Street. For its construction Langdon turned to Daniel Hart, a joiner who had served in Langdon's independent military company during the 1770s and became his chief ship joiner for the construction of continental warships. Hart, in turn, employed Michael Whidden to assist him, especially with the interior finish joinery.

Inside and out, the house is a traditional 18th-century Portsmouth elite dwelling dressed up in elaborate rococo garb. It continued the use of a high hip roof with dormers that remained popular in this city from the 1750s through the earliest decades of the 19th century. The front portico, probably derived from ideas in Abraham Swan's *A Collection of Designs in Architecture* (London: 1757), is integrated into the normal five-bay façade by downward-sweeping panels on either side of a French window on the second floor and by additional panels flanking the doorway. The three dormers in the front slope of the hip roof echo the pediments that Daniel Hart's father, Samuel, made for the Moffatt-Ladd House 20 years earlier.

The public quality of the Langdon's life is, perhaps, especially apparent in the width of the central hallway and the size of the north parlor that occupies the whole depth of the large house. The Langdon mansion was the first elite house in the Piscataqua to have such a double room and its scale bears comparison with Benning Wentworth's "Council Room" at Little Harbor

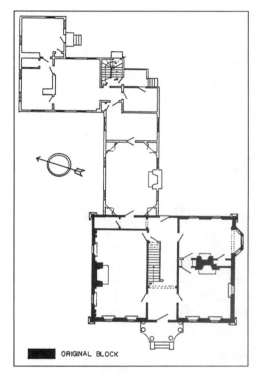

ORIGINAL BLOCK

Drawing by Judy Quinn after HABS.
First floor plan, Langdon House.

[see Wentworth-Coolidge Mansion] It must have been especially impressive to visitors when the warm putty paint of the woodwork set off the plain pink imported wallpaper and a dozen upholstered lolling chairs that the Langdons ordered for the room.

Garvin has identified the architectural elements of the staircase and entrance hall as probably the work of Ebenezer Clifford, a master-joiner from Exeter who later designed several elite Portsmouth homes. But it is the interior ornament, rich with the most lavish display of rococo carvings in any house along the Piscataqua before or since, that makes the interior so noteworthy. These carvings, on the north parlor fireplace and that of the small southwest parlor, were the work of Ebenezer Dearing and his son William. Their designs were drawn, with more or less fidelity, from plates 48 and 54 in Abraham Swan's *The British Architect* (London: 1745).

In 1836 this house became the home of Charles and Anne Burroughs. He was as Episcopal minister, who had the southeast rear sitting room remodeled in the Greek Revival style and a bay window added overhanging the raised cellar wall like a pulpit. At the end of the century the house was purchased by a New York descendent and namesake of John Langdon's brother, Woodbury Langdon, for his mother. After he inherited the property it was enlarged as an in-town summer home. In 1905-06 the firm of McKim, Mead & White, replaced the original service wing with a new dining room, modern kitchen, pantry and servants quarters. Kevin Murphy has discovered that the client demanded that the dining room be a copy of the octagonal room from Woodbury Langdon's 1785 Adamesque brick house on State Street. *[see Rockingham Hotel]* The architects were self-conscious of it becoming known they were undertaking a strict replication. John Howard Adams, draftsman in the firm's New York City office, however, exploited details from measured drawings of that room to also design new elements like the ceiling medallion. The recreated woodwork was furnished by Irving & Casson of Boston, who also took drawings of the old State Street room for motifs used in the dining room furniture.

Brick offices: At the front corners of the Langdon house are two brick one story structures which appear on the 1812 map of the city. While that next to the driveway has been substantially altered, its plan as a two room office with a missing chimney between is clear. Under the present roof is evidence of an earlier skylight. The larger brick flanker facing Pleasant Street near the original northern edge of the property (the mid 18th-century Penhallow House then occupied the corner lot) also contains two rooms. In 1816, lawyer William M. Richardson advertised that he had moved "to the Brick Office in Pleasant street, near Gov. Langdon's." These are the only two remaining detached one-story commercial buildings of the dozens which once dotted the streetscape of this era.

RMC

Sources:

Garvin, *Academic Architecture.*

"A Noble & Dignified Stream" The Piscataqua Region in the Colonial Revival 1860-1930, ed. by Sarah Giffen and Kevin Murphy.

DOWNTOWN PORTSMOUTH
CIVIC AND RELIGIOUS STRUCTURES

The Portsmouth Book (1890)
Queen's Chapel

New Hampshire's ecclesiastical beginnings were tentative and episodic, but began with Anglican services for fishermen and others of the earliest trading company. As early as 1638 a small Church of England chapel may have been erected on Pleasant Street. It did not last and it was not until 1732, when the oligarchy of royal governors established their control of patronage and politics, that a permanent Queens Chapel was established on Church Hill. Renamed St. John's in 1791 and rebuilt after the fire of 1806, it remained the sole Episcopalian church structure in Portsmouth until 1832, when a small Doric Temple (now lost) was built next to the parsonage on State Street. Christ Church, a second Episcopal Church (also lost) was built on Madison Street at the end of Austin Street between 1880 and 1883. After it burned in 1963 the congregation rebuilt in the growing west part of the city on Lafayette Road

The proximity of the Bay Colony and the annexation of the Piscataqua settlements and governing of them by Massachusetts governors, brought Standing Order congregational polity and theology to New Hampshire. Communities were allowed but not required to fund a minister and meeting house from public taxation. In Portsmouth the presence of a Puritan minister dates to the rise of Massachusetts-oriented leaders in the mid-17th century in opposition to royal governors. The first public meeting house in Portsmouth, built just below the south mill dam, was constructed in 1659 although a church was not gathered until the

Gleason's Pictorial Magazine (July 1853)
Episcopal Chapel (left) built 1832 by William Tucker and South Church (right), 1824 State Street.

first regular minister was ordained in 1671. [see 6] The "logg" structure was to be made "40 feet square with 12 windows well fitted, 3 substantial doors and a complete pulpit."

The Portsmouth Book (1890)
North Meeting House after 1854 sketch.

South Meeting House.

Like other growing communities Portsmouth eventually divided into two parishes, after a meeting house location and control controversy so common in New England towns. The new North Parish constructed a meeting house at the eastern edge of the glebe lots, now Market Square, in 1711. The second new church for this congregation was built on the same site in 1854. *[See North Church]* The old meeting house, now known as South Parish, was replaced in 1731 by a new meeting house located on what came to be known as Meeting House Hill above the south mill pond. In 1796, the congregation voted to paint "the out side of the Meeting House, the Walls of House of a light stone colour, & the Roof of a chocolate colour." The exterior may have had trim and other details picked out with red or brown, and the interior was probably white with blue highlights. Joiner-architect Bradbury Johnson assisted with this remodeling. A few years later the meeting house was given "a handsome projection of a semielliptical form" in its gallery to accommodate singers, its "ill looking braces" were replaced by wooden knees, its ceiling was coved, its posts cased, its interior painted, and a porch added. The congregation occupied the building until 1826 when they moved into a new granite edifice on State Street. *[see South Church* On the site of the 18th century meeting house stands the later South Ward room, now the Children's Museum *[See South Ward Hall]*.

Compared to the experience of some of its neighbors, Portsmouth's response to the Great Awakening was mild. Whitefield visited but found the townspeople "spiritually unconcerned." By 1757, however, members of both parishes withdrew and eventually formed an Independent Congregational Society under the Separatist and Baptist Samuel Drown. They built a meeting house on Pitt Street, now Court Street, between Pleasant and Washington Street (now replaced). After 1764 followers of Robert Sandeman met in town, espousing an anti-Calvinism that caused much concern to the growing number of New England Baptists. The Sandemanian meeting house of 1764 was on the site of Col. Thomas Thompson's 1784 house next to the John Langdon house on Pleasant Street *[see map p. 2]*, although Sandemanians were still meeting as late as 1801 in a private house.

After the Revolution the geographic parishes became more distinct in theology, a common pattern in large communities in New England. The South began to be identified with Arminian and finally Unitarian theology, while the North remained both Calvinist and Trinitarian. In 1829 a group withdrew from the North Church and formed the Independent Congregational Society *[see Pleasant Street Church]*, but this schism was short-lived. Together with the Episcopalian churches, the North and South churches were attended by the most influential and wealthy members of the community. Both North and South congregation added chapels – the former at the east side of Middle Street near Islington, the site now occupied by the Salvation Army, the latter on the site of the Court Street meeting house, now occupied by the First Pentacostal Church.

Throughout New England the early national era saw religious societies emerge to represent a variety of views unthinkable before the Revolution. These included both anti-Calvinist groups as well as increasingly evangelical ones. Benjamin Randall began the spiritual quest that resulted in the founding of the Free Will Baptists in nearby New Castle, and adherents to his new faith were found here at the end of the 18th century. They did not form a religious society until 1832 and reorganized in 1851. In 1858 they erected a church opposite the Portsmouth Steam Factory on the corner of Hanover and Pearl streets, recently the "72" restaurant.

John Murray, founder of New England Universalism, visited Portsmouth as early as 1773. Early converts met in a schoolhouse and the Sandemanian meeting house before building off Vaughan and Hanover streets in 1784. In 1808 they built a new meeting house on Pleasant, south of Court Street; when it burned in 1896 they rebuilt in a brick Gothic style which also burned in the 1940s. Their first building subsequently served several congregations beginning with the Methodists. Jesse Lee, among the most effective of the Methodist itinerants, visited Portsmouth as early as 1790; a society was formed in 1808 and purchased the former Universalist meeting house. In 1827 they built a brick church for themselves on State Street *[see Temple Israel]*. When they began Methodists were subject to much criticism throughout New England, but by the mid-19th century were quite well-established and deemed respectable.

Elias Smith was responsible for the eventual establishment of a distinctive church known both as the Christians and Baptists, but unassociated with either group. Meeting first in Jefferson Hall above the Brick Market, they were incorporated in 1806 as the First Baptist Society of Portsmouth. Their 1804 first meeting house was located on Chestnut Street *[see Music Hall]*. The group changed their name to the First Christian Church in 1838, and a group subsequently bought and removed to the Pleasant Street Independent Church. By the 1850s the denomination had no meetingplace of its own, apparently rotating among church buildings in town. In 1862 they purchased the one story Brodhead Methodist Church on Court Street near Haymarket Square and in 1899 remodeled it. In 1954, when they purchased the adjacent Granite State Insurance Company building for a new home as the Central Baptist Church, their older building became an annex. More traditional Baptists organized in 1826 and built a church at the western intersection of State and Middle streets in 1828, a new church in 1852, with a chapel around the corner on State Street after 1883. The congregation, the Middle Street Baptists, rebuilt in the 1950s on the original site of John Peirce House which they moved and remodeled. William Miller found believers in Portsmouth, meeting first in a small chapel on Hanover Street before building their own in 1853; they relocated to Summer Street in 1941.

While for many ears only Protestant groups established societies and parishes in Portsmouth, renewed European immigration brought diversity with it in the mid and late 19th century. Although small numbers of Roman Catholics were long present

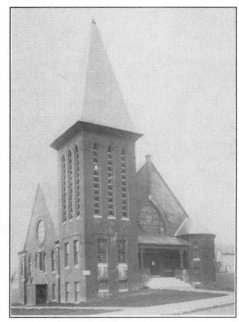

Courtesy Portsmouth Athenæum
Universalist Church, (1896).

Courtesy Strawbery Banke Museum
Central Baptist Church, Court St. (1891).

From J.H. Bragdon, *Seaboard Towns* (1857)
Hanover Street Chapel.

Sources:

Ahlstrom, Sidney. *Religious History of the American People* (1972)

Dedication of the Advent Christian Church. 1941

Laurence R. Craig, *Three Centuries of Religious Living,* 1966

Alexander Munton, *125 Years as a Parrish Church 1852-1977,* 1977

South (Stone) Church, 1824-26.

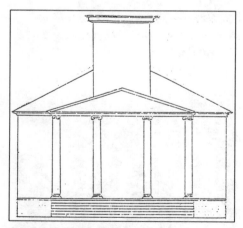

Courtesy Earle Shettleworth

Proposed First Parish Church, Portland, ME, ca. 1826 by Chief Justice Prentiss Mellen after South Church, Portsmouth, NH.

[*see Imaculate Conception complex*], they remained unorganized and unchurched until early in the 19th century. A mission in 1836, Portsmouth did not become an independent parish until 1851; its first church on Summer Street, between Middle and State streets, was completed two years later. The parish added a school in 1867 and rebuilt its church in 1871 and again in 1934. As Portsmouth expanded to the west after World War II, new parishes were formed to serve the area: St. Catherine of Sienna in 1951 and St. James in 1958. Establishment of a Jewish congregation dates to 1905 and the group purchased the Methodist Church in 1912. Having met in homes and rented spaces since the turn of the twentieth century, the Greek Orthodox community purchased the Cabot Street School from the city in 1932, and formed St. Nicholas Church. In 1971 they too moved west to Alumnae Drive.

CWD

South Church/Unitarian-Universalist

Built 1824-26
292 State Street
Jonathan Folsom, joiner
architect: 1858 addition and remodeling: S.S. Woodcock, Boston

Although often misattributed to Alexander Parris, the South Church (built between 1824 and 1826) was probably designed by Jonathan Folsom, a joiner originally from Exeter who is credited with so many brick landmarks built in Portsmouth after the 1813 fire [*see Custom House, Long-Ladd House, Larkin Rice House*]. Folsom undoubtedly acted as architect as well as master builder for the South Church. While Parris [*see St. John's Church*], introduced the Greek Revival into New England first at Boston's St. John's Church in 1819, he seems to have derived his 1827-28 Congregational church in Quincy, Massachusetts, in response to plans of this Portsmouth model shown to him by the church committee. South Church, a large granite structure with a short square tower and a Greek Revival portico of four Doric columns, was promoted by the *New England Galaxy* as "a model for the next church in Boston" because of its beautiful architecture. Several New England church proposals, including one for Portland, Maine, derived direct and indirect inspiration from its design.

Upon completion the church had only one balcony in the rear of the building for the choir, a departure from the usual church design with side galleries. The organ was concealed within the rear wall so only the front of it was visible from below. A high pulpit was originally installed, then replaced in 1841 with a lower one not only because of changing stylistic tastes but also "for the safety of the pastor's health & for the convenience of hearing and thus for the benefit of the whole parish."

Some thirty years after completion, the Stone Church, as it was familiarly known, underwent significant alterations. Masons carefully disassembled the rear stone wall of the building, built new side walls, then reassembled the rear wall seventeen feet from its original location. This addition allowed for a larger organ and choir in the rear of the pulpit as well as complementary service areas. Interior changes included new Corinthian capitals and entablatures for the existing fluted pilasters, an arched ceiling paneled with ornamental moldings, and a "rich scroll work canopy, supported by fluted columns and rich capitals." Under the supervision of Boston architect S.S. Woodcock, plastering and stucco work were done by John Mack of Lowell; carpentry by Geo. Hanson of Malden; and masonry by Thos. J. Whidden of Boston. On Christmas day of 1858 South Church was reopened and rededicated. In 1987 the interior of the church was again renovated by the local preservation contractors Dodge, Adams & Roy.

EF

Sources:

Peter Benes & Phillip D. Zimmerman, *New England Meeting House and Church: 1630-1850*. Boston: Boston University, 1979.

New England Galaxy, 9 (July 21, 1826): 2.

James Garvin, Academic Architecture: 504-8.

Portsmouth Journal, 8 Nov. 1858; 1 Jan. 1859.

Earle Shettleworth, "The Emergence of the Greek Revival in Portland, ME, 1825 to 1840," unpublished paper, 1971.

Edward Zimmer, The Architectural Career of Alexander Parris (1780-1852). 3 vols., Ph.D. diss., Boston University, 1984: 544-546.

North Church/Congregational

Built 1854
Market Square
architects: Towle & Foster, Boston

The North Church had its beginnings in the division of the earliest congregation into the north and south parishes in 1712. The group that followed the minister to the new building, at what is now the corner of Congress and Pleasant Streets, became the North Congregational Church. *[See Market Square]* The original building on Market Square was:

> *seventy feet long and three stories high, with two galleries and three tiers of windows set with diamond-shaped glass in leaden sashes... the pulpit occupied the middle of the western side, and was surmounted by a large sounding-board.*

There were three entrances on the north, south, and east sides. A tower with an open belfry and a steeple one hundred and fifty feet high was added soon after the building's completion. The north bell tower and steeple is generally believed to be a 1730 addition, but in 1723 the town voted to plaster the upper galleries and create inside doors "at the Steple End." In 1749 a clock, given to the town by several prominent citizens, was placed in the steeple.

In 1834, plans to remodel the old meeting house went awry resulting in the resignation of the minister who felt that the building was inadequate for both his and the congregation's needs. The next year the building was remodeled and "converted into a respectable looking meeting house of more modern style." During this renovation the meeting house was reoriented and transformed into a church. From a later photograph of the structure, one can see that large windows replaced several small ones. On the east side of the building alone some twenty small windows on three levels were supplanted by three large round headed windows each three stories high. At this time the three entrances were replaced by one entrance on the west side.

In 1854 the old building was finally replaced by a new $30,000 structure, designed by Towle & Forster of Boston, reflecting an urban design recommended by the Congregational church

Courtesy North Church Collection, Athenæum
Remodelled North Meeting House 1837-54.

Sources:

William H. Pierson, Jr. "Richard Upjohn and the American Rundbogenstil." *Winterthur Portfolio*. 21 (Winter 1968):235-237.

North Church, 1854. Towle & Foster, architects.

Methodist Church and the end of Penhallow Street, ca. 1850–1860.

in *A Book of Plans for Churches and Parsonages* (1853). The architects' 17-page printed building specifications specifically cited their earlier Shawmut Church of Boston as the standard for the new Portsmouth structure. They also described the desired appearance of the new church's exterior as

> *painted with three good coats of the best of English white lead and best of Dutch linseed oil. Each of the two last coats will have blown in them sharp clean sand. The color of the outside will be in imitation of freestone, dark color. The outside wood work is all to be painted within ten hours after it shall have been applied to the edifice....The doors, both outside and inside, to be grained in oil in imitation of oak....Sashes outside to be painted a bronze color. Inside stained in imitation of Cherry.*

James Moses III, the builder, contracted with the firm of Johnson Hathaway & Stone of Worcester, Massachusetts for ten terra cotta double window caps with consoles for the side windows, six single caps for the front windows, and one center window cap with consoles. An addendum to the contract adds two single window caps for the tower with consoles at the cost of $25.

While 1854 interior specification also detailed the frescoing of the pulpit wall and a portion of the ceiling, this work may have not been done. In 1872 the *Portsmouth Journal* noted that "the interior of the North church will probably be greatly improved by frescoing the walls and ceiling," and Charles J. Schumacker of Portland, Maine, was employed to complete the frescoing. Schumacker, an immigrant from Prussia who arrived in the United States in 1853, is known for painting landscapes on canvas, undertaking fresco paintings in buildings, and running an art store in Portland with his brother before moving to Boston in 1882. Interior frescoes in "trompe l'oeil" were extremely popular for public buildings *[see Rockingham Hotel]* during the second half of the century. The church was further embellished in 1890 with the addition of a new organ and memorial windows.

EF

Temple Israel formerly the Methodist Church

Built 1827
200 State Street

The Methodist Society, organized in Portsmouth in 1808, began by meeting at a private home on Washington Street. From there the society moved to the "Cameneum" on Vaughan Street, formerly home to the Universalists before the erection of their Pleasant Street building . Finally, in 1827 with the appropriate Masonic ceremonies, the cornerstone for the Methodist's own church was laid. When completed at a cost of $9000, the brick building rose two-and-a-half stories high, gable end to the street, with a projecting pavilion topped by a brick and wood cupola. Separate staircases for its three doors were connected by fencing. During 1853-54 "the church was completely renovated" and the church was covered with paint and sanded in imitation of brownstone like that of the North Church. Simultaneously, quoins were applied around the front doors, the outer corners of the building, and along the pavilion. Photographs show the front steps were altered to one long set of stairs running almost the length of the building. [see photo] Around 1890 a street-level doorway was added on the east side of the building leading to the basement level. By about 1900, the paint and sand mixture had been replaced by light-colored paint.

In 1912, the building became home to a Jewish congregation who renamed the structure the Temple of Israel. About 1920 the Temple removed the cupola and substituted a painted replica of the Ten Commandments for the shuttered window in the gable. A brick-faced concrete addition to the 1827 building was completed in 1967. The building was stripped of its paint and refurbished in 1991/92.

The building's interior has undergone several alterations. Although we do not know the appearance of the original balconies, we know that they were removed in 1861 after being declared unsafe. This change set in motion a major interior remodeling, including the installation in the rear of the pulpit of a larger organ to replace one of 1837, a complete rebuilding of the altar, and the introduction of new pews. The basement, always a problem, was further water-proofed and repaired although it was not used for Sunday School classes until 1890. A balcony was remodeled at a cost of $30,000. New features included a basement, a heating system, an electrical system and light fixtures, and two school rooms. Both the interior and exterior were painted at that time.

EF

Courtesy Whalley Museum and Library
Methodist Church, ca. 1860-70.

Source:

History of Methodism in Portsmouth: 1790 – 1976. First United Methodist Church, Portsmouth, NH.

St. John's Episcopal Church

Built 1807
Chapel Street
architect: Alexander Parris, Portland, Maine

There were two predecessors to the present St. John's Church. The first was a the Church of England chapel and parsonage on Pleasant Street, erected about 1638. The church's plate and service books were brought from England by the earliest Portsmouth settlers. Following the dismissal of an early pastor and due to conflicts within the church and the influx of Puritans from Massachusetts Bay Colony, services were held only on an intermittent basis for many years.

In 1732 a small group of congregants built a large wooden building some sixty feet long and forty feet wide. Six round-headed windows adorned each side of the building. On the western end was a tower with an open belfry and spire. Under the stairs on the north side was the vestry. There was a large carved wooded canopy bearing the royal arms which sheltered two large carved chairs for the governor and later visiting dignitaries such as George Washington. The structure was named Queen's Chapel, in honor of Queen Caroline who had given the church silver stamped with

Courtesy Strawbery Banke Museum
St. John's Church.

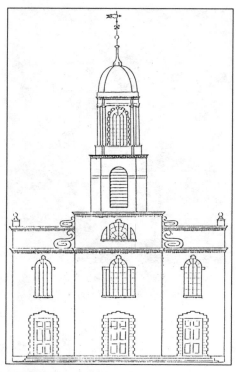

drawing by James Garvin

St. John's Church, Reconstruction of 1807 front façade and modern elevation.

Sources:

Robert E. McLaughlin, *On Church Hill.* Portsmouth: St. John's Church, 1982.

Philip Zimmerman, *Ecclesiastical Architecture in the Reformed Tradition in Rockingham County, New Hampshire, 1790–1860.* Ph.D. diss., Boston University, 1985: 112-117.

C.S. Gurney, *Portsmouth Historic and Picturesque.* Portsmouth, 1902.

Garvin, *Academic Architecture* (1983): 418-31.

James L. Garvin, "St. John's Church in Portsmouth: An Architectural Study." *Historical NH* (Fall 1973): 153-175.

the royal arms, and gave its name to Chapel Street. The church's bell was brought from Louisburg in 1745 where it was captured from the French. The bell was to be recast twice, once by Paul Revere in 1807 and again in 1896.

In 1791, after the American Revolution, the Church was renamed St. John's. In 1806, a fire destroyed the building despite an attempt to cut down the steeple to save the structure. Three days after the fire, seventy-four subscribers met and petitioned the parish to build a brick chapel with a bell, organ and other necessary furniture at their own expense on the lot where the old church had burned. They would be reimbursed later by the sale of pews.

The subscribers hired 26-year-old Alexander Parris of Portland, Maine, to design their new church. He was paid $24 to journey from Portland in April of 1807 and an additional $50 for his church plan. St. John's was the one of the first houses of worship in New Hampshire built of brick. Parris' innovative design for St. John's combined Boston influences with English book design concepts. The architect's plan for the exterior of the church was derived from Plate 39 of Asher Benjamin's *American Builders's Companion* illustrating the congregational meeting house at West Boston and the cornice at the top of the belfry was copied exactly from Plate 12. Originally, the church also had baroque scolled volutes on either side of the parapet probably derived from plate 38. The lantern was possibly derived from Bulfinch's 1805-6 cupola on Faneuil Hall in Boston. Parris also made extensive use of William Pain's *Practical House Carpenter* (Boston, 1796). He copied Plate 133 for the design of the oculus and blind arch, the pulpit, altar piece, and possibly the vestibule plan. The greater influence of Benjamin's *The American Builder's Companion*, as Garvin has shown, was Parris' use of Grecian molding profiles, those based on conic rather than circular sections, that can be seen on both interior and exterior moldings of the church.

The new church attracted enormous attention in the region. Some 5000 people attended the laying of the cornerstone in 1807, a number equivalent to the entire population of Portsmouth. The construction gave employment to Portsmouth's best craftsmen and exposed them to Asher Benjamin's new ideas. The fifteen joiners who worked on the building spread the new styles to subsequent Portsmouth projects. The total cost of the church was $30,000, at the time Portsmouth's most expensive structure and certainly its most stylish.

Later alterations to the church include the removal of the box pews in 1867, and the removal of the wine glass pulpit and the sounding board. In 1848 Daniel M. Shepard of Salem, Massachusetts was paid $923. to execute a "trompe l'oeil" painting on the lower walls and ceiling of the sanctuary. Stained glass windows began to replace clear glass windows in 1885. Church history states that in 1863 the original soft exterior bricks were replaced by hard ones.

EF & MS

New Hampshire Colonial State House

Built 1758-60; alterations 1764-6, removed 1836
original site: Market Square at the head of Congress St.
Phase I Overseer: Daniel Warner; chief joiner, James March
Phase II Overseer: Mark Hunking Wentworth; chief joiner,
Michael Whidden III

A remnant of the original State House frame, moved to Court
Street and remodeled into a house in 1836, the New Hampshire
Division of Historical Resources by Adams & Roy Consultants and
Salmon Falls Associates in 1988. Like other New England state
houses, it had a council chamber, at the eastern end of its second
floor, a chamber for the house of representatives in the center and a
court room on the western end. The first floor was one large
unheated space, with turned columns to support the upper floor,
undivided until 1813 when the Proprietors of the Portsmouth
Library asked to partition off a space for their books.

The major timbers of the frame were hewn and the floors
framed with sawn 2" x 8" planks used as joists. This method of
framing with sawn lumber was common in the 1760s; it can be
seen in the Moffatt-Ladd house and in the Wentworth-Gardner
House even the posts and girts are sawn. The original building was
designed to have a cupola, although this was delayed until the
second building phase in 1764-66. It may have been like that in
Boston, but no image of this part of the structure is known. The
reconstruction of this element, as well as the particular dormer
configuration, is frankly conjectural.

Only the eastern (council chamber) end survived after 1836,
but the one known interior description captures the opposite end of
the building. William H. Hackett, whose father was a lawyer who
knew the room after 1822 while the building served as a county
court house, wrote in 1890:

> *In the second story of this building...was the court-room with its
> elevated bench, its bar with its circular table covered in green
> baize, held fast by the round-headed brass tacks which the present
> generation never sees. The elevated boxes where sat the dignified
> and consequential high sherrif and the humble though no less
> indispensable crier, where the dock was flanked on either side
> with a box in which the deputy of the sherrif constantly sat with
> argus-eyed care on the prisoner, showed conclusively to the
> spectators that no guilty man could escape.*

Later county courts were housed first in a wooden Greek
Revival temple form building, designed and built in 1837 by joiners
Henry T. Vaughan and William Tucker, located on the site of the
old almshouse on Court Street. From 1891 until the court was
moved to Exeter in the 1960s a brick Romanesque Revival courthouse on State Street, designed by C.W. & C.P. Damon of
Haverhill, Hassachusetts, continued Portsmouth shiretown function. A county jail and jailor's house, designed by William A. Ashe
in 1891, was built behind the courthouse on Penhallow Street.

JLG

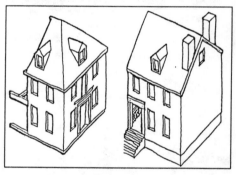

drawings, Salmon Falls Associates
Reconstructed New Hampshire State House
Top: 1759-64
Center: 1766-1817
Bottom: Fragment 1836 remodelled as
tenament, Court St.

Sources:

James L. Garvin, "The Old New Hampshire
State House," *Historical New Hampshire*, 46:4
(Winter 1991):203-230.

Adams & Roy Consultants, Inc., "Historic
Structure Report, Old New Hampshire State
House, Portsmouth, NH," 1988.

BUILDING & MARKET
1804 –

1   2   3   4   5   6

Sise Building.

Athenæum and stores altered ca. 1860.

Sheafe Block after 1883.

REBUILDING SQUARE –1904

KEY:
1. State House
2. Peirce Block
3. Portsmouth Bank
4. NH Insurance Company
5. Rundlet Store
6. Sheafe Block
7. Pearse Store
8. NH Bank
9. Brick Market
10. North Meeting House

7   8   9   10

Drawing by William Paarlberg

Reconstruction of Market Square In 1813.

Pearse Block (left), NH Bank (right) remodelled 1885.

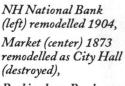

NH National Bank (left) remodelled 1904,

Market (center) 1873 remodelled as City Hall (destroyed),

Rockingham Bank (right) built 1857.

North Church and Market Square.

Courtesy Portsmouth Athenæum

89

Eliza McClennen, after Hales 1812 map
Market Square area, 1812.

COMMERCIAL PORTSMOUTH
DANIEL AND MARKET STREETS, MARKET SQUARE

Touring the commercial center can begin at either Penhallow and Sheafe Streets *[see Old Custom House]* or at Market Square. Looking east down Market Street, Merchants Row is the long brick block that terminates the vista. It was begun in the late 1790s. It faced "Fore Street" (now Market Street) on one side and Ceres Street with its wharves along the river on the other. An 18th century public market was located here at Spring Hill, the junction of these streets with Bow Street. The two blocks of Market Street from Spring Hill to the colonial state house was formerly called "Paved Street," being the only such roadway in the town. It was lined with timber framed dwellings, although one early brick house was also located here. These structures, many with cellar and ground-floor shops, contained the largest concentration of English and other dry goods stores and homes of many merchants.

After 1799 the commercial center shifted from the waterfront to the old "Parade," the open land opposite the Eastern end of the State House and North Meeting House, when the old Spring Hill Market was moved to the waterside and used exclusively for a fish market. In 1800 the town chose the Parade site over Haymarket Square for a new arcaded Brick Market (on the site of the present Fleet Bank) that was built with a public hall above. The area thus became Market Square and attracted additional commercial building,

Courtesy American Antiquarian Society
Portsmouth Fire, 1813.

especially after Market Street was destroyed by the first of Portsmouth three major fires which occurred in 1802, 1806, and 1813. In 1803 the street was widened and soon lined with new brick buildings four stories in height. The centerpiece of this new construction is the long row of stores on the western side of the street that curves to form the northern wall of Market Square. Its owners, the apex of the mercantile community, combined to erect a building for the NH Fire and Marine Insurance Company and rented the hall above to their Masonic Lodge *[see Portsmouth Athenæum]*. After the old State House became the county court, law offices filled the upper stories of many nearby brick blocks. The early national city also was a center of banking and in the first half of the 19th century began to concentrate along the block of Pleasant Street on either side of the Brick Market.

Portsmouth's brick commercial district grew out of its fires. Replacement in fireproof materials, not only brick but composition roofs of tar and gravel, was immediate. In 1814, moreover, the state provided legal authority to mandate brick building throughout the urban core. The large 1813 fire zone was rebuilt slowly and many lots did not have new buildings until well after 1825, when

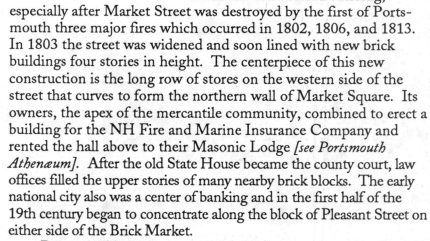

Courtesy Strawbery Banke Museum
Mid 19th century remodelling, Haven Block, Market Square.

the brick building law was replaced by other fire laws. Subsequent fires on Market Street in 1845 and spot fires in the 1860s destroyed only single buildings or small groups of structures.

These masonry blocks along Market and neighboring streets illustrate a full range of New England commercial building types of the first half of the nineteenth century. The Athenæum and its neighbors facing Market Square largely retain their original four story height and fenestration. The roofs, however, have all been changed to higher pitches that replace their original flat back-sloping roofs. The row of three buildings built for Edward Parry memorializes the 1803 fire in a plaque on the least altered store (A& P Paints) that still retains its sloping flat roof above the low-studded top story. Within the heart of the 1813 fire zone the old U.S. Custom House at the corner of Daniel and Penhallow Street was developed in conjunction with the brick row along Daniel Street as well as the brick rowhouses on Sheafe Street. Many 1805-1820 commercial and mixed use buildings in the fire zones used a standard brick vocabulary. Masonry keystones, watertables, and lintels set off the warm salmon brick, while buildings located at the junction of two streets employ rounded and recessed brickwork to turn the corner. Smaller examples of commercial building in brick, like the Congress Street building housing Winebaum's newspapers, reflect brick building legal requirements after 1814. At the lower end of Market street near Bow Street are good examples of Boston granite storefronts of the 1830s and 1840s, with solid slabs of granite posts and lintels forming the ground story of the brick blocks, like those flanking Boston's Quincy Market.

Mastic, brackets and quoins: By the mid-1840s the city was linked to Boston by the railroad and in 1848 Portsmouth legally became a city. Over the next dozen years Market Square and adjoining portions of the brick commercial core adopted a new image of a progressive manufacturing and commercial center. Its details derive from mid-century interpretations of historical European styles but reflect even more the popularity of brownstone in American urban building. At the heart of this change was the 1854 North Church, designed by Boston architects Towle and Foster and almost identical to other examples of their work from Boston to Bangor. The city employed the same architects to design a new public high school (1855) at the corner of Daniel and Chapel streets. Together with the Boston-area architect S. S. Woodcock's design for a new city hall (1858), these outside architects established a new architectural vocabulary for local practitions to follow. This included either mastic or red-brown paint over the brick surface, the use of new building materials in ornament, and wide bracketed cornices and corners defined by the use of quoins. The remodeling of the Methodist Church on State Street followed this pattern, as did the refacing of the building immediately east of the Athenæum. Remnants of the use of mastic, quoins and brackets can be seen in John S. Dodge's 1871 redesign of this Market Square curved row building as well as on several other commercial blocks throughout the downtown.

Terra-cotta: Among the earliest use of architectural terracotta

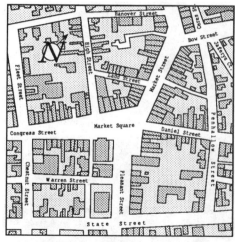

William Paarlberg, after 1892 NH Atlas
Market Square area, 1892.

S.S. Woodcock, proposed design for a new City Hall, 1858.

Photography: Robert Kozman
Cast-iron staircase, U.S. Custom House.

in New England, the arched window caps of North Church were specified by the architects and supplied by the Worcester firm of Tolman, Hathaway & Stone. From 1848, when Henry Tolman, Jr. began supplying Worcester architect Eldredge Boyden with terra-cotta ornament, Worcester supplied professional architects with this new building material that helped reinforce their claims to specialized architectural knowledge.

Cast-Iron: The present Portsmouth Brewery (56 Market St.), was a dry-goods store completed in 1860 using cast-iron in both its façade and interior. The original storefront had two entrances, one for the store and another to the stairway, which was replaced by the present configuration in the late 19th century. The iron work was selected by local architect-builder James Moses III, who had also superintended the construction of North Church. One of the leading manufacturers of architectural cast iron, Daniel Badger of New York City, was born in the middle of the Piscataqua River on Badger's Island. While his iron works was noted in 1858 by the local press, no local examples of his products have been documented. Two later cast ironstore fronts along Market Square (Cafe Brioche and Eberle's), however, are identified in their bases as products of the Portsmouth Machine Company (1883-1897) which occupied the remnant of the textile factory on Hanover Street (see Portsmouth Steam Mill) after it burned in 1880. Those on the Exchange Block may also be from this local company.

Landscape: When the town took 10 feet from the properties on each side of Market Street to widen the "Paved Street" after the fire of 1802, it did not add new Durham flags to the pavement.

> *This arrangement of the street left a carriageway through the centre, flanked by sidewalks of most ample breadth. The ladies, who as a matter of course promenaded there chiefly in fine weather, generally walked on the smooth and cleanly swept gravel near the stores, while the school-boys...ran along the flagstones...*

Market Square and the first block of Pleasant Street had a variety of trees at different periods. The earliest trees mentioned is an apple tree on the eastern side of the Square and a row of elms, lining the eastern edge of Pleasant Street along the fences of the John Fisher and Nathaniel Adams homes. These were burned in the 1813 fire and replaced by lombardy poplars during the early 19th century craze for that species. Mid-century photographs show replantings along both Market Street and the Square, only to be removed in the late 19th century as building owners sought to capture more light.

Public improvements to Market Square in the 1970s used federal funds to make the commercial core more pedestrian. Carol Johnson Associates, Landscape Architects of Cambridge, Massachusetts, designed the brick and granite sidewalks and public spaces in a manner like that developed for an urban renewal/preservation project that renovated the Federal core of Newburyport, Mass.

19th and early 20th-century changes: After rebuilding from its early fires, the commercial core remains largely intact until the 20th

U.S. Branch Bank and Piscataqua Bank, Corner Pleasant and State streets.

century. Pleasant Street between the square and State Street is a catalog of 19th- and 20th-century specialized commercial forms: The Stephen Pearse block (1803) at the corner of Daniel Street is the oldest and smallest. The row of five stores with offices above the corner of State and Pleasant streets is The Exchange Block, a business investment built by James Sheafe after the fire of 1813, remodeled in 1893 with new dormers and "Bedizened with cheap show of copper ornament" – its window caps – "and of gaudy paint." At its corner with State Street is the former home of several banks, including that where the Jacksonian Bank War began in 1829; at the other end of the Exchange Block is the 1857 Rockingham Bank. The granite Beaux Art building and adjoining block (1904) are merely the latest remodelling of the old New Hampshire Bank (1805). Fleet Bank's Market Square offices (1911-12) were constructed in the "colonial" style that replicated the blind arcade of the old Brick Market that had served as the City Hall since the 1860s. Across Pleasant Street stands the granite US Custom House (1858-60) and 1854 North Church that replaced the 1712 North Meeting House.

RMC

Portsmouth Athenæum

Built 1805 for the N.H. Fire & Marine Insurance Co.
Bradbury Johnson, architect; ovals and capitals carved by
   William Dearing
Reading Room, James Nutter, joiner; remodeled 1892, Henry B.
   Ball, architect; chimneypiece made by W.F. Ross, Boston

Construction and Original Use: Designed in 1804 as the headquarters of the New Hampshire Fire and Marine Insurance Company by architect Bradbury Johnson, who had earlier designed the public Brick Market across Market Square, the structure formed the centerpiece of a curving commercial row constructed after the fire of 1802. Its brick walls and flat, rear-sloping, composition roof (still extant in the attic beneath the pitched roof added in 1824) were part of a unified response by merchants to the danger of fire, as was the formation of a new insurance company. Its façade was ultimately derived from Adam's Royal Society building in London, by way of such popular expressions as Bulfinch's central pavilion for the ill-fated Tontine Crescent in Boston (the first home of the Massachusetts Historical Society). The use of two story pilasters above the ground floor was similar to that of many other urban commercial buildings, like that by Alexander Paris in 1803 for the Maine Fire and Marine Insurance Company in Portland, Maine. The arched door and window openings of the ground floor façade repeated the arcade of Johnson's Brick Market across the square, reproduced in the walls of Fleet Bank which replaced the old building in 1912. In this case, however, only the lower floor was devoted to the insurance company; the ornament of the upper floors signified the spaces rented by Masonic lodge which had its own door to upstairs on the rear wall. Only when the insurance company went out of business in 1823 did it transfer the property

Sources:

Susan McDaniel Ceccacci, "Architectural Terracotta in the United States Before 1860," MA Thesis, Boston University, 1991.

Portsmouth Journal, Sept. 4, 1858, "Iron Stores"; Nov. 4 and 25, 1893.

Portsmouth Morning Chronicle, Jan. 11, 17, and 21, 1860; Sept. 25, 1893.

[Tobias Miller], "Traders in Old Paved Streat," *Portsmouth Morning Chronicle,* Nov. 27, 1852.

R. Clipston Sturgis, "Architecture of Portsmouth," in *The Portsmouth Book,* Boston: 1899.

Cast iron research by Jane Porter

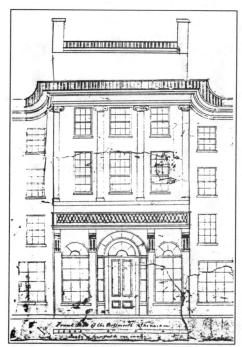

Unrealized proposal to add a bracketted balcony to Portsmouth Athenæum façade, 1848, William Tucker.

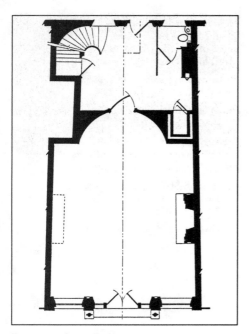

Drawing by James Garvin
First floor plan Portsmouth Athenæum.

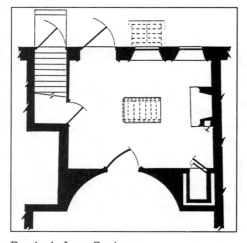

Drawing by James Garvin
Reconstruction rear stairs 1805-1823.

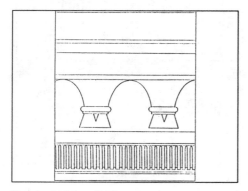

Drawing by James Garvin
Detail reading room cornice, 1805.

to the Portsmouth Athenæum, a private proprietary library, which reconfigured the rear staircase and occupied all three floors.

The Insurance company issued fire insurance for only a few years and by 1810 was one of two local companies writing marine insurance exclusively. Both were closely associated with local banks. The Portsmouth Bank, for example, abutted the New Hampshire Fire and Marine office and its stone vault actually occupied part of the cellar under the insurance office that occupied the rear room of the ground floor. Here a tall writing desk, a few chairs, and a small fire-proof vault provided all the necessary equipage for a type of business formerly done in coffee houses. The large front room, lit by large round-arched windows with decorative fan glazing, served as a subscription reading room where ship-owners, captains and other businessmen could read newspapers form distant points of call. So integral to marine insurance was a newspaper reading room that in 1816-17, when the short-lived Union Insurance Company occupied ground floor rooms beneath the N.H. Union Bank, it also devoted its "front hall" to a subscription reading room. Conditions of the 1823 transfer from the New Hampshire Fire and Marine to the Portsmouth Athenæum assured that its stockholders be given shares in the private library and that the lower front room remain a reading room.

The Portsmouth Athenæum: One of a series of libraries once serving Portsmouth, the Athenæum is the only early collection to survive the free public library movement's 1897 renovation of the Portsmouth Academy (1809) into the Portsmouth Public Library. Like its model, the Boston Athenæum, it was designed as a social center for the study of literature, the arts, and science. It collected ancient volumes as well as modern books, paintings and memorabilia of historical association, as well as a cabinet of curiosities donated by mariners who brought back all manner of natural and man-made objects for a "museum" begun in the 1820s. Today the Athenæum functions as a specialized research library. Its manuscript and photograph collections have grown dramatically since 1982 when the library expanded into the upper floors of an adjacent new building that provided new rare book and special collections vault, new stacks, and public access to the research library.

The Reading Room: This 1805 interior was finished by local joiner James Nutter and his cornice, dado, door and window trim survive. The high-ceilinged oval-ended room originally contained two small fireplaces on opposite walls. When first remodeled in 1852 these fireboxes were closed, a stove installed, and the walls painted in fresco work of arched panels to bring the room up to the most modern standards of interior decoration. In 1892 most of the mid-century changes were swept away and many historical artifacts brought down from the attic to create an atmosphere of elite gentility and association that matched the member's self image.

This 1892 remodeling of the Reading Room of the Portsmouth Athenæum is especially well-documented. James Rindge Stanwood, an antiquarian and secretary for the committee supervising the remodeling, kept letters and notes on the restoration that illustrate the aesthetic choices made by the committee and their architect. Henry B. Ball, of the Boston architectural firm of Dabney and Ball, originally came from Portsmouth. His architectural competence and stylistic bias was already known. In 1891 he designed a new colonial revival house on Middle Street for Athenæum proprietor Wallace Hackett (now the Masonic Lodge) and would later design the Cottage Hospital (now city hall) atop the knoll at the end of the vista seen from the Athenæum's front door. Ball's father had been a shareholder in the Athenæum and the architect offered his services gratis. Stanwood sought professional help in restoring the room "as far as possible upon the architectural ideas prevalent at the time" of its construction. The architect agreed to keep "the spirit of the charming old building intact in the re-decoration and other alteration." After his draftsman took measurements, Ball returned to Portsmouth with "elaborate drawings showing the alterations proposed" for a "head piece" to be placed over the room's rear curved door that was never executed. The old fireplace, "cherished by many former members" was to be "reopened and enlarged, surmounted with heavy mouldings, ornamented with rich figures and carvings" which to Ball, reproduced "the characteristic features of the room." The new fireplace, two feet wider than the original, was constructed with Philadelphia brick instead of tiles as Ball first suggested.

But the restoration committee and Athenæum members balked at "painting the walls in anything like a terra-cotta shade." Instead, "a shade of Colonial Buff (numbered 13 in Sampson's sample-book of colors from T. Strahan & Co.)" was selected for the walls with ivory-white woodwork and cornice, the latter lightly touched with Roman gold, and the ceiling a light shade of cream. Ball's plans also included "a border of frieze enriched with ornaments of sculpture and deeply inlaid with gold" for which no evidence survives to prove if it was installed.

All this decorative work set off a mixture of old and new furnishings. A center table was donated and made by the Davenport company, perhaps from Ball's designs. Another member donated the "pair of ornate andirons" also still in use. Iron newspaper racks were nickel-plated and "confined to the westerly side" of the room. "Mahoganized" newspaper reading desks replaced those from the early nineteenth-century then moved to the attic. A search in the attic located six old fire-buckets inscribed `Fire and Marine Ins. Co.' and an 18th century set of elk horns. Installation of the horns as decoration (rather than scientific specimen in the Athenæum's cabinet of curiosities) invested them with historical and distinctly domestic associations. Like firebuckets hung near the stairs, ancient antliers were still found in some of the best colonial mansions of the city, including the Warner and Moffatt Ladd houses.

Between 1894 and 1895 several of the Athenæum's historical artifacts were also restored, donated or reproduced to link the Athenæum's proprietors to past heroes, events, and old families. Smibert's eighteenth- century portrait of Sir William Pepperrell at

Courtesy Portsmouth Athenæum
Reading Room, ca. 1885.

Drawing by James Garvin after Ball
Reading room fireplace, Henry Ball, architect, 1892.

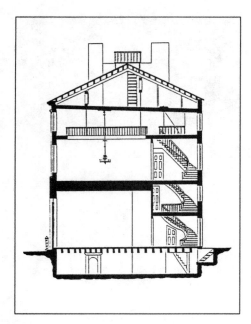

Drawing by James Garvin

Section, Portsmouth Athenæum
after 1824-26 stair and roof changes.

Sources:

Garvin, *Academic Architecture..*, 380-398.

Exerpted, in part, from Giffen & Murphy, eds., *"A Noble and Dignified Stream"*

the Essex Institute was copied by local artist U.D. Tenney and the Athenæum's own companion painting of Sir Peter Warren was repaired. Two small cannons captured from a British vessel at the Battle of Lake Erie (owned as garden ornaments behind the Haymarket Square Peirce mansion) were installed on either side of the front door.

Mezzanine and Library Room: The old office behind the reading room was converted to a hallway in 1824 when the rear window and doorway were reversed to accommodate the curved staircase that replaced the entrance and stairs to the Masonic lodge. An intermediate landing between the main floors of the building, with closets in the corners of the curved rear wall of the high ceilinged Reading Room, contains mementos of the 1905 Treaty of Portsmouth which ended the Russo-Japanese War and won Theodore Roosevelt the Nobel Peace Prize.

The room above is a rare survival of an early 19th century library with its original plaster busts, grained book shelves, and the book collections. The gas light was installed in the 1850s and extended when the third floor was cut through to create a balcony in the 1860s. After central heating was installed as part of the 1897 renovation (the furnace in the cellar still works), the sidewall chimneys were removed to make way for more shelving. Gifts of two private libraries at the turn of the century were shelved in special alcoves. That of Charles Levi Woodbury, a Boston and Washington lawyer who was the son of NH Governor and U.S. Supreme Court Justice Levi Woodbury, includes much of his father's library as well as remnants of his own interest in rare book collecting. The Tredick Library is a mid-19th century Philadelphia gentleman's library bequeathed by a Portsmouth- born merchant who made his fortune in that city.

The Attic: Access to the original roof, which now serves as the floor to the attic, is up a dangerously steep stair from the rear of the balcony. The pitched roof was added in 1824 to solve leaking problems of the composition roof and provided access (until the recent installation of a modern skylight) to a balustraded deck above the ridge. Party walls containing the chimney flues were extended to hold the ends of the purlins and the rear wall raised to provide low windows that provided the only natural light.

RMC

James Rundlet Store
now Portsmouth Flower Shop

Built 1804-5, remodeled 1863-4
16 Market Street

James Rundlet moved from Exeter to Portsmouth in the 1790s where he began as a commission merchant for a Boston firm and then dealt as a retail and wholesale dry goods merchant on his own account. When the store he rented from Col. John Langdon was destroyed in the 1802 fire, he was one of a group who built a new store in this row.

Rundlet may have designed his own "Fireproof Brick Store" in the coordinated rebuilding effort.   Besides the basic cost of land and materials his accounts show that he paid Mark Simes $ 70.95 for "Marble Window Crowns & Sills" that year. In 1805 he contracted with joiner John Miller to add a "walk on top of Brick Store" and the next year credited joiner James Nutter with "2 days work in Store." The few details of the interior are accounts for 1805 when he bought a "Rittenhouse stove" and "paper & border for [his] Counting room." Well into the 1840s he kept counting room in the second story of this Market Street building (reserving the right of passage through the rented store). According to a local memoir:

> *A merchant in those times, meant a man engaged in whole-sale business, not perhaps in country towns and villages, but in sea ports.... He was supposed to have an office and not a store. When he spoke of going to business, he would say that he was going to his counting house.*

Chambers in the two floors above his office were undoubtedly rented like those in all the brick stores. In 1811, when William Simes advertised to rent his store, he also offered the "Chamber over the same, suitable for an attorney's or any other public office." According to local lore, Daniel Webster had his office in Rundlet's commercial building during the beginnings of his career.

Unlike other merchants he engaged in little exporting , although in 1806 he did engage in 'broken voyages' which transformed West Indies goods into American products for reshipment to Europe. In 1819, a dozen years after he built his house on Middle Street *[see Rundlet-May house]*, Rundlet reduced his stock of textiles and retired from active sales at age forty-seven. More successful was his contract to supply the U.S. Army with woolens manufactured in a factory at Amesbury, Massachusetts, in which he invested heavily. From then on he was primarily engaged in investments in textile factories and in 1822 he became the major investor in the Salmon Falls Manufacturing Company up the Piscataqua River in Rollinsford, NH.

Alterations: Except for a brief period when the store was rented to his son in the late 1830s, it was occupied by long-term tenants W. B. Lowd, book binder, and John W. Moses, tailor. In fact Moses continued beyond Rundlet's death in 1852. On June 5, 1863 the Rundlet heirs agreed with their long-term tenant, J.W. Moses, that he might "alter and rearrange said building so that it shall consist of three stories" into a lower floor 12' high, a new 9' second story, and a third story to "extend to the top of the present fourth story" (8'3").   Moses also promised to "make an entrance and staircase to the second story" inside, all in accord to plans dated 1863 signed by Isaiah Wilson, a local builder architect *[see South Ward Hall].* In 1864 a newspaper reported that the store of Mr. J.W.Moses "is now completed...internally and externally...The height of the building remains the same but the four stories are now divided into three...and with the iron front. For 22 years Mr. Moses has been an occupant of the same rooms..." While little

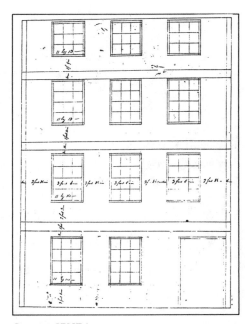

Courtesy SPNEA
Original elevation, James Rundlet Store, ca. 1804.

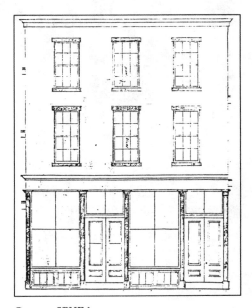

Courtesy SPNEA
Elevation, proposed alterations to Rundlet Store, 1866.

evidence remains of the former openings on the façade, where the original marble window caps and sills were lost, but the rear wall shows bricked openings of earlier windows. Wilson's drawing shows also that the cast-iron storefront remains much as it was designed in 1863, although the glazing system has been changed throughout the building.

Rundlet's building is only the best documented of the many other early four story brick stores along Market Street gutted to alter them into three story buildings. The few original fourth floors that survived into recent years were barely five feet high where the slight slope of the flat roof joined the rear wall. The desire to convert older commercial properties into buildings with internal volumes that matched the ceiling heights of newer blocks was, therefore, overwhelming.

RMC

Sources:

E. Rundlet MSS, SPNEA

Portsmouth Journal 18 June 1864

John Lord, *Beacon Lights of History,* NY: William Wise & Co., 1921 ed.quoted in Szasz, Fenenc M., "John Lord's Portsmouth," *Historical New Hampshire,* 44:3 (Fall 1989): 148-149.

Jacob Sheafe Block

Built 1807
corner Market and Daniels Street

Across Market Street, Jacob Sheafe's new brick row emphasized its prominent location with a slightly recessed rounded corner and low hipped roof. Along its street side Sheafe's building looked much like James Rundlet's four story commercial and office block. Designed as an income property, his brick row had shops at ground level but a pair of three-story dwellings in the upper stories. An 1807 contract to finish these apartments "from the Garret to the Cellar" specifies the joiners work for "chambers, Kitchen, Entries, iron railings, etc." The wrought iron rail ornamented the window of what Sheafe's probate appraisers listed as the "Bow Room" in this fourteen room "Mansion House" which he came to occupy after the loss of his own home to fire in 1813. In the same way, Charles Peirce combined a bookstore and house across Daniel Street from Sheafe's block:

Courtesy Portsmouth Athenæum
Portsmouth Athenæum (left) 1805, Sheafe Block (right) 1807. Photograph ca. 1860.

> *The House (which is separated from the store by a brick partition and an iron door) has ten finished rooms, besides a large unfinished store room; an excellent cellar, a wood-house that will hold 20 cords of wood; a smoke house, &c. The upper kitchen, has Count Rumford's Cookery works, also an excellent well of water and pump; and the lower kitchen, has the aqueduct handy.*

Sheafe's 1829 will left to his wife Mary "that part of the brick

98

dwelling" adjoining then occupied by Capt. Wm. W. Thompson. The corner shop of the ground floor was Haseline's jewelry store and Charles Howard's lottery shop. During the 1820s the next three shops were rented to different dry goods merchants, smaller versions of Henry Haven's at the corner of commercial alley or James Rundlet's across Market Street. In the 1830s two of these disappeared in favor of bookstores, as James M. Shores took the corner stand and Foster's bookstore located just down the street.

Like many Market Street buildings, it was reconfigured in to three floors within its original shell about 1881 when the upper floor now occupied by the Warwick Club became the home of The Knights of Pythias. The cast iron front of the ground floor (Alie's Jewelry) was installed in 1893.

RMC

Old Custom House & Sheafe Street Row

Built 1816
corner of Daniel and Penhallow streets
attributed to Jonathan Folsom

In 1815, joiner Jonathan Folsom and real estate developers Langley Boardman and John Abbott, acquired part of the area destroyed in 1813. They laid out a new 18'-wide lane for access from Penhallow Street to the rear of new brick buildings erected along Sheafe Street and Daniel Street. Over the next few years they constructed small brick rowhouses on the Sheafe Street lots, side stairhall plans with kitchens behind a front sitting room and one-story service ells behind. The idea of narrow brick row houses, like those in larger coastal American cities of the early republic, did not become widespread in Portsmouth. Semi-detached or duplex houses and other multiple housing forms like those of the 1820 and 1830s along State Street were popular methods of rebuilding in brick after the 1813 fire, but did not become common elsewhere in town.

U.S. Custom House: Built by these developers in 1816, this corner structure was sold to the U.S. government in 1817 as a custom house to replace rented quarters in other buildings like Merchants Row. Its central doorway is a reproduction based on 1937 HABS measured drawings of the applied columns supporting a Gothic entablature over the fan-lit arched opening. The second story Palladian windows set in blind relieving arches are similar to other examples in Portsmouth, especially that in the ca. 1810 "Benedict House" *[see Thomas Morton house].* These originally lit a single room on the 10' high second story, later partitioned for an antechamber and stairway to the custom hall. The architectural geometry of the northwest corner curved wall with its Palladian window was echoed by a curved wall on the northeast corner that hid the vault. The third floor was divided into several small chambers which once held the Portsmouth Athenæum, before it acquired the NH Fire & Marine Insurance Office, and the Union Insurance Company's subscription reading room.

RMC

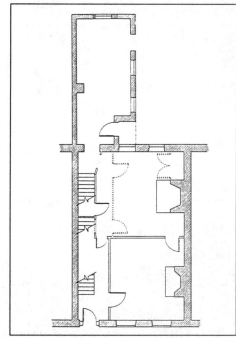

Measured by B. Herman and R Candee, drawing by Gabrielle Lanier
First floor row-house plan, 17 Sheafe St.

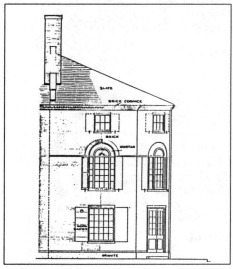

HABS
Elevation, Custom House, Daniel St.

Courtesy Portsmouth Athenæum

Rockingham Bank, S.S. Woodcock,
architect, 1857.

Rockingham Bank

now the Piscataqua Savings Bank

Built 1857
15 Pleasant Street
S.S. Woodcock, architect, Boston, Massachusetts
first floor alterations, 1925, Alden & Parker, architects of Boston

The Rockingham Bank," which eclipses every other business building on the square," was the first major new commercial building to Market Square and Pleasant Street after Portsmouth became a city. Towering 16 feet above the old Exchange block, it was the point of reference for architectural reformers who commented on its beauty and promoted its stylistic qualities. It was designed by S.S. Woodcock of Boston and erected in 1857. The first floor of the building, now occupied by the Piscataqua Savings Bank, was remodeled for that institution in 1925 to designs by Boston architects Alden & Parker.

Why S.S. Woodcock, who advertised his Boston practice in the 1850s Portsmouth directories, received this and other local designs is uncertain. Like others he may have originated in the local area or had relatives nearby. He was the architect of the Stone Church renovation in 1858 and proposed a design to either rebuild or replace the 1800 brick market next to the bank [see p. 91]. His designs incorporated ornate cast iron window lintels and a cupola with brick walls covered in mastic above a granite arcade that continued to serve as the market. Instead, the city remodeled the market to its own tastes in 1873. One observer thought it looked "like a donkey with elephantine ears."

Woodcock also designed the Rice Library in Kittery and in 1882 was responsible for the alterations to the 1805 New Hampshire bank next door to the Brick Market, then occupied by the First National and Portsmouth Savings Banks. The two banks were entirely remodeled once again and faced in granite between 1902 and 1904.

U.S. Custom House

Built 1857-60
corner of State and Pleasant streets
Ammi B. Young, Architect of the Treasury

A variant on customhouses designed in 1855 for Chicago and in 1854-57 for Providence (and a 1856-61 court house and post office in Indianapolis, Indiana) this granite palazzo is typical of medium sized federal buildings designed in the 1850s by the Supervising Architect of the Treasury, Ammi Burnham Young. Its use of structural and ornamental iron, as well as its adoption of the Italianate form and style, reflects a high degree of standardization that Young used to achieve economy and efficiency in governmental construction. The three-story, five-bay block contained a new post office on the ground floor, custom offices and judicial chambers on the second, and a court room on the third. Unlike other

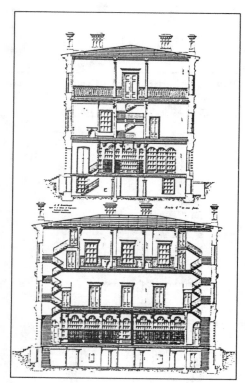

HABS after Portsmouth Public Library

Sections, U.S. Custom House,
Ammi B. Young, architect, 1858.

cities, where high property values forced new governmental building some distance from the commercial center, the site adjacent to Market Square was selected over those "rather far up town" a block or two away. Many hoped the building would replace the old brick market, whose altered form was seen as an architectural monstrosity. Young, however, rejected that site in favor of the opposite corner location.

When completed Charles Brewster compared it to the Rockingham Bank to its detriment:

> The new Custom House also stands forth in much beauty — but its elevation above the surrounding buildings has a rather depressing effect upon those in the neighborhood.

However, "the building itself looks very finely, much better than the plan did on paper."

In 1860 Captain Alexander Bowman, the Treasury engineer, described the building as "an ornament to the place" but noted that it was "largely in advance of the wants of the city, and it will be a long time before its available space will be required for public services." Others saw the structure "perhaps adapted to what Portsmouth is to be, rather than what it is now." In fact, the first and only major addition was not made until 1927. With the completion of a new federal office building on Daniel Street in 1966 the old post office was declared functionally obsolete and surplus property.

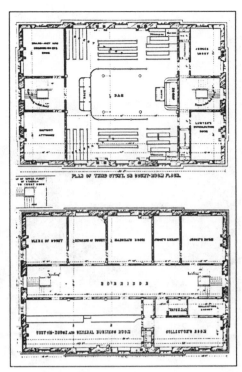

HABS after Portsmouth Public Library
Second and third floor plan, Custom-House.

CONGRESS STREET

The street running inland from Market Square, Congress Street, was rebuilt with larger commercial blocks over the 19th century as the railroad stations pulled the center of business activity westward from the riverfront. Rebuilding after the fires led several brick structures to be built among 18th-century wooden houses along Congress Street, of which Winebaum's News Service [72 Congress] is one of the last to survive later rebuildings. A series of fires, especially in the late 1870s, provided sites for some of the city's largest commercial buildings. Across the street until an 1879 fire, for example, stood Langley Boardman's brick Franklin Hall (1819) and the older Franklin House hotel.

National Block

Built 1878
46-50 Congress St.
building contractors: Foster & Dutton of Waterville, Maine

Frank Jones bought and remodeled the old Cutter house as the City Hotel in 1867. When it burned in 1877, he employed Foster & Dutton of Waterville, Maine to construct the present National Block the next year. The building remained in his estate until purchased in 1919 by the Odd Fellows, who maintained their lodge rooms beneath its Mansard roof until only a few years ago.

Sources:

Charles Brewster, *Rambles About Portsmouth.* I: 229; 318-19.

Geoffrey P. Moran, "The Post Office and Custom House at Portsmouth, New Hampshire, and its Architect, Ammi Burnham Young," *Old-Time New England,* 57 (April-June 1967): 85-102.

Daniel Bluestone, "Civic and Aesthetic Reserve: Ammi Burnham Young's 1850s Federal Customhouse Designs," *Winterthur Portfolio,* 25 (Summer/Autumn 1990): 131-156.

Morning Chronicle, 16 June 1859.

Franklin Block

Built 1879
75 Congress St.
architect: Arthur H. Vinal of Boston

Congress St., Franklin Block (center).

The largest of the city's 19th century commercial blocks, the Franklin Block was erected for prominent local merchant Alfred Stavers after an 1879 fire destroyed the earlier buildings on this block of Congress Street. It is the earliest known commercial design of Boston architect Arthur H. Vinal, who is known for later commercial blocks and opera houses throughout northern New England as well as for designs rejected for the Boston Public Library while he was City Architect (1884-85). The new "Franklin Buildings" incorporated multiple functions: six shops on the front, three smaller ones on each side, a large restaurant, and two "amusement halls" in the upper floors of the wings. In 1902 one of the public halls was removed for offices and the theater remodeled for a vaudeville and later movie house.

RMC

The Kearsarge Hotel

Built 1866
104 Congress, corner Chestnut Street
building contractor: Benjamin F. Webster

At the southwest corner of Chestnut Street in 1865 an old home was removed for a block of brick buildings that then marked the western edge of commercial development. Its Mansard roof, like many built in the 1860s and 70s including those of a few of the most costly Civil War homes *[see William F. Parrott and Jones-Sinclair houses]*, provided a residential image with impeccable Boston pedigree, was topped with a cupola later relocated behind 56 Market Street. The brick bow front appears to have been planned as "a large and elegant double tenement," modeled after those constructed over the past two decades in Boston's South End, with a pair of mirror image plans divided by a brick party wall. Yet, from the start the upper floors were leased as one hotel with shops and offices in streetfront spaces on either side of a central front entrance. In the 1870s the hotel was named in honor of the Portsmouth-built ship *Kearsarge*. Its owner, Col. Joshua W., Peirce, was agent of the Salmon Falls Manufacturing Company, founded by James Rundlet and other Portsmouth investors in 1825, until 1838. He occupied an estate in Greenland, NH, for the next thirty years before moving to the 18th century house immediately west of this commercial block, which was intended to provide support for his wife and daughters after his death.

RMC

Kearsarge House.

Music Hall

Built 1877
corner Chestnut and Porter streets
architect: William A. Ashe

The site of the Music Hall was originally retained by the town for a prison when the Glebe Lands were divided in 1715. In 1803 it became the site of Elias Smith's new Baptist Meeting House, built by 1804 from plans drawn by house carpenter George Nutter. After forty years of religious occupation, the church and its land was sold to a group of businessmen who in 1844 enlarged and totally rebuilt the old church into an ampitheater of 1000 seats, based on a Salem, Massachusetts, prototype, for religious services as well as a lecture and concert hall known as The Temple. In 1847 it was sold for a brief time to the Portsmouth Washingtonian Total Abstinence Society. After thirty years as a place of public entertainment, The Temple burned in 1876. The land was acquired by the Peirce estate, which owned the neighboring Kearsarge, and the new Music Hall was erected later in 1877 to designs by Navy Yard architect William A. Ashe. In the decade before WW I, the Music Hall shifted from large theatrical productions to vaudeville and silent pictures. Remodeled in 1947 as The Civic Theatre, it was run as a movie house until 1984.

Rockingham County Deeds
The Temple of the Washingtonian Abstinence Society.

Abraham Shaw House

Built between 1808 and 1811
379 State Street

The site of this house was originally part of Woodbury Langdon's estate, advertised in 1808 as "A very complete building lot." The L-plan house was erected by Captain Abraham Shaw, a master mariner and privateer, before 1811. Its later occupants have often had a strong historical interest. An 1842 visitor to the Rockingham House next door was introduced to this house by Mrs. Edward Cutts:

> *She is one of those ladies who delight in displaying their own eccentricities & tastes and treasures to all who may have the honor of ten seconds acquaintance with her. She had us all over her house before we had been ten minutes in it, showing us old chairs & china sets, and couches, and pictures & rooms, with complete history of their character as she called it. Some had belonged to old Sr. [Wm] Pepperrell & some to the ancient Quincy family, to which she was cousin in some out of the way degree, and some had been imported from China, where, she assured us several times, the custom of the people do not change.*

In 1873 new owners made several changes, including the granite steps and new front porch. These changes may have included new balusters applied to the original circular staircase inside the front entry and the unusual arched window cap above the exterior Palladian window over the entrance.

RMC

Courtesy Strawbery Banke Museum
Abraham Shaw House.

Sources:

Research by Jane Porter.

NH Gazette, 28 Jan. 1812.

"Journal of a Tour of the White Hills': An 1842 Chronicle by Samuel Johnson," Bryant F.Tolles, Jr., ed. *Essex Institute Historical Collections.* 120:1 (Jan. 1984): 4-5.

The Rockingham Hotel

Built ca. 1785, enlarged 1870-1871, burned 1884
401 State Street
architects: Gridley J.F. Bryant with Louis P. Rogers (1870);
Jabez Sears 1885-1887 renovation

The expanding railroad system and the establishment of hotels were inextricably intertwined. Between 1870 and 1900 Portsmouth's leading industrial magnate and millionaire brewer, Frank Jones (1832-1902), rebuilt several area hotels for both the commercial traveler and the summer tourist. A near Horatio Alger career transformed this New Hampshire farmboy into the "King of the Ale makers," Mayor of Portsmouth and sometimes Democratic Congressman, a director of many of the city's manufacturing corporations, as well as the Eastern Railroad, and ultimately president of the Boston and Maine Railroad. Jones's hotels promoted his ale and railroads while providing an opportunity for lavish entertainments expected of the richest man in the area.

Courtesy SPNEA
Rockingham House ca. 1850
(Woodbury Langdon House).

At the core of the Rockingham Hotel was the Woodbury Langdon house, built about 1785 to replace the earlier home of Governor John Langdon's brother, a merchant and judge. The first Portsmouth dwelling to be constructed of brick since the MacPheadris -Warner house, the house is also considered as the earliest to use new Adamesque decorative ornamentation. Its floor plan, as reconstructed from written sources, appears to have been an ell-house with one large west room (with joinery derived from the works of William Pain) , a central hall, and a range of ground floor spaces on the east. On this side of the first story was a front sitting or dining room with closet and a side staircase that separated the front room from an inner kitchen; an outer kitchen as well as a ground floor kitchen chamber and a second chamber appear to lie in the slightly offset rear ell. Beyond was a wood house and a brick stable; in front were two brick flankers, one of which may have been the "office" listed in Langdon's 1805 inventory. The large three story mansion set the style for the merchant elite along Court and State streets, and down Middle Street beyond Haymarket Square in the late 1790s and first two decades of the next century. The brick edifice was converted to a hotel for boarders and travelers in 1830 and run as the Rockingham House for forty years.

Rockingham Hotel, after 1970.

Frank Jones purchased the Rockingham House in 1870 and hired the Boston architectural office of Bryant and Rogers. Gridley Bryant was well known as a hotel architect who had already designed at least one Portsmouth home, the brick Mansard pair of houses on Middle Street for William F. Parrott in 1864. Their design for Jones doubled its length, capped the old hotel with a "French" or Mansard roof and enlarged it with a major annex to 130 rooms. Philip Butler, a Boston painter who decorated many of the major buildings of this period in Portsmouth, added Victorian appointments. In 1871 The Rockingham reopened as a commercial hotel.

In September 1884 the Rockingham was nearly destroyed by fire and Jones turned to a Boston architect with local connections, Jabez H. Sears, to enlarge and remodel the hotel. The result of this $300,000 rebuilding was "the most elegant and superbly furnished establishment... outside Boston" and was described by its architect as "a palace open to the traveling public." Sears' redesign of the Rockingham combined a variety of sources for "the rooms occupied by Mr. Jones en suite" as a second story private residence. The parlor cornice of this apartment was said to be "modeled from an example in the Louvre" while the painted ceilings were "frescoed in designs of the romantic school."

For the first time in this hotel's remodellings, the design echoed its location in an historic town. The western "dining room" from the original Woodbury Langdon house "was saved from the fire by great exertion," and its woodwork was now "painted white, with abundance of gold decoration" picking out its old neo-classical detailing. Furnished with "beautiful and artistic" furniture, the room was then "used as a private dining room for social parties, whose convivial enjoyments are increased and heightened by the historical reminiscences clustering about its ancient and time honored walls." The white and gold finish of the Langdon Dining Room is a particularly early expression of "colonial" reuse in the mid-1880s, especially amidst commercial decoration derived from English Queen Anne and other sources used in this urban commercial palace. [also see John Langdon Mansion]

Jones' association with Langdon was made even more explicit in the two façade gables above a new fifth story. These were embellished with "two busts in terra-cotta of heroic size," depicting Woodbury Langdon and Frank Jones, by Professor F. Mortimer Lamb of Stoughton, Massachusetts. Lamb, whose drawing of the new Rockingham interiors was published in *The Decorator and Furnisher* in May 1887, was also responsible for the "hunting scene in terra-cotta around a massive horseshoe" fireplace in the registration lobby. The "artistic" embellishment of the striking fireplace for this commercial living hall owes much to the American version of the aesthetic movement. Yet of this room's seven foot high mahogany wainscoting and fireplace, the architect said:

> the architectural treatment ... partakes of the Colonial, with its small moldings and carvings ... reminding one of 'ye olden days,' with its yule logs, cheery fires, and weary travelers refreshing themselves from tankards of fur [sic] or mugs of 'flip.'

The hotel continued in use until 1973 when Stahl/Bennett, architects of Boston, redesigned it for condominiums.

RMC

The Decorator and Furnisher (May 1887) *Rockingham Hotel lobby, 1885.*

Sources:

Ray Brighton, *Frank Jones, King of the Alemakers* (Portsmouth; Peter Randall Publisher, 1976).

James Garvin, *Academic Architecture*: 286-304.

William H. Withey, *The Rockingham: The House that Jones Built* (Portsmouth: Rockingham Condominium Assoc., 1985): 17-46, 89.

Susan Mackiewicz Evans, *F. Mortimer Lamb (1861-1936), A Master from our Midst*, (Brockton, MA: Brockton Art Center, 1975)

Jabez H. Sears, "The Rockingham House at Portsmouth, N.H.," *The Decorator and Furnisher* (May 1887): 48.

Giffen and Murphy, "*A Noble and Dignified Stream*"

The West End
Detail Portsmouth Bird's Eye, 1877.

THE WEST END

The development of Portsmouth's West End began in the final years of the 18th century, accelerating in pace during the first two decades of the 19th century, followed by two additional waves of growth, during the 1840s and 1850s and again in the 1910s. As the town grew in population it expanded from the riverside to the interior and increasingly into the distinctive urban fringe. In the decades on either side of 1800, pasturage was sold and subdivided to create new neighborhoods distinguished by larger lots and lower densities wherever a builder/owner could afford to do so. After mid-century, the rise of manufacturing and brewing, along the railroad corridor to the north and in the new fringe zone further to the west, and the westward expansion of the downtown brought successive waives of development to the area.

Development in these periods corresponds to spurts in the town's population growth, and was accomplished by specific members of the community in styles and forms that signify their intentions. In Haymarket Square, along Middle Street, and the first block of Austin Street can be found an important cluster of housing for the mercantile elite. These were built primarily for newer residents who came from surrounding country towns after the 1790s and first decade of the new century and invested the profits of neutral trade, privateering, and auctioneering to expand and rebuild the port town. Into this area wealthy and middling citizens moved in search of more room, more distance between their homes and their workplaces at the waterfront or the emerging commercial center.

At the same time, parcels north and south of Middle Street were subdivided into smaller lots by and for a community of artisans, especially joiners and other woodworkers, as well as a portion of the town's black community. Remnants of this pattern can be seen along Cabot and Union Streets, where early 19th-century artisan housing survives among small houses of mid-century textile workers and infill duplexes and boarding houses built at the turn of the 20th century. Although certain streets retained an elite appearance, Portsmouth's wealthy families were never isolated into exclusive neighborhoods separate from their clients or their employees. The development of State, Summer, and Winter streets tells a slightly different story: a few moderately sized houses from the early 19th century followed by two decades of similarly scaled infill.

North of Islington Street along streets crossing the Hanover-McDonough Street spine, still another pattern emerges. This is a landscape of densely fitted homes of primarily small and multiple-unit building types in what became the town's earliest industrial and manufacturing zone. Here a variety of gable-front side-entry house, duplexes, and wooden rowhouses of the mid-19th century mingle with older houses remodeled into tenements and boarding houses. The area remained industrial even after the textile mills burned and new industries emerged to the west. By the early 20th century two- and three-deckers, New England's most common multi-family building form, began to be built on a few remaining empty lots.

CWD

107

S.R. Cleaves House, Glen Cottage.

The open garden of Glen Cottage, at the corner of State and Middle streets, . . . low and open fences show that the owners wish for the world to enjoy with them the beauties which nature by their training richly displays.
Portsmouth Journal Sept. 19, 1846

ACADEMY CORNER

The intersection of Middle and Islington streets includes elements of each phase of West End development. Purcell House or "John Paul Jones House" and the Buckminster House represent the last surviving pre-Revolutionary houses in the area. Although the hay market was gone by 1850, the area gradually developed as an institutional core. The construction of the Portsmouth Academy dates to 1806, as Portsmouth's elite sought to provide college preparatory training for its young men. The Academy was soon joined by the Baptists in 1828 and the Christians after 1862. In 1895 the Academy was converted into the Portsmouth Public Library. During the 20th century this institutional focus was affirmed by the construction of the Portsmouth High School (1903 by John Ashton of Lawrence, Mass.) and the former North Church chapel (now the Salvation Army). Little remains of one of Portsmouth's handful of Gothic cottages built in the second quarter of the 19th century.

The original appearance of Glen Cottage, 56 Middle Street, built in 1845 for S.R. Cleaves, a soap factory owner, can be seen in a painting at the of the Rundlet-May House. Glen Cottage is now obscured by the addition of a ca. 1920 Tudor design, and remodelled for offices.

CWD

Painting Purcell House & Glen Cottage 1853 painting by William H. Titcomb.
Glen Cottage (left), the Purcell-Lord (now John Paul Jones) House and Rockingham Hotel (right).

Portsmouth Public Library

Portsmouth Academy

Built 1809 to plans of James Nutter
carved capitals, William Dearing; chief joiner, John Miller
remodeled 1895-1896 as the Public Library, William A. Ashe,
architect
addition 1975, Stahl-Bennett, Architects, Boston

Thomas Morton House
Built 1810-12
Library Annex

Long incorrectly attributed to Charles Bulfinch, the building
records for the Academy reveal the designer to be James Nutter
assisted by the chief joiner John Miller with carving provided by
William Dearing. While the exterior remains essentially un-
changed, the interior was gutted during its conversion to serve as
the town's public library. The architect of this change, William
Ashe, was active in the city from the 1870s to 1915 *[see William
Ashe, Architect],* and many of his commissions were for alterations
of existing buildings like this one. His alteration created a large
and open reading room, with galleries at the level of the former
second story serving as stacks. By 1975 when more space was
required, the expansion of the building was achieved through the
annexation of the adjacent brick dwelling known as Benedict
House, and the construction of a new building linking the two.
More accurately described as the Morton House, this three story,
single pile house was constructed in 1808-10, facing onto Middle
Street across a passage known as George Street. An 1812 ad for the
building names the following rooms "An excellent Cellar and lower
kitchen, and on the lower floor, a Parlor, Keeping room, Store
room, Kitchen, Scullery, &c. In the second and thirds stories are
eight Chambers." Its interior includes a room on either side of a
circular stair on each of the three upper stories, and ells that once
extended from the north and west have been removed. The new
portion of the building serves as the entry area from both the east
and west sides of the building and the circulation area between the
reading room and the storage and administrative offices in the
annex.

CWD/RMC

John Paul Jones House,

Portsmouth Historical Society
Built ca. 1758, remodelled during 19th century, restored 1920.
43 Middle Street

Now owned by the Portsmouth Historical Society, this large
gambrel-roofed double house was constructed for Capt. Gregory
Purcell in about 1758 at the edge of what was then the compact
part of the town. Operated as a boarding house for many years,
Jones made his home here during the construction of the "Ranger"
at a Portsmouth ship yard during the Revolution. The house was

Courtesy Portsmouth Athenæum
John Paul Jones House before restoration.

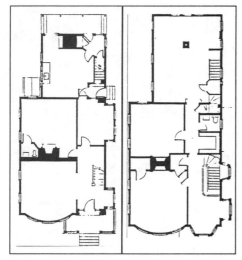

Drawings by Philip Tambling, architect
First and second floor plans, Bodge-Chase House.

Sketch by Philip Tambling, architect
Bodge-Chase House.

in the 19th century long the home of the Lord family. Ells and a barn were added along the east and north walls, including a polygonal two-story Queen Anne porch designed by Boston architect William Ralph Emerson. Keeping the house in Portsmouth, when its sale to the Metropolitan Museum of Art in New York City was threatened, was one of the city's early preservation efforts. The present configuration was achieved during the restoration by Joseph E. Chandler when the house was opened to the public in 1920.

CWD

Bodge-Chase House

Built 1842-43
43 Middle Street

William Bodge, a wood and lumber dealer turned grocer, built a gable-front side-entry house that still shows its Greek Revival window trim along the south wall. When built it may have looked much like the row of three buildings on the north side of State Street nearest Middle Street. Its façade and north wall, however, have been much altered as has its interior. It remained in the family until just before WW I, although from 1901 to 1905 Albert A. Sheafe — listed as a cabinet maker after 1903 — also occupied some part of the house. As property taxes were abated for the Bodge heirs after 1900, few if any of the major changes were probably accomplished until the house was sold to Dr. Julia Chase in 1914. Mrs. Chase was an osteopathic physician who had her doctor's office in the front room of the house. As the first person to have an office here, it must be she who had the unusually informative lighting identification system installed that documents the name of each room and other spaces. The house has been an architects office in recent years and now serves as a design center assisting individuals to remodel or design their own homes.

RMC

Central Baptist Church

Built 1924 for the Granite State Insurance Company.
Corner State and Middle street

Facing Middle Street, the present meeting place for the Central Baptist congregation was built in about 1924 for the Granite State Insurance Company. This insurance company was formed in 1885 by Frank Jones, whose dissatisfaction with the insurance industry dates to the succession of fires at his Rockingham Hotel. His efforts at reform resulted in the so-called valued policy law, which in New Hampshire guarantees payment of the full face value of a fire insurance policy in the case of total loss, and lead to the exodus of other insurers from the state. The building is of masonry and built with fireproof materials and structural systems.

This congregation has its beginnings in the preaching of Elias Smith, one of New England's most innovative and radical preachers and theologians of the turn of the 19th century. Smith's preaching began in Portsmouth began in 1803, and his congregation, and its meeting places, were called both Baptist and Christian. Smith is most closely identified with the restorationist movement of the period that emphasized simplicity of dogma, requiring only the teachings of the New Testament as its base, and known in other parts of the country through the teachings of Barton Stone, James O'Kelly, the Campbells, and elsewhere in New England by Abner Jones. The group built its first meetinghouse at the site of the present Music Hall, and owned the southern most of the Pleasant Street meetinghouses as well for a time. The congregation suffered some division, and its small size and budget sent them to a variety of meeting places during the middle of the 19th century. In 1862 they purchased the small two year-old house of another congregation facing Court Street behind the present house of worship. Much of its present appearance dates to a remodelling of 1891, from 1889 designs of local architect Henry S. Paul, that included the raising of the original structure above a new vestry [p. 81]. The congregation purchased the insurance company in 1954. In spite of its present name the congregation is not affiliated with either of the national associations of Christians, the Disciples of Christ or the Churches of Christ, nor any of the various Baptist affiliations.

CWD

HAYMARKET SQUARE AND MIDDLE STREET

The rapid development that characterizes the first decade of the 19th century is perhaps nowhere better seen than along the east end of Middle Street. At the end of the 18th century few houses or barns were found in the open fields that marked the urban edge. [see map p. 2] Here stood the town Hay Market where fodder and other farm products were retailed. In rapid succession a few large landholders began to sell off parcels of houselots, some to owners who would build for themselves and occasionally sub-divide, others to more speculatively oriented developers. The Jaffrey heirs had their land platted in between 1795 and 1799; the western blocks of Court Street and all the lots facing the Haymarket and eastern Middle Street were purchased from this estate. More than 30 new houses were built here and along the first block of Richards Avenue [see Richards Ave.] between 1798 and 1812. Throughout most of the early 19th century a significant minority of these large houses were rented, especially after the War of 1812 when real estate rapidly declined in value and "a large house rarely rented for more than $200." Although a few houses around Haymarket Square were replaced over the next century, most of those on the 1813 Hales map still survive today.

In their construction of homes along the major radial thoroughfares of Islington, Middle, and Pleasant streets, Portsmouth's mercantile and professional elite employed patterns of building that connected them to broadly similar patterns of that era and to

Sources:

Historical Report 1802-1952, 175th Anniversary, Central Baptist Church (1978).

Sanborn Map Company, Portsmouth, NH 1920 and later overlays.

Morning Chronicle, 5 January 1889.

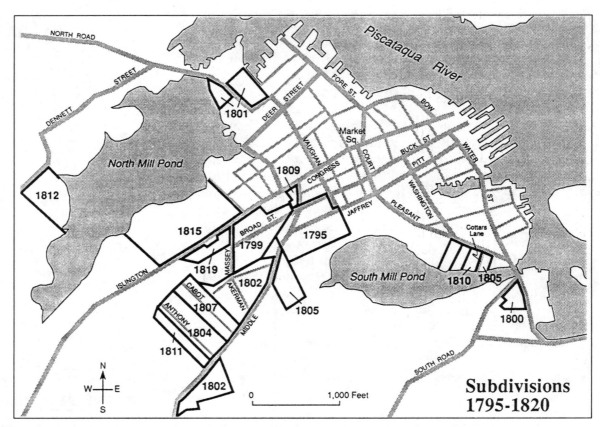

Eliza McClennen, cartographer

*Platted land divisions, Portsmouth, NH
1795-1820.*

Sources:

Broadside, *Independent Electors of the Town of
Portsmouth*, March 1816

Research by Richard Candee

narrower solutions of New England. A small number constructed large rural estates, but more commonly homeowners chose generous lots. In either case it was not uncommon for owners and promoters to control the character of their neighborhood and the value of their investments there. Jeremiah Mason's deeds included a restriction against "any dwelling house or buildings in which any mechanic trade shall be carried on" for 60 years. Daniel Austin's deeds, by contrast, required dwellings to "be three stories in height or shall be as large as the house now occupied by William Stanwood." Nowhere can this desire for architectural control be better seen than in the Brick Act of 1814. It was first thought that only those sites burned in 1813 should be rebuilt in brick, but "certain gentlemen, who owned land in the west part of town," proposed extending the boundaries to Cabot Street. This effectively encompassed the whole urban core. Thus, after passage of the amended Brick Act, all new buildings within the brick zone were supposed to meet its construction standards. In practice, only the wealthy could do so, and after public controversy the town overlooked many violations and ignored the Cabot Street boundary for a line east of the center of Summer Street. Most lots in this area had been developed by then, but evidence of the act's influence can be seen nonetheless.

Where cities in other regions had a tradition of truly urban forms in their choice of lot sizes, house types, and levels of density, New Englanders seldom built initially to these patterns. Like those in other cities of this region, the elite that expanded into these neighborhoods selected large free-standing dwellings, often surrounded with not just front yards and deep service spaces to the rear, but ample side yards and high solid fences to insulate them from their neighbors *[see the Rundlet-May House]*. The largest homes of the decades on either side of 1800 continued to favor the double house or georgian plan and three story height; the five bay, center-entry façade remained popular, with the third story housed in a low-studded full story (like the largest houses of the 1760s) rather than behind a fenestrated attic of most colonial and post-colonial examples. Further evidence of the emphasis on a taut façade over a plastic one can be seen in the generally flatter execution of moldings at the cornice, windows, and entries. The preference for low hip roofs complemented these choices, although a surprising number of high hip roofs continued to be built on such houses well past the first decade of the new century *[see Hart?-Briard Houses]*. On the interior these largest houses occasionally partook of the era's preference for more inventive floor plans, and, while oval, round and octagonal rooms or bays were relatively rare in the Piscataqua, the town's housewrights warmly embraced the round and elliptical stair, and occasionally placed that stair in an offset niche that opened up the broad central hall. Two of the finest houses with these features are the John Peirce Mansion and the Langley Boardman House.

CWD

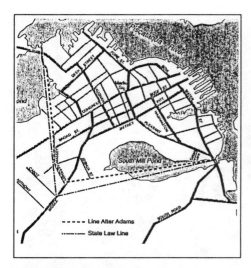

Eliza McClennen, cartographer
Brick Act boundaries, 1814.

Eliza McClennen, cartographer
New construction after Brick Act, 1814-25.

Construction Types:

■ Brick
○ Stone
▲ Wood
▫ Brick & Wood

0   1,000 Feet

1814
- - - Brick Act Boundary

Courtesy Portsmouth Athenæum
John Peirce House, on original site.
Photograph ca. 1860.

John Peirce House

Built 1799
Remodeled as annex to the Middle Street Baptist Church, 1955
Haymarket Sq.

The first of the mercantile mansions to be built along the Middle Street axis was built by John Peirce (1746-1814) in 1799. Situated in the intersection known as Haymarket Square, the house is an early example of the large three story Federal mansion house that became the preferred building mode. Although Woodbury Langdon had constructed his large brick house further east a dozen years before, this is the earliest house surviving that combines elaborate Adamesque ornamentation with the new planning modes preferred by New England elite builders during this decade. Much of the house was, of course, not new: its three story, center hall, double pile form, or its belvedere or cupola, for example. But in its level and amount of exterior and interior finish, and in its use of an elliptical stair, its off set position, it marks a distinctive phase within New England building. The exterior of the Peirce House, in particular the treatment of its central three bays, employs a common 1790s combination of an arcade supporting pilasters, supporting the roof line cornice, with the added embellishment of oval plaques in the tympana of the arches, patera above the capitals in the frieze, and a central oval and flanking rectangular spandrel panels. On its interior, the house demonstrates the use of William Pain style elements for door and window surrounds, mantels, cornices and wainscotting, including elements used with particular frequency in the Portsmouth area, such as clusters of three colonnetts flanking either side of the mantel and over mantel, and frieze elements including the drapery motif and the arched modillion block. The craftsmen employed here combined elements from Pain with those advocated by Benjamin to substitute combinations of small wood pieces in the place of carved moldings.

Construction of the colonial revival Middle Street Baptist Church dates to 1955 when the congregation relocated from the southwest corner of Middle and State streets. The present church was designed by local architect Maurice E. Witmer.

CWD

Walter H. Kilham Sketchbook, 1889
Boardman fanlight and door.

Langley Boardman House

Built 1803-1806
152 Middle Street

In the Langley Boardman House can be seen elements of design and ornament more commonly associated with Salem, Massachusetts to the south. Boardman was an important craftsman and real estate developer, and though he built this house, it appears that he did not live in it until after 1815. Once again the house takes the three story, center hall, double pile plan, with offset elliptical stair in the rear hall similar to that built for Admiral Hull at the Naval Shipyard. But the façade's treatment is more austere, with the elegant flushboard façade and ornament otherwise limited to the treatment of the center door and window above with the interlocking visual elements of the Palladian window with recessed relieving arch, a fan and sidelit door, and a semicircular door with Ionic columns that recalls the Gardner-Pingree House of Samuel McIntire. The interior of the house further confirms the Salem elements in the treatment of the parlor mantel with sheaves of wheat, central fruit basket, and vine-entwined Ionic columns with Scammozi capitals. The left rear room was expanded and redecorated in the middle of the 19th century and exhibits Greek Revival detailing that is generally uncommon within the city except for updatings such as this one. The front right room was redecorated later in the century and boasts of the paper wall treatment Anaglypta, designed to resemble Lyncrusta and other expensive Artistic wall treatments.

CWD & MFC

Ell Houses

A significant variation found in Portsmouth as in other large New England communities is the house form known as the "L-house." When merchant Charles Treadwell hired Robert Lapish, a country joiner from Durham, to build a house (replaced in 1889 by the Sise Inn on Court Street nearest Haymarket Square) he specified:

> Said house is to be an Ell house so called of the following dimensions that is Main body Forty two feet in length & 22 in breadth, the Ell 20 [long] by 18 [wide], & it is to be understood that the House before described is to be three storry & to have a hip'd roof and the Eaves to Cove Eight Inches on the frount [&] to be ornamented with Medalions [modillions] same as the House now building for Edwd Parry.

Surviving houses on Court, Middle, and Austin streets demonstrate the plan's popularity among elite home-owners and tenants. While it shares all the characteristics of the front half of a double house, a perpendicular rear ell replaces the second tier of two rooms and the back hall. On the largest houses such ells are commonly two or three stories in height and on corner locations ells of full height are placed so as to appear as a double house along both streets. An elaborate ell house built in 1801 by Ebenezer Thompson, a merchant and shipowner from Durham, NH, was occasionally rented to others [#2 on map p. 116]. It takes advantage of its site on Haymarket Square and the passageway between this lot and the Peirce house so that the two walls are fully in view, rather than hiding the ell along an interior lot line, and these two façades are treated with equal elaboration. James Rundlet rented here while building his own house [see Rundlet-May House] and later purchased it for one of his children. Just across the street from Thompson's 1801 house a new house was also going up for shipcaptain and mariner Richard Shapleigh [#3]. Although now partially obscured by a later semicircular entry porch, its doorway demonstrates the popularity of the Pain-Benjamin motifs of a century earlier. After Shapleigh's death the house was owned by his son; he leased the house to Elisha Crane who

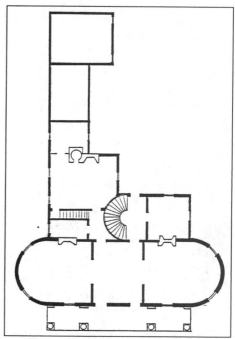

Drawing by Amy Amidon after John Locke
Isaac Hull House (Quarters A) Portsmouth Naval Shipyard. L-house plan with elliptical staircase, John Locke, 1814.

Courtesy Portsmouth Athenæum
Charles Treadwell House, 1798.

Courtesy Portsmouth Athenæum
Richard Shapleigh House, before porch additions.

Key to map (upper right)
1. *John Peirce House, 1799*
   Haymarket Square
2. *Ebenezer Thompson House, 1801*
   145-147 Middle Street
3. *Capt. Richard Shapleigh House , ca.*
   1800-1803, 116 Middle St.
4. *Gains House, site of Parrott Houses*
   1866, 132-134 Middle St.
5. *Langley Boardman House, 1803-06*
   152 Middle Street
6. *Ham- Briard House, 1804-06*
   159 Middle St.
7. *Samuel Larkin House, by 1808, ell*
   1809, John Locke, housewright
   160 Middle St.
8. *Joshua Wentworth House, 18th century*
   (destroyed) site of Larkin-Rice House
   (1815), 180 Middle St.
9. *Stanwood House, ca. 1799*
   199 Middle
10. *George Long House, 1811, Jonathan*
    Folsom architect-builder, corner Middle
    St. and Richards Ave.
11. *Hunking Penhallow House, ca. 1810*
    298 Middle
12. *Hardy - Haven House, ca. 1806*
    240 Middle St., corner Austin
13. *William Garland House, 1810-11*
    282 Middle St.
14. *Hart-Briard House, 1810, burned*
    1822, rebuilt or replaced by 1825.
    314 Middle St.
15. *Rundlet-May House Built 1807-1808*
    346 Middle St.
16. *Rindge-Lyman House, ca. 1804*
    (destroyed)
17. *Daniel Austin House, ca. 1800*
    enlarged as Pickering-Kimball houses
    ca. 1867, 43-53 Austin St.
18. *Amos Dow House, ca. 1803*
    85 Austin, corner Summer St.

A. *site of Haven-Decatur House (Octagon),*
   1813, replaced by Jones-Sinclair House,
   1866, 241 Middle St. corner Richards
   Ave.
B. *site of A.P. Peabody House, 266 Middle*
   St.
C. *site of N.K. Walker House, 1857,*
   remodelled ca. 1900, 171 Middle St.

J. G. Hales 1813 map of Portsmouth
Haymarket Square and Middle Street – Austin Street houses.

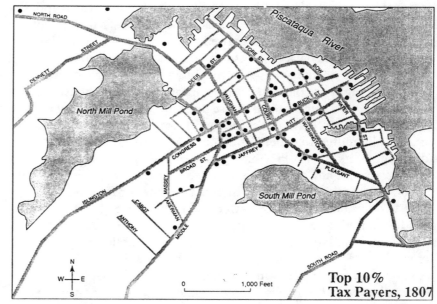

Eliza McClennen, cartographer, for Richard Candee
Urban residence of those in the top 10% of the 1807 tax list.

improved the property before buying the house. The side doorway was designed by local designer Oscar Vaughan in 1931.

Next to Thompson's house in 1804 William Ham III, trader, acquired a lot on which his new ell-house was soon built [#4]. After he sold it to Oliver Briard, the property was improved with a large garden and orchard along Middle Street that was not built on until 1857, when the land was subdivided for N.K. Walker's new home. Across the street is the first Samuel Larkin house, constructed in 1808 by the joiner who designed the Universalist meetinghouse and who later designed and built the Admiral Hull's quarters at the Naval Shipyard. Its rear ell was added in 1809 as evidenced in the purchase of land by Larkin from Boardman for this purpose. Further west, subdivisions by Daniel Austin led to the construction of the Hardy-Haven House in 1806 [#8], the William Garland House in 1810-11 [#9], the Hunking Penhallow House by 1810 [#10] all three-stories high. Along Middle and Austin streets ell houses outnumber the full double pile examples. Others are located along Pleasant and Islington streets, though many there have been destroyed or altered by subsequent auto-related development, and in occasional examples on the secondary streets surrounding them.

RMC & CWD

Courtesy Portsmouth Athenæum

N.K. Walker House, 1857, before colonial revival alterations; William Stanwood House (right).

Courtesy Portsmouth Athenæum

Middle Street houses on Austin lots left, Penhallow House, center, Garland House, right, corner Peabody House.

RICHARDS AVENUE

Joshua Street, as Richards Avenue was known before its extension beyond Parrott Avenue, was the first street to be developed south of Middle Street. Surveyed into lots of 60' frontage in 1805, all but the corner lots facing Middle Street were purchased by Langley Boardman. Over the next six years Boardman sold these lots outright and with mortgages to other skilled artisans. Most of the artisans who mortgaged their land back to Boardman agreed to pay the cabinetmaker with work or products of their trade. Five men promised "joiners work" and other artisans paid him in goods that he might otherwise have used in his cabinetmaking such as upholster's work and bed-bottoms made of sailcloth. By 1813 there were 11 houses on Joshua Street and another was added the next year, just as Folsom's octagon was being erected on the western corner lot. Most houses are center-entry types that face the street, but a narrow three-story house advertised for sale in 1813 by mariner John Sullivan was sited on a subdivided lot gable end to the street. Only one three-story center-hall plan house was built, about 1807, for cabinetmaker Samuel Wyatt. Other artisan houses were typically two stories high with end and rear-wall chimney plans like those built at the same time throughout the city.

JMcB

MIDDLE, AUSTIN AND SUMMER STREET TRIANGLE

This triangle of land was laid out by Daniel Austin by 1802 as a real estate development designed to extend the Haymarket Square neighborhood and benefit from its elite character. Austin viewed

Courtesy Portsmouth Athenæum

Rindge-Lyman House, ca. 1804 (destroyed)

Courtesy Peter and Nancy Beck
Austin-Pickering Houses.

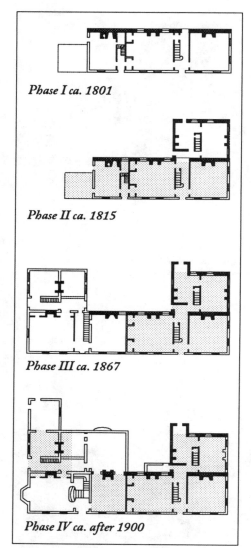

Phase I ca. 1801

Phase II ca. 1815

Phase III ca. 1867

Phase IV ca. after 1900

Drawings by Robert Kozman,
after Bernard Herman and Richard Candee
43-53 Austin St. evolution, 1801-1990.

his original house as the center of a new elite neighborhood. From 1802 to 1805 he advertised "House Lots For Sale, within a few minutes walk, or a quarter of a mile distance from the state-house" being located "near Middle Street opposite" his own "mansion house." Among the first new homes here was the John Rindge house (ca. 1804), formerly occupying the corner of Austin near Middle Street. It was a high hip-roofed center-hall plan house, but only its rear stable or carriage house (misdated "1782") survives. To control the visual character of the work of two joiners to whom he sold lots, Austin placed deed restrictions that "the first dwelling house which shall be erected on said lot shall be three stories in height or shall be as large as the house now occupied by William Stanwood." To the west, Amos Dow built the three-story L-house, 85 Austin Street, later owned by shipmaster John Lake. These houses, and the one pre-1810 house across Austin Street, met the three story requirement of Austin's deed restrictions. Moreover the Stanwood House at 199 Middle Street survives to illustrate Austin's alternative model. This house was built quite early for this neighborhood, between 1799 and 1806, and takes a smaller and less stylish form than its neighbors. Two-and-a-half stories in height under a common gable roof, with a fan-and-pediment entry treatment, it is a fine example of the smaller double house popular during the 18th century. Stanwood was a hairdresser who occupied this house until his death, when it was sold to Timothy Upham; it was later occupied by the Prescott sisters [See Prescott Park].

RMC & CWD

Austin-Pickering Houses

Built 1801-03, additions 1815-1867
43-53 Austin St.

Austin moved to Portsmouth from Charlestown, Massachusetts about 1800 after his wife Mary inherited several tracts beyond Haymarket Square. Although it was subsequently altered into a double house, the house Austin built for himself was an unusual mansion house. Estimated to have cost $10,000, the 3-story house originally extended three rooms across its façade, but was only a single room deep. By 1816 it was owned in common by two lawyers and a large brick ell was constructed behind the east end, following the directives of the Brick Act. When these tenants divided it in 1825, the east room and entry in the front pile as well as the new additions went to William M. Richardson, while the center room, kitchen, and another secondary western entry went to William Clagget. Richardson sold his eastern half to David Kimball in 1833 who eventually recombined the house as one in 1858. About 1867 the west side of the house was expanded and reconfigured for Commodore Charles W. Pickering, USN, upon his retirement after the Civil War. The exterior appearance of today, two connected houses, each a full five bay façade, was then achieved. The exterior ornament of the 1860s, like the roof, was all new on the far western end.

RMC

MIDDLE STREET AFTER 1813

Middle Street also allows consideration of the work of Jonathan Folsom, the craftsman who introduced some of the most unusual forms of building to the town in the 1810s. His more traditional buildings, borrowing on the convention earlier established at the Portsmouth Athenæum and the Peirce Mansion, are the Larkin-Rice House and the George Long House at the corner Middle St. and Richards Ave. The broad proportions of the second house built for Samuel Larkin, from profits made by auctioning privateer spoils during the War of 1812, with its generously spaced openings, and the floor-to-floor shift from palladian through recessed arch to simple rectangle, has prompted comparison to the Edward Shippen Burt House (1801-2) in Philadelphia by Benjamin Latrobe. In addition to the 1816 Custom House on Daniel Street and rowhouses on Sheafe Street, the 1824 South (Unitarian) Church on State Street, and the Joshua Haven House on Islington Street, Jonathan Folsom was the architect-builder of a long-demolished "octagon" house that stood opposite George Long's house (at the corner of Middle with Joshua Street, later Richards Ave.) with its pilasters and one-story porch.

Drawing by George H. Higgins and Edwin J. Hipkiss, 1917.

Larkin Rice House, 1815, attributed to Jonathan Folsom.

These blocks of Middle Street remained an elite residential area into the 20th century and a few buildings of equal substance were later built as infill or as replacements. In addition to the character-defining Federal houses, ambitious buildings can be seen in the Italianate, Mansard, and Colonial Revival modes. Open garden lots began to be subdivided for new housing in the 1850s *[see the Peabody house]* By the 1860s Portsmouth began to patronize Boston architects for larger commissions, and two Middle Street houses *[see Parrott and Jones-Sinclair houses]* illustrate this trend.

Elsewhere on Middle Street can be seen large frame houses, constructed with locally preferred forms and ornament. The N. K. Walker House, 171 Middle Street, built in 1857-60, was originally of this local type. This hatter, built his new house in the west garden of the Ham-Briard House next door. Its colonial revival remodelling that dates to its purchase in 1910 by Oskar Aichel, brewmaster at the Portsmouth Brewing Company.

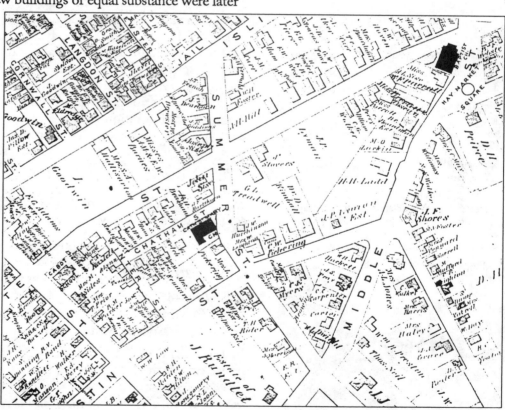

Detail of Beer's Map of Portsmouth, 1876, Library of Congress

Haymarket Square to Cabot St.

CWD

119

Downing, *The Architecture of Rural Cottages* (1850)
Gervase Wheeler, Timber-Frame Villa.

Courtesy Strawbery Banke
A.P. Peabody Cottage Villa, 1852.

Sources:

Dell Upton, "Pattern Books and Professionalism," *Winterthur Portfolio* 19:2/3 (1984): 107-150.

Patricia Anderson, *The Architecture of Bowdoin College* (Brunswick: 1988): 153-155.

Vincent J. Scully, Jr., "Romantic Rationalism and the Expression of Structure in Wood: Downing, Wheeler, Gardner, and the 'Stick Style' 1840-76" *Art Bulletin* 35 (1953): 121-142.

Andrew P. Peabody, "Fires in American Cities," *International Review* (January 1874).

Courtesy Portsmouth Athenæum
Parrott Houses.

Andrew P. Peabody Cottage Villa

Built 1852
266 Middle St.

This house shows the adaptation of pattern book designs by local builders, for it is one of many houses derived from Gervase Wheeler's design for an "English Cottage" or "Plain Timber Cottage-Villa" first published in 1849 in *The Horticulturalist*. Subsequent publication by A.J. Downing occurred in 1850 and a variant by Lewis E. Joy in 1852. As Wheeler noted, the building he illustrated was "slightly modified from one erected by the writer at Brunswick, in Maine," in 1849. This house was constructed in 1853, for the Rev. A.P. Peabody, the minister of the South (Unitarian) Church who came to Portsmouth in 1833, and previously lived in the Garland House next door west. A young man of 22 when he took over this pulpit, Peabody went on to a scholarly and literary career that included multiple lectures, part ownership of the *North American Review*, and, after leaving the stone church, returning to Harvard as Professor of Christian Morals. Although much of the exterior massing of his house resembles the popular pattern book house, there were alterations in initial construction as well as in later remodellings. Not the least of these altered the plan and reversed the rear ell from the right to the left side. No Gothic Revival ornament can be seen in old photographs. The interior was remodelled using Colonial Revival ornament around the turn of the century, but retains fireproof walling that Peabody derived from English sources. "I built a house . . . in 1853," he wrote, "using for the interior wall of every partition bricks laid edgewise." Surviving brick-filled interior partitions confirm that he also adopted a more common configuration than that proposed by Wheeler's plan. The entry hall is narrower, with a stair in the more usual orientation running from front to rear, and the chimneys are located between the rooms in the front and rear pile, without the sliding doors of the plan or the single large open parlor suggested by Wheeler. Peabody and his carpenters did not adopt the model in all its aspects, but borrowed from several sources selectively.

CWD & RMC

William Frederick Parrott Houses

Built 1864-65
132-134 Middle St.
Gridley J.F. Bryant, Boston, architect

In 1864 Capt. William F. Parrott purchased the early 19th-century house east of the Boardman house. It was then *"cut in two and rolled away...to different parts of the city... half, of this wooden mansion...contains the front door and the old central staircase."* Over the next two years a fine example of an expensive double brick house was constructed, common in larger cities but rare among the houses of Portsmouth. Parrott lived on the east side, his mother and sisters on the west. The design can be assigned to Gridley J.F. Bryant, based on a checklist of his office drawings. Bryant's was then the largest architectural firm in Boston, and its commissions were numerous and high profile. Many were executed, as were the Parrott houses, in what he described as "the modern style of Renaissance architecture."

CWD & RMC

Jones–Sinclair House

Built 1865-67; remodeled 1889
241 Middle Street

One of the few large villas in Portsmouth replaced Folsom's octagon built for Thomas Haven and later sold to Admiral George W. Storer. The Jones-Sinclair house, 241 Middle Street at the corner of Richards Avenue, was constructed in 1865-1867 for Admiral Storer's daughter and her husband Albert L. Jones. It was leased after his death in 1870. A room-by-room inventory of his estate and that of the next owner who died in 1889 confirms the present elaborate floor plan existed before the house was bought by Frank Jones as a wedding present to his daughter, Emma, and her husband Charles A. Sinclair. Sinclair established the Islington Street Morley Button Company, manufacturer's of papier-mache buttons and button sewing machines. Domestic improvements made that summer included new plate glass in the white and gold decorated west parlor, exotic wood finishes and frescoes on the first floor and mahogany trim throughout the second story. The embossed and gilded lion head wallpaper of the vestibule makes symbolic reference to Jones's favorite bronzed lions in front of the Rockingham Hotel. A large stable, since removed for the elderly apartment complex next door, and the granite and cast-iron fence were added the next year.

CWD & RMC

MIDDLE STREET AFTER 1890

Continued infill and moderate levels of replacement characterize Middle Street at the turn of the century period. Colonial Revival designs are most numerous, as builders sought forms they felt appropriate to the old town. Among the most ambitious was the house at the corner of Miller Avenue *[see Wallace Hackett House]*, built in 1892 to a design by the Boston firm of Dabney and Ball, responsible for resort residences down the coast in York as well as the Portsmouth Cottage Hospital and other buildings *[see Portsmouth Athenæum]*. In 1920 the building was converted to use by the Masons, who constructed the Classical Revival annex on Miller Avenue. Across the street, John W. Emery built a house at 338 Middle at the corner of Summer after acquiring the land in 1903. The architect, Robert Coit of Boston, borrowed and altered the idea of the staircase at the Mill-Whipple house.

The most recent addition to this section of Middle street was the Margeson Apartments, built as HUD co-sponsored housing for senior citizens in 1973. The site was formerly occupied by the brick

Courtesy Portsmouth Athenæum
Thomas Haven "Octagon" House.

Courtesy Portsmouth Historical Society Collection, Portsmouth Athenæum
Jones-Sinclair House in 1897.

<u>Sources:</u>

Ray Brighton, *Frank Jones, King of the Alemakers* (Portsmouth: Peter Randall, 1976).
Boston Herald, 12 Dec. 1897.

Courtesy Portsmouth Athenæum
Samuel P. Long House (destroyed).

Hart?-Briard House, after addition of roof dormer.

From Frank E. Wallis, *American Architecture, Decoration and Furniture of the 18th Century* (1894)
Doorway, Hart?-Briard House.

Sources:

Nathaniel Adam, *Annals of Portsmouth* (Portsmouth: 1824): 377

Portsmouth Oracle May 26, 1821

Fireward's Records, vol. 1: 1806-1834, Portsmouth Athenæum

carriage house of the Jones-Sinclair House, which, with a small gas station and showroom, also served as the Pontiac Cadillac dealership, and by the Samuel P. Long Gothic Revival cottage. The developer of the turn-key project, which includes 137 one-bedroom apartments and a range of recreation and dining facilities, was Crown International; the architect was George Earl Ross of Braintree, MA. The project was plagued by labor and financial difficulties, including an unsuccessful bombing.

CWD

Hart?-Briard House

Built 1810, burned 1822; rebuilt 1825
314 Middle Street

On May 26, 1821 the newspaper noted that dwelling house built by housewright Benjamin Locke in 1810 for Jeremiah Hart "was consumed ... and threatened several elegant houses in the neighborhood." City firewards stated that "the Fire made its appearance first in the lower room at the north east corner of the House which in the course of an hour was entirely consumed." The lot was within the westernmost corner of the line controlled by the Brick Act of 1814 and it may not be coincidental that there was no house listed here until 1827, two years after the controversial act lapsed. It was owned and sometimes rented by Captain William A. Briard who sailed out of New York harbor.

This would seen straightforward if certain elements like the high hip roof and the staircase balusters did not so resemble other houses of 1800-1810 date. The doorway, with its unique paired colonnettes, the surviving mantelpieces, and the ornament of the interior arched doorway between the front and rear halls all appear consistent with the 1820s. Yet, during recent renovation, a layer of black consistent with soot was found beneath later paints in several parts of the hall and east room. It is unclear whether the L-plan form is that of the 1810 house or whether any parts of the existing building may have been salvaged and reused in the 1820s rebuilding.

RMC

Rundlet-May House

Built in 1807-08
346 Middle Street

Exceptional in both its size and its siting since its construction, and even more so now in its intact survival, the Rundlet-May House is an excellently documented property that provides important insight about the Federal town. Built in 1807 in a newly opening portion of the town by a newcomer to the upper reaches of the merchant community, both James Rundlet and his house embody key characteristics that distinguish them from their fellow city merchants. When Rundlet died in 1852 the house was inherited by his two single children, Caroline (1797-1880) and Edward (1805-1874), and after their deaths by James Rundlet May (1841-1918), the son of their sister Louisa Catherine (1817-1895), who had married

George Hall May. In 1881 James R. May married Mary Ann Morison, whose family lived at the Purcell House prior to its acquisition by the Portsmouth Historical Society. Mrs. May was very interested in all aspects of the Colonial Revival movement, and many of the furnishings came into the house through her family or through the collecting efforts of her sister. Their only son Ralph May (1882-1975) was the last family owner, and after his death the house went to the Society for the Preservation of New England Antiquities.

James Rundlet was born in Exeter in 1772 and came to Portsmouth in 1794 shortly after completing his secondary education at Exeter Academy. He married Elizabeth Hill the next year and the couple lived in rental property for a dozen years before building their substantial mansion. During that time six of the couple's thirteen children were born, they inherited property from her father Elish Hill, and Rundlet expanded his operations as a retailer of textiles and commission merchant. Rundlet's rise through the town's ranks is amply documented in his changing position within town taxpayers. When he came to town he was situated within the second quarter, five years later in the second tenth, in 1805 and 1810 within the highest tenth; from 1815 he was the tenth highest taxpayer in the town, and until his death in 1852 he never fell from this wealthy ranking. Rundlet accomplished this accumulation through a distinctive combination of business dealings, and through investments in new enterprises aimed at the traditional goals of maintaining capital. After accumulating substantial wealth through importing and selling textiles, particularly by provisioning woolens to the Army during the War of 1812, Rundlet left retailing in 1819. For the next 20 years he lived on an income of approximately $4000, the interest and profits from approximately $135,000 in investments divided into three primary categories. The largest third or about $45,000 was invested in real estate, including his house on Middle Street, stores in Market Square, a farm at Sagamore Creek, and a small number of other houses he rented out, often to members of his family. He also owned tracts of open land that surrounded his estate, guaranteeing the rural quality of its setting. In this he differed from other local merchants who invested in shipping rather than land, as well as from those who like Langley Boardman acquired lands, or like Daniel Austin used inherited land, for real estate development. Rundlet held his property as an estate and invested in bank stocks

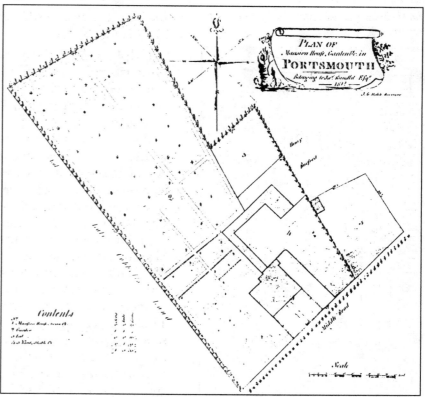

Courtesy SPNEA

"Plan of Mansion House garden &c... belonging to Ja' Rundlet, Esq'. 1812" by J.G. Hales, surveyor.

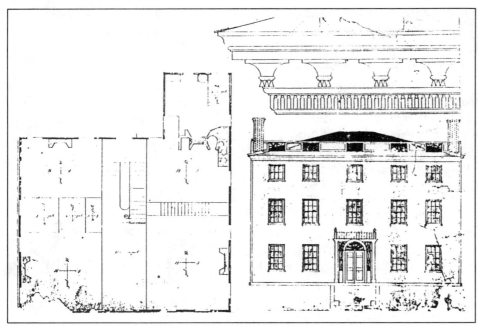

Rundlet Proposed elevation, plan & cornice detail.

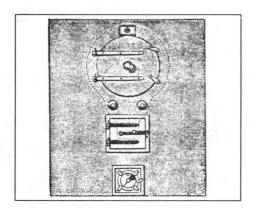

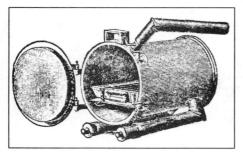

and U.S. stocks, as well as a number of municipal improvements including turnpikes, bridges, saltworks, library, academy, and aqueduct.

His most distinctive enterprise however was to shift his personal attentions from retailing to the manufacture of textiles. He began in 1813 to invest in the Amesbury Wool and Cotton Manufacturing Company with Paul Moody and Ezra Worthen, and continued to supply the Army until competition from Philadelphia area manufacturers and declining quality lost him the commissions, and he began to look for a buyer for his stock. In 1822 he invested in a second wool manufacturing enterprise, this one on the Salmon Falls River in Somersworth NH. Again he searched for technically knowledgeable employees and advisors, and this time found fellow investors in Portsmouth. His inability to sell his Amesbury stock forced him to sell his Salmon Falls holdings only a year later. The Amesbury property was purchased by Boston Associate Amos Lawrence in 1830, who eventually purchased Salmon Falls in 1844.

Building the House: Within the family papers held by SPNEA is the fortunate survival of a first floor plan, elevation, and cornice drawing, the schedule of workers, and bills paid for the construction of the house. While some details of the drawing were not executed, it is important as evidence of the use of Benjamin's *American Builder's Companion.* The survival of a "Labor Schedule" in addition to a set of bills to workmen, wholesalers, and retailers provides exceptionally detailed information on the house and its builders. On this chart workers are listed by name and their work on the site indicated in units of a day, a fraction of a day, or an absence; six-day weeks were the norm. The construction of this large dwelling began in the spring of 1807 and that building season continued until December. The largest number of billable labor costs were accumulated during this season, totalling over 2500. The briefer second season employed fewer men and ran from late March through early November of 1808. Bills associated with this work continue through 1809. Although all laborers cannot be matched from schedule to bill, nor all bills definitely distinguished between labor and materials, tiers of wages can easily be identified. Most general labor and joiners work is paid by the day or a fraction thereof ranging from as low as 90 cents to as high as $2.00 per day, but most commonly clustering at $1.20 to $1.40. Only specialized tasks or products are distinguished in reporting and hence in mode of payment. Rundlet paid a larger proportion of the cost of the house on the labor of many craftsman, including more than $5000 on daily wages and transportation, nearly $600 for boarding some of the workers, nearly $200 for their rum, and more than $1000 on named construction tasks. These last include what appear to be the most specialized tasks completed by the many workers, including the frames for the house, woodhouse, and stable, as well as a variety of finishing tasks including turning and carving. A conservative division of bills between labor and materials indicates labor equalled about $6800 and materials $5500. The bills complement the labor schedule and suggest a fairly predictable sequence of work on the house, with digging the cellar, constructing the foundation and chimneys, the frame, during the first season, followed by interior finish the second, and decorating during the third.

The Rundlet-May House is representative of the later phases of Federal period construction, when exterior ornamentation became more limited and standardized. Its cornice follows the arched modillion block seen in the earlier Peirce House and interior of the Portsmouth Athenæum, and its front entry is treated with a fan and sidelights and a Tuscan portico. Its plan includes the classic double house plan of four rooms on either side of a central stair hall, with a tier of service spaces between the rooms on the west side and a service stair between those on the east. With the exception of the ell, the plan is repeated on each of the upper two stories, although on the second floor a narrow corridor runs along the east wall allowing access to these rooms from the service stair. Many of the furnishings of the house when built remain in the house, and examples from the shop of Langley Boardman can be seen here. In the east parlor, the original wall paper and border, Peach Damask and Paris Flock Border remain on the walls. The treatment of the mantel here provides contrast with that in the west parlor at the Boardman House, including several similar elements, the basket and the wheat sheaves for example, executed in a very different fashion. A piece of the west parlor wall paper called Green Worm can be seen between the front windows there, while the mantel exhibits the inset figured panels that are characteristic of Portsmouth Federal detailing. The kitchen was fitted with a Rumford Roaster and three boilers that remained in use as late as 1858. The rear ell was planned from the start, providing extra heat sources for a scullery or summer kitchen.

Alterations to the plan as drawn are focused in two areas. The rear ell was expanded in two phases to both the east and the west. On the east, the small pantry room was apparently added by 1813, the wellroom by 1852; on the west, the ell was widened to expand the scullery by 1813, including the addition of a rear hall by 1852. The service spaces between the front and rear rooms on the west side were reduced in size when the rear or north wall of the west front parlor was moved back to enlarge that room. This change is undated but is believed to have taken place shortly after the completion of the house.

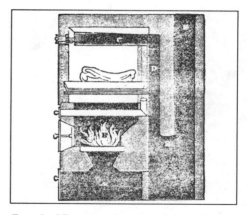

Rumford Roaster, elevation, perspective, and section from Benjamin Thompson, Count Rumford, On the Construction of Kitchen Fire Places and Kitchen Utensils (London: 1802).

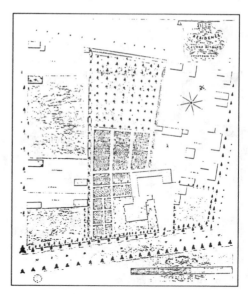

Courtesy SPNEA
Plan of site 1853.

125

Plans of the house lot were completed in 1813 and again in 1852, when the large holdings on the opposite side of Middle Street was drawn as well. The scullery is connected to the long L-shaped array of wood-shed, privies, and pig stye that connect the house to the carriage house, an exceptional survival in an urban context. The barn that Rundlet owned was sited on one of the adjacent parcels. Rundlet purchased an array of plants and fruit trees for his garden, the remnants of which include the pathways and the form of the rose bush supports. The present plantings of the garden primarily reflect the efforts of Mary Ann May, and the former orchard at the rear of the property is now a denser shade park, while the beds nearest the house are more ornamental and abundantly planted than originally. Though Rundlet had purchased vast acreage to assure himself a rural retreat, his children and heirs eventually sold all but the large nearly two acre house lot. The first lots across the street to be sold were three toward Wibird Street in the 1860s, but the largest parcel was sold in 1872 to the real estate developer Benjamin F. Webster. Lots directly opposite the house were sold in 1889 and a lot on the west to Mrs. D. Montgomery by 1886 *[see Montgomery-Eldredge House]* and that on the east side was sold to W. Emery in 1902.

CWD

Sources:
James Garvin, *Academic Architecture.*
Research by Claire Dempsey.

Winthrop P. Hoit House

Built 1818
corner of Middle & Union

Courtesy Portsmouth Athenæum
Winthrop P. Hoit House.

In 1817 the *NH Gazette* advertised *"Land on Union (or Anthony) Street, near Akerman's Rope-Walk, measuring forty-five feet on said street, and fifty deep, adjoining the land of Mr. Winthrop P. Hoit and Mr. Francis Wingate,"* belonging to the estate of Daniel Marden, that had been purchased in 1816 from Boardman and Abbott. Sally Marden, whose brick house on Cabot Street Rundlet was to soon purchase, sold the lot that year to the joiner Winthop P. Hoit and he erected the house on this and part of his adjoining lot. In 1818 Hanson Hoit sold the mortgaged property, "lately occupied by W. P. Hoit," back to Boardman & Abbott and they held it as a rental until 1824. Not until the later 19th century was there any addition to the main block, when a store was added to the west end. Thus, the house is a good example of the work of an Austinborough joiner's rear wall chimney house plan.

RMC

Mills-Whipple House

Built ca. 1760
599 Middle Street
original owner, John Mills (before 1761);
Joseph Whipple, 1766-1806

This two story house with hip roof, relocated in 1969 from its original Glebe lot at the NE corner of State and Chestnut streets, is a modest 30' x 35' exclusive of its early 19th century wing. Its five-bay façade, embellished with triangular pediments over the ground story windows. projecting caps above those on the second, and a central Corinthian frontispiece around its now-recessed doorway, belies the unusual floor plan. Its original west elevation (now east) is marked by an arched window for the staircase landing of the large corner entry hall Built by the English immigrant turner John Mills sometime before 1761, the house prefigures, on a smaller scale, the plan and detailing of the stair at the Moffatt-Ladd house on which Mill's son, Richard, likely did the turnings. These two houses are the sole colonial examples in the Piscataqua to devote nearly a quarter of the floorplan to the stair hall. In this case, it is the unmistakable boast of a turner and joiner who, in his own house, could indulge his craft to a degree impossible in the normal central-hall house of that day. Unlike the Moffatt-Ladd staircase, the balustrade rises against the rear wall of the room and thus presents the staircase broadside to the visitor to compensate for the hall's smaller size. The window that lights the landing is treated as an aedicule, with Ionic pilasters (with capitals attributed to Dearing) and a full entablature. The run of stairs rising to the second floor is placed so that both sides are enclosed by a balustrade — probably the only example in this region.

Although much altered, the plan can be reconstructed with a rear room behind the stair entry through a door at the foot of the staircase and a front sitting room or parlor in the opposite front corner. The break-out or projection of room cornices over all the doors and windows, common to many colonial and post-colonial houses of the Piscataqua, provides clues to the original fenestration and door location, although what the projection of the cornice around the inner corner suggests about the access to the rear kitchen corner is anybody's guess.

Later additions and alterations: In 1766 the house was sold to Joseph Whipple, a merchant and developer of extensive lands in northwestern New Hampshire as well as collector of customs throughout much of the early Federal period. It was apparently Whipple who made a one story addition to the original east (now west) end of the house, perhaps after the fire of 1802 destroyed his Market Street store. After his death the property was leased, "reserving the chamber over the store house where certain papers belonging to the estate of Joseph Whipple are kept." This wing was remodeled with a Greek Revival portico in the mid-19th century and later raised to a full two story height with a matching colonial revival extension of the cornice. Subsequent owners in the early 19th century were likely responsible for the addition of federal mantelpieces in the upper and lower rear rooms, and modern owners have further altered the house for use as a boarding house and later apartments.

RMC

Courtesy Portsmouth Athenæum
Mills–Whipple House, on original site, State Street about 1900.

Sources:

Mss Lease to James H. Pierpont, Portsmouth Historical Society Collection, Portsmouth Athenæum.

James Garvin, *Academic Architecture* (1983)

"Journal of a Tour to the White Hills': An 1842 Chronicle by Samuel Johnson," edited by Bryant F. Tolles, Jr., *Essex Institute Historical Collections*, 120:1 (Jan. 1984): 4-5:

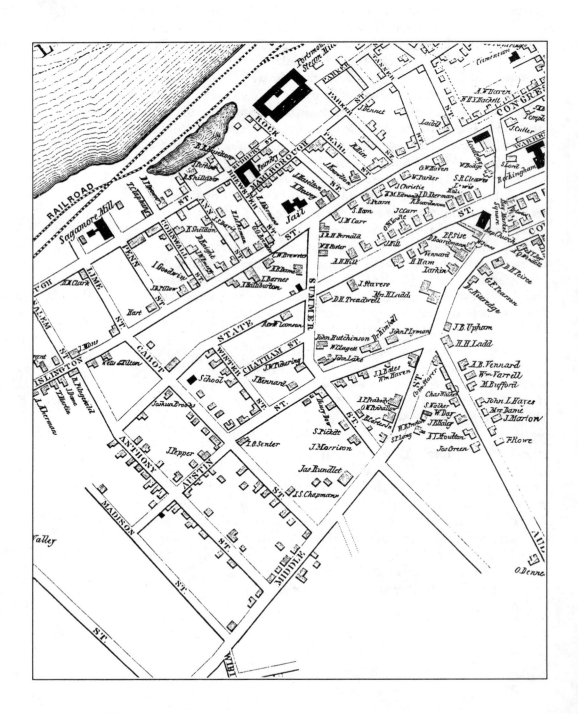

Map of Portsmouth, 1850

Detail, West End.

Note: Anthony Street now called Union Street.

AUSTINBOROUGH: CABOT, AUSTIN, AND UNION STREETS

The development of the cross-streets between the Middle and Islington Street thoroughfares occurred incrementally as local real estate speculators like Langley Boardman, John and Butler Abbott, and Daniel Austin repeated the process Boardman tried first on Cottars Lane and Joshua Street. From 1806 to 1816 Boardman sold and mortgaged empty houselots on Cabot Street to more than 20 craftsmen, many again to be paid in craft work or products. While neither the Abbotts nor Austin followed this practice, they too provided mortgages to many brickmasons, cabinetmakers, and joiners. While some may have planned to build and sell new homes here, with the slowing of construction in the decades after the War of 1812 many lots remain open and some homes were lost for debt.

In 1844 the Reverend Andrew P. Peabody, minister of the Unitarian South Parish, noted there were "hardly more than 500 men who are mechanics or manufacturers," but that the "most numerous class of mechanics is that of house carpenters, whose structures invest much of the earnings of the town in a permanent form." Yet, he estimated, "the repairs and the new buildings of the last ten years would hardly balance the deterioration of buildings that are waxing old." A substantial number of these woodworking mechanics still lived and worked in the West End streets of "Austinborough" around the dead-ends of Union, Austin and Cabot streets as well as new streets of the 1840s *[see Winter St.]*. These artisans included John Perkins, whose small Cabot Street house was immediately west of the Rundlet fence, James Coffin and Oliver Manson on Union Street, and the Nortons (Thomas, Benjamin, and John) who lived and worked near Austin and Union streets. Many built their own homes, such as James Coffin (179 Union) in 1828, 119 Union Street *[see Oliver Manson house]* in 1840, and Benjamin Franklin Webster (292 Austin Street) in 1851. Others built for specialized markets, such as Thomas Norton who prefabricated house-frames in his workshop at the corner of Union and Austin streets and shipped them to San Francisco during the 1849 Gold Rush. Working in Norton's Austin Street shop was Moses Yeaton, a joiner whose purchased Rundlet land and subdivided it to many carpenters who built Winter Street houses. Yeaton also bought lots on State and Union Streets in the 1850s and 60s onto which he moved one house and sold lots for others.

Until the 1840s most of the homes in Austinborough were small in scale and value. An 1830s house owned by Benjamin Garland [see p. 9] was once a one-story rear-wall chimney cottage north of Manson's house on Union Street. The two Perkins houses on Cabot Street were also small; one may be imbedded in the small cottage along the rear property line at 33 Cabot Street, behind a pair of stick-style houses. Their workshop was across the street, and many carpenters had small barns, separate workshops, and other buildings on otherwise empty lots as far west as Madison Street. Across Cabot Street is also the c. 1810 brick house of

James Coffin House, 179 Union St., 1828; doorway (left) is from an earlier house moved here ca. 1865-70.

Photograph 1977
Samuel Jennings House, 214 Union Street.

Sources:

Research by Johnna McBrien, Richard Candee, and Beth Hostutler

Andrew Preston Peabody, *The Wealth, Industry, and Resources of Portsmouth*, Lectures at the Portsmouth Lyceum, Nov. 12, 1844 (Portsmouth: 1844).

Courtesy Portsmouth Athenæum
Union Street Homes, ca. 1890
left. William Pollard (destroyed)
center. Liberty Carey
right. Samuel Jennings.

brickmason Daniel Marden (at 64-68), one of those in favor of the Brick Act.

There were also a number of African-American families whose homes clustered at the end of Union Street near Middle Street. Here truckman Ceasar Whidden early acquired a number of empty house lots and, while he never lived on Union Street himself, may have played a role in attracting other persons of color to this corner. Two small houses of this group survive. The earliest may be the ca. 1814 western half of 214 Union Street, originally a two-story single cell house with an end chimney bay that was constructed with intermediate studs made from shaving thin sapplings. At some later date, perhaps as late as the early 1870s, the house was enlarged to the east by incorporating the remnant of another federal building that shows evidence of once having a hip roof over the second story. The house was apparently built for Samuel Jennings, a black mariner, whose widow Dinah was living here in 1840. Across the street was the home of another black mariner (no longer standing). The one-story house next to Jennings (226 Union) was owned by Liberty Carey from at least 1821 to 1828, and later rented to John Fogg, a black hairdresser, in the 1830s.

Stocking Weavers of the West End: A small house formerly on the site of Regan Electric next to Liberty Carey's was in 1850 the home of William Pollard, a "stocking weaver." Many of the homes of Austinborough were tenanted by men in this occupation during the 1840s and 1850s. Until the 1840s Portsmouth's only textile industry was a small hosiery factory that spun yarn and knit stockings and underwear. The stocking "weavers" operated hand-powered knitting frames that used yarns spun by water-powered factory production and "put-out" to these weavers. The Portsmouth Stocking Factory, established in 1835 at the west end of the North Mill Pond, employed some 50 hands in the mill with a putting-out system that employed three times that number — largely, but not exclusively, women — seaming and finishing the knitted materials at home. While female home workers are difficult to identify, the factory hands and a number of English-born male stocking weavers can be located from city directories. The American-born factory managers occupied homes along the far end of Islington Street near the mill. A half dozen identified English weavers either lived near the factory or clustered in West End streets with the blacks, joiners, and other tenants of Austinborough. The 1850 census shows their numbers had increased to at least 140 men and 213 women, also clustered in the West End near the mills and the earlier English weavers.

Hosiery weaving in Portsmouth was carried on at several different scales of industrial organization. Several small companies of English-born weavers worked in or near their homes similar to the small workshop systems in Great Britain or Germantown, Pennsylvania. For example, in 1850 Thomas Moore, a 36 year old English stocking weaver employed four men (at a total labor cost of $12 a month) and a dozen women ($50 a month) in his shop somewhere near the corner of Middle and Cabot streets. This small group of hand weavers produced 3600 stockings and 1760 shirts and drawers annually on Moore's modest $1000 capital investment. Nearby on Austin Street, Daniel Pepper, a 55 year old English stocking weaver had a similar small shop. Next door lived his son, John Pepper, a 27 year old machinist who began working as a stocking weaver in Newburyport at age 11 before the family moved to Portsmouth. At age 23 he discovered a system to finally put "the common loom in operation by machinery instead of manual power," so it could be run by steam or water power. Three experimental looms were set up in the Portsmouth Stocking Factory in 1847 and tested for two years. A single female operative produced 23 pairs of stockings and 22 pairs of drawers in one day. By comparison, a journalist in 1849 wrote, the best common stocking hand loom produced 2 ½ dozen of shirts and drawers per week.

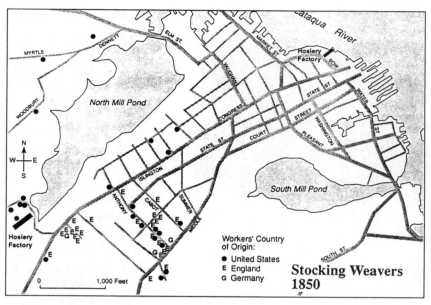

Eliza McClennen, cartographer

Stocking Weavers from 1850 U.S. Census with country of origin.

> *The invention, which we have just seen in operation, is unlike in appearance to any other stocking looms we have ever seen, occupying just half of the space of the improved looms, and will probably not cost half as much as those invented two years ago.*

The old hosiery factory, then owned by Boston investors under the name of the Rockingham Steam Mills, had 80 to 100 primarily male workers in the mill, including those operating 51 hand "stocking looms" and seven powered knitting looms. It also employed "weavers who work their Frames at home" plus 175 to 200 females "living in the city and neighboring towns" who were "employed for a part of their time at their Houses finishing and Seaming." The company annually produced $100,000 worth of shirts, drawers, as well as ladies and men's hose and by 1850 their machine shop manufactured Pepper's power looms.

There was also a smaller steam-powered hosiery factory on Bow Street, with a separate weave building for 15 hand looms. When the owner had to mortgage the contents in 1848 (perhaps to help finance his investment in Pepper's power looms) the factory had in the store house "seven hundred dozen hose of all sorts and sizes, seventy five dozen frocks and Drawers, fifty dozen children's Mittens, two dozen Shawls, four dozen Comforters" as well as 1500 pounds of raw wool and an equal amount of woolen yarn. The waterfront, especially along Bow Street and Mechanic Streets, was a traditional manufacturing location with both iron and brass foundries, this second hosiery factory, a steam planing machine and window sash manufactory — all using new steam engines. The stocking weavers who worked here, however, still lived in the West End.

RMC

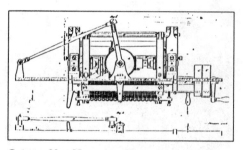

Courtesy New Hampshire Historical Society

Pepper knitting frame patent drawing.

Sources:

Portsmouth city directories, 1839/40, 1851.

Portsmouth Personal Property Mortgages, vol. 1, mss City Clerks Office, City Hall.

1850 U.S. Census Enumeration, Portsmouth, NH.

S.D. Chapman, "Enterprise and Innovation in the British Hosiery Industry, 1750-1850," *Textile History* 5 (Oct. 1974): 14-37.

William Felkin, *A History of the Machine-Wrought Hosiery and Lace Manufacturers* (NY: Burt Franklin reprint, 1967): 542-3n.

Philip Scranton, *Proprietary Capitalism: The Textile Manufacture at Philadelphia, 1800-1815.* (Cambridge: Cambridge Univ. Press): 224-271.

Norris-Chapman House, ca. 1810 with additions.

Courtesy Strawbery Banke Museum

John Pepper "Cottage House," 1848. 217 Austin St.

Edward Coffin House, 1862.

Mid 19th-century Infill and Replacement along Union, Austin, and Cabot Streets: This area was part of a T-shaped industrial zone along the railroad to the north and stretching west to the breweries and a later button factory. Empty lots were quickly filled in the decades after 1840 to provide new and larger housing for the city's increasing population. New building on Cabot, Austin and Union Streets replaced many smaller dwellings, either by engulfing them in later additions or by complete replacement. An interesting example of this is a rear-wall chimney house at 39 Cabot Street, built about 1810 for ropemaker Benjamin Norris, who probably worked at the Akerman ropewalk across Middle Street (modern Wibird Street). By 1846 Ira Chapman, a spinner at hosiery factory, owned the house that he enlarged to be able to take in five boarders. While he worked at the Rockingham Mills as late as 1851, he is listed as a carpenter after 1857 and a note in the 1861 tax list that he had "no house, money" explains his removal. Across the street at 54 Cabot in 1847, mason Robert H. Marden was among the first in this area to erect a 2-story gable end, side entry, house with Greek Revival detailing. He advertised the house for sale in 1850 as "within five minutes walk of the Portsmouth Steam Factory, or seven of Market Square," unsuccessfully trying to appeal to two groups of potential buyers like those building nearly identical houses on Summer *[see Hutchinson house]* and State *[J.S. Sise house]* and Middle Streets *[Bodge-Chase house]*.

At the corner of Cabot and State streets John S. Trickey got himself in financial trouble building a seven room Gothic Revival cottage that he advertised in 1847 as "now finishing and nearly completed" with "4 chambers, 2 parlors with sliding doors, and kitchen." When auctioned in 1850 it went to Joshua Brooks, who began as a railroad conductor but ended up owning a large grain business along the waterfront. In such ways the woodworkers and stocking weavers of Austinborough were joined by a number of businessmen as well as new groups employed in the nearby factories.

John Pepper, inventor of the powered knitting machine of stocking frame, was among this latter group. Perhaps the projected success of his patent gave him confidence to build a house near his father Daniel. In 1848 John brought an Austin Street lot from his father and erected a 1 ½-story "Cottage House" with twin facade gables along its side. Mortgaged to J. Fisher Sheafe of New York, the younger Pepper's home was auctioned off to his father in 1852, the year he became a non-resident taxpayer on this and other rental properties. Daniel Pepper continued to own it as an income property until his death in 1870, even after John returned from a dozen years in Holderness and Lake Village, NH. An elaborate porch (not yet enclosed) and its noteworthy corner entrance, were most likely alterations made after the property was sold in 1871.

Edward D. Coffin, a painter living on Union Street at the home of his mother, Ann Coffin, (widow of the joiner James), bought the front half of a lot sold in 1809 to laborer Daniel Dearborn. Bounded by "Coffin's Alley" (now Court), in 1823 Dearborn has a house here in Austinborough worth $50. Coffin built a new house at 74 Cabot Street in 1862 valued at $8,000. Three years later he acquired the rear half of the lot on which the barn was later built. The gable front five-bay, center-entry plan is essentially identical to L-houses of the earlier 19th century, but here dressed in Italianate ornament and employing manufactured building materials.

RMC

Oliver Manson House

Built 1839–40
119 Union Street

Oliver Manson (1814-1906) is one of the few mid 19th-century carpenters about whom we can be specific. His accounts of daily employment at both house and ship carpentry from 1838 to 1869 provides enigmatic clues to his work while his two homes suggest something of the life he led. Born in Kittery, Maine, he came to Portsmouth in 1830 "to learn the carpenter's trade," and his accounts show he worked on the Eliot, Maine town house and other projects in 1838. He may have apprenticed with joiner John Norton, whose house and shop were on Union Street just north of Austin Street, whose daughter he apparently married "early in life." Norton provided Manson his earliest known jobs and sold him a house lot adjoining his own in 1839. While steady employment was in ship carpentry at both private shipyards and the Portsmouth Navy Yard, Manson continued to work for individuals repairing or remodeling older houses. For example, he worked 28 1/4 days for Lewis A. Bruce on his house on Jaffrey Court in 1842 and in 1842-43 worked for John Norton "on the mill," in his shop making doors, and on an unspecified meeting house. In addition to Norton, other nearby joiners and builders who provided him work include Rand V. Reed on Cabot Street and Moses Yeaton on Austin Street, as well as speculator Benjamin Cheever and the builder James Moses III. In the 1860 census he is listed as a "House Carpenter" and, as ship-building waned, he returned to this trade, working off and on from January 1866 to April 1867 building a new house and a green house for A.L. Jones *[see Jones-Sinclair house]* on the corner of Middle Street and Richards Ave. He spent the end of 1869, from September to December at $3 a day, "House Carpentering" for William P. Jones at 82 Court Street, probably on the "outbuildings" first taxed the next year.

He began to build his own house in December 1839 and continued to March of 1840. Meanwhile he lived in a rented house at 110 Austin Street at the corner of Summer Street, a narrow two-story home set with its end toward the street, overlooking the back of James Rundlet's orchard. The new 1-story house that Manson erected for his new wife, also set gable end to the street, has end chimneys and a side entry hall leading to a staircase between the two ground-floor rooms (a front parlor with kitchen behind). The parlor retains wide Greek Revival fluted trim around the mantel and windows, as does an upstairs fireplace. The inset front doorway

Private collection
Oliver Manson, carpenter (1814-1906).

Courtesy Portsmouth Athenæum
110 Austin Street (left).

Oliver Manson House.

has distinctive Greek Revival trim with a rectangular plaque above the opening similar to other doorways at 12 and 21 Union Street and on other cross streets north of Islington Street. In 1850 Manson, a member of the Middle Street Baptist Church, was living here with his 31 year old wife, Elizabeth (Norton), and their 8 year old son Alvah. Ten years later he had been widowed and remarried to Charlotte Parsons Manson (1828-1903) of York, Maine. They lived here with the second son of his first marriage, Herman, age 9, who later became a local painter. Oliver Manson lived here until his death in 1906.

RMC

Sources:
Portsmouth Herald, May 12, 1906
Oliver Manson Account Book (1838-1869), NH Historical Society

Odiorne House, 32 Union Street.

Union Street from State to Islington Streets: Because the land was originally owned by the Haven family, the last block of Cabot and Union Street between State and Islington Street were the last to be developed. Moses Yeaton moved and built houses at State and the west side of Union, just as other builders did on the east side and along Cabot Street in the 1850s. In the 20th century many of these West End homes have been divided into apartments.

The Odiorne house at 32 Union Street (1865) is one of a group of prototypical smaller gable front side-entry house built or possibly moved to this end of Union Street after an 1850s land division. This house reflects the many early 20th-century alterations common to so many West End homes. Entry to the main block is into a short stairhall, behind which is a small room which may have originally served as part of a larger kitchen across the rear half of the house. The rear ell containing the present kitchen was a later addition. The stairhall has two door, the first of which leads to the parlor. Since the early 20th century, the parlor is separated from the dining room only by low built-in bookcases. When the rear ell was added both rooms were opened and redecorated as a connected parlor - dining room; a room behind the stairhall may have been partitioned at that time. On the second story other early 20th century additions include the insertion of a bathroom at the top of the stairs, a back staircase to the new rear ell, and a dormer and windows that light a side bedroom.

EH

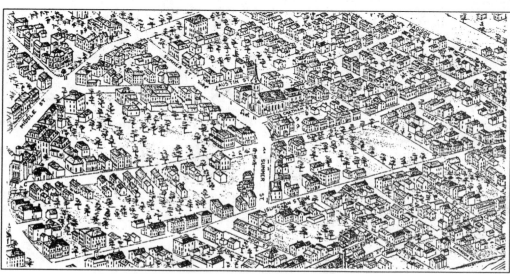

State Street detail, 1877 Bird's Eye looking South.

STATE STREET

The development of the State Street area during the first half of the 19th century provides a contrast to the patterns of elite building identified for Middle Street and the artisan development of Cabot and Union streets. On State Street development was confined to the east end of the street during the first period of growth. Near the junction of State and Middle streets, a small group of houses was constructed resembling in some ways the developments observed on Franklin and Cabot streets. State Street was extended west in 1805, one of several streets radiating from Haymarket Square and Middle Street providing building sites for the city's artisans and businessmen, as part of the development of Jeremiah Mason's estate. There moderate-sized versions of common period forms were built, primarily before the passing of the Brick Act in 1814. A hiatus in construction followed, with few buildings added during the decades of the 1820s and 30s. But during the mid-19th century this area grew rapidly, and builders and owners along these streets choose forms that included a handfull of the period's larger homes and small and inexpensive homes, but larger proportions of houses of moderate size.

In the dozen years after Haines built his house nearly all of the parcels on the street east of Summer Street were constructed. On the north side of the street at the east end a group a similar gable front houses were built, including the three that remain today and three more that once stood in what is now the empty lot next door. Of the remaining houses, that at 495 State Street, one of two residence owned by James Odiorne, appears on the tax list in 1844. The next year 481, long the home of cabinetmaker Thomas Lewis, appears on the tax rolls, and 487 a house owned by joiner William R. Hall was declared "unfinished." The Joseph D. Akerman house at 505 State Street was not taxed until 1848, when it was valued at $2000 or twice as much as its neighbors. Each has had later alterations. Larger Greek Revival versions of the double house were constructed here as well. The Stavers House (608-10 State St.), since converted into a duplex, is sited in the gable-end-to-the-street, entry-on-the-side configuration. John Stavers was a prosperous grocer and shoe merchant who erected this house in 1846 and in 1850 lived here with his wife and four children, plus 20 year old Ellen Lock. Opposite it, on the large lot now occupied by the Whipple School, once stood the similar Aaron H. Hill House. Hill was a principal in the Hill and Carr shoe store, and his partner lived down the street in a house now demolished. Hill also had a maid in his household, while Carr boarded a shoemaker. This building was moved in 1889 and can now be seen in its new location at the southwest corner of Cabot and Austin streets. A smaller version of the Greek Revival house can be seen at 567 State Street. First occupied in 1843 by shipmaster James M. Hill, it is a variation of the L-plan house with a single pile gabled front pile and a rear ell for service space.

In addition to those houses already mentioned, a number of other changes have altered the streetscape here. At the corner of

Courtesy Portsmouth Athenæum
Baptist Chapel and Akerman House.

State and Middle streets stood the church of the Baptists. A small meeting place was built here in 1828; a new brick church was built in 1852, remodeled in 1868 and enlarged in 1899 with financial help from Frank Jones. It remained until the church moved across Haymarket Square in the 1960s. A small chapel associated with this congregation was constructed across State Street in 1883; greatly altered, this building survives within the office building at 507 State Street. The construction of the large Whipple School (1889) at the corner of Summer Street was undertaken to replace the city's small and declining neighborhood schools with "modern school houses with modern improvements." Built by Charles W. Norton for nearly $26,000, it was the city's most expensive school-house. In 1980 the building was converted into 17 condominiums by Jerry F. Weiss of Cleveland and Portsmouth. The large lot now occupied by 600 State Street was open throughout the 19th and much of the 20th century, owned and left undeveloped by its owners who lived in the Larkin-Rice House on Middle Street whose lot adjoins this one.

The fabric of State, Summer, and Winter streets is typical of the residential neighborhoods built in increasing numbers in commercial villages and towns, and within streetcar suburbs of cities throughout the region. While neighborhoods of this type are commonly believed to be among the earliest examples of segregation by class, and more particularly of the rising new middle class, Portsmouth's experience provides an important cautionary example and contrast to such an interpretation. Reported occupations in period directories and the population census of 1850 reveal a varied mix of artisan, retail, and professional employment within this small six block area, demonstrating the continued popularity of large corner lots among the more prosperous residents, but a broad mix along the blocks. Of the 50 households, 18 include only members of what appear to be nuclear families. Sixteen appear to be more complex in their structure, though in many instances the individual appears to be the mother of one member of the married couple. As many as 14 households have one or two young females within the household, with differing surnames that suggests they were employed as maids; of these women, 6 were born in Ireland, 5 in New Hampshire, 2 in Maine, and one each in Nova Scotia, Washington DC, and Antwerp. In four households apparently unrelated young men may be apprentices, including two joiners, a shoemaker, and a merchant's clerk. About a third of the residents were renters here rather than homeowners. State Street demonstrates that in Portsmouth, at least, many artisans remained of "middling" status through the 19th century even as a white collar community grew.

CWD

Vennard House

Built by 1813
536 State Street

The Vennard House provides an excellent example of the creative ferment that characterized period building in the region. The two story house has the common gable roof and pedimented entry of the period, but its plan illustrates the adaptation of center chimney planning to the new conditions of the Federal period. The plan includes three primary first floor rooms, one each side of the small entry in the front pile, and a single large room flanked by small service spaces in the rear pile. As other plans illustrate, removal of the center chimney was not always accompanied by the use of a through passage. The house makes use of such ambitious period embellishments as an arched doorway to the right front room and an offset circular stair. The builder and earliest owner of this house is not yet known, though during the 1830s it was owned and occupied by Jacob and Mary Haven Sheafe Jr., each an heir to a Federal era merchant dynasty. Through most of the middle of the 19th century the house was owned by Matthew B. Vennard, shipmaster, who lived here with his wife Sarah and their four children.

CWD

Vennard House.

Abner and Miriam Greenleaf House

Built 1811-12, ell added ca. 1838
552 State St.
Josiah Gains, joiner

The Greenleaf house is a 3-story example of the real-wall plan oriented perpendicular to rather than facing the street. It is one of a pair of back-to-back houses erected after coppersmith Abner Greenleaf subdivided a lot purchased of joiner Josiah Gains in 1811. Gains had acquired the land from William Varrell, painter, in 1807, only a year after Varrell had purchased a somewhat larger lot from Jeremiah Mason. It was described as "the mirror image" of an adjoining back-to-back house that Varrell sold in 1812 to watchmaker Supply Ham. Until it was demolished in 1933, the Ham House stood next east to the Greenleaf House, constructed at about the same time and in the same form, with its back just two feet from its neighbor. Both houses were sited gable end to the street with only two feet between the rear walls, and had circular staircases opposite their fan-lit center entries. The walls of the Greenleaf house staircase are also curved and contain an interior oval window lighting a rear stairhall at the second story. Back stairs also run from the original kitchen to the third story.

Greenleaf's copper foundry was located immediately east of the Stone [Unitarian] Church on State Street and produced copper fastenings for the hulls of locally-built ships. Greenleaf became a school master by 1821, and would become post master in 1830 and the first Mayor of the new city in 1850, although he sold this house

Greenleaf House.

in 1825. In 1835 Ebenezer Haines purchased the house and between 1838 and 1839 added the rear ell. He was living here in 1840, but by mid-century the house was a rental property supporting the "quiet but harmless" insanity of Ann Elliot. It was then occupied by a family of English-born stocking or hosiery weavers who had come to Portsmouth by way of Canada and New York state. From 1867 to 1884 it was the home of widow Caroline S. Walker, who took in gentlemen boarders, and from 1886 to 1982 the home of the Griffin family.

RMC

Sources:
research by Martha Fuller Clark
Portsmouth Herald 25 Oct. 1933

Haines-Fonda House

Built 1836
557 State Street

The Haines House of 1836 marks a significant break in the designs chosen within this neighborhood, and throughout the town and region. Like several of the earlier houses, this house is oriented with its gable end to the street, but now the entry is located along that wall as well. And on its interior, the house employs the side plan seen only rarely before this time, but rising to great popularity during the next two decades. Its single story Greek Doric porch and flushboard façade would be seldom seen in Portsmouth again, but its use of the entablature portion of the Doric order to embellish the cornice and entry of the building, and of Doric pilasters at the corners would became commonplace by mid-century. This part of State Street was subdivided when Jeremiah Mason [*see Mason House*] left Portsmouth, selling much of his property to Daniel H. Treadwell. This house sits on lot #2 of this subdivision, purchased by Haines for $150, who sold it a year later to James Bufford, painter, for $550 with a house. The building was probably incomplete as he sold it for $1200 the next year to George W. Towle, who rented it out. In 1859 it was purchased by Ira B. Fonda, who operated a Market Street millinery shop and whose descendants held the house until 1908.

CWD

Haines-Fonda House.

Source:
Research by Portsmouth Advocates.

Jeremiah Mason House

Built 1808
Remodelled and attached to the Advent Christian Church, 1941.
634 State Street

Jeremiah Mason was the member of the town elite to build an estate in this area, having purchased a large tract in combination with John Peirce, Jonathan Clark, and John Haven in 1799. Mason eventually bought several of the other owners out and he received three quarters of the parcel when they subdivided to provide each with a broad area on which to build. Mason's land included a large portion of the land on the south side of Broad Street as State was then known, as well as a section across the street; Haven received an upper section near Summer and Islington streets. Mason's house followed the form established on Pleasant, Islington, and Middle streets: a large, three story, double pile house of central hall plan, ornamented on the exterior by a fan and sidelights at the door screened by a portico. Mason employed deed restrictions in 1811 when he began to sell off lots from his large parcels, prohibiting any artisan activities from the lots. The pace of his sales accelerated after he moved to Boston to further his legal career after 1832. His house was then purchased by Daniel H. Treadwell who with his descendants owned it for many years.

By the 1940s, the estate was available for purchase and the Advent Christian Church saw the large house and its adjacent yard as ideal to their needs. This congregation has its beginnings in the middle of the 19th century when William Miller calculated the Second Coming of Christ for 1842. When the date came and went, many turned away from the Millerites but those who remained formed a number of Adventist Churches. In Portsmouth these groups met in a meeting house on Hanover Street between Vaughan and Bridge streets, now part of the urban renewal area, that was known by various names including Hanover Street, King's, and Lord's Chapel. In 1853, when this building had been converted into a fire engine house, they purchased the lot next door and constructed a nave plan frame building with a façade treatment of shed-roofed vestibule and corner entry tower. The building committee included Robinson Berry, a joiner who built a house on Winter Street. Though the congregation had hoped to build in the same location once they had raised a sufficient building fund, the site proved unacceptable for the new, large building they had planned. They purchased this lot from the Treadwell estate and employed Arland A. Dirlam of Malden, Massachusetts to design the church, A.F. Smiley of Pawtucket, R.I. as contractor. The colonial revival design is wood frame with brick veneer.

CWD

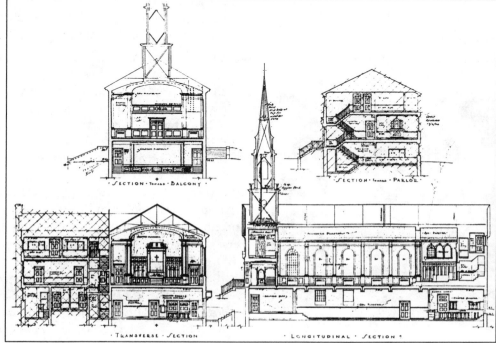

Courtesy Dirlam Collection, SPNEA
Section, Advent Christian Church and Mason House,
Arland A. Dirlam, architect
1940.

Courtesy Strawbery Banke Museum
Kindergarten School, Summer Street.

SUMMER STREET

Summer Street and its continuation toward Islington, once called Massey Street, were laid out in 1802. At its southern junction with Middle Street it bordered part of Daniel Austin's elite subdivision. Larger houses were built on northern corner lots while smaller artisan houses were built from 1810 to the 1840s. By 1890 the shingled double house near the corner of Middle Street is shown in the 1890s as a kindergarten school.

John W. and Betsy Hutchinson House

Built 1845
119 Summer Street

The Hutchinson house follows the form that rose to popularity in Portsmouth during the second quarter of the 19th century and can be seen in multiple examples in this area, particularly along State Street. Hutchinson bought the lot, described as "a part of the garden formerly owned by Jeremiah Mason" for $400 in 1845. Its configuration of Greek Revival ornament at the entry, corners, and cornice, the openings on the main block, and the presence of the service ell follow the pattern believed to be the most popular of the side entry, gable front houses. In plan the first floor includes the entry/stair hall, with two parlors flanking, a small room behind, and a kitchen and pantry in the ell. John Hutchinson, a mason, was in his thirties when he built this house, and in 1850 lived here with his wife Betsy and their four young children, and a young woman of 23 named Elizabeth Dame.

J.W. Hutchinson House.

Immaculate Conception Church Complex

Built 1925–33
98 Summer Street

Dominating the rise of Summer street today is the complex of church, rectory, and school that characterizes large and urban Roman Catholic parishes throughout New England. Roman Catholics were few, but not unknown in New England prior to the mass migration that resulted from the Irish potato famine of the 1840s. After the Revolution, priests from Boston visited throughout the region, and the first northern New England parish was established in Maine in Damariscotta in 1808. Portsmouth Catholics met in private homes before the parish St. Mary's was organized in 1851, the third in the state. The parish historian credits the growth of the town in the ante-bellum period to the increased numbers of Catholic "laborers, carpenters, spinners, hosiery weavers, laundresses" in the town, and numbers the early parish at about 300. When the first lot was purchased at the corner of Chatham and Summer streets the area was known as the Circus Field on Mason's Hill. The first church was built with the assistance of labor from parishioners, and resembled "most of the church structures built in New England." The parish's first school was located

Courtesy Portsmouth Athenæum
Roman Catholic Church (1871).

on State Street next to the Methodist Church [*see Temple Israel*] in 1867, and teaching sisters lived next door. In 1871 the first church burned, and the parish met in the Music Hall. When a new Gothic brick church was built, it seated over 1000; at the same time the parish was renamed. During the end of the 19th century the parish expanded its plant through the purchase of land on Chatham and Summer streets, for a parochial school, convent, and rectory. Both of the latter residences were originally housed in older homes purchased by the Church, but were later rebuilt, the rectory on the corner in 1925. The original school here was built in 1887 but during a major expansion in 1904 it was "virtually obliterated;" in 1915 twelve sisters taught 500 children at the school. In 1933 the parish decided to rebuild their church and dismantled the existing building and attempted to salvage what they could for the new one. The interior was remodelled in 1955 and again in 1973 to meet the new requirements of the second Vatican Council.

CWD

WINTER STREET

The buildings of Winter Street provide a useful contrast to the others in the area, including a concentration of buildings dating to the 1840s. In 1843 James Rundlet sold the last parcel of land he owned on the north side of Austin Street to the joiner Moses Yeaton. By 1850 all of the houses on this short street had been constructed except for the house at 30 Winter Street, and by 1876 there were three houses of gable front form along Chatham Street, as well as one on the opposite side of Winter Street. Perhaps one of these was moved to this site when the church expanded to hold the entire block at the turn of the 20th century. The group of houses serves as a catalogue of sorts, of small and moderately-sized housing of the second quarter of the 19th century. Throughout his mid-19th century career, Yeaton bought land in the West End and subdivided it for development by himself and other joiners.

His Winter Street activities are particularly clear. Yeaton's own house (171 Austin St.) was built in 1843 and remodelled 20 years later. He sold the first and largest lot at the corner of Austin in 1844 to joiner Robinson F. Berry, "next to land of mine connected with my dwelling house". Berry's lot was bounded by "a new street recently laid out but not yet named" that soon became Winter Street. Berry built a house for himself on the corner that does not survive, and a second house along Winter Street in 1848. This he sold to widow Sarah Ann Anderson as "a new story and a half dwelling house," though the tax record show each of them in possession of half the double house. 22-24 Winter Street is a small duplex with a small version of the side passage plan including two rooms in the main block and a rear ell kitchen. Sarah Anderson operated a boardinghouse during the mid-century. In addition to her three children, Mrs. Anderson was joined by Joseph and Abby Peirce and seven single females between 16 and 22 years old. The entire house eventually returned to Berry's ownership and at the turn of the 20th century Dr. James White used the building as his home and office.

Sources:
Alexander Munton, *125 Years as a Parish Church*, 1941.

Moses Yeaton House, 171 Austin St.

Anderson House, 22-24 Winter St.

Pickering-Lynn House.

Also in 1844 Yeaton sold the next lot to the north to joiner John H. Whidden, who constructed a house by 1846. The next year the house was sold to Josiah Cheney and Sterrett Anderson, and two years later Cheney sold his half interest to Anderson. This house, 40 Winter Street, is an example of a sparsely treated gable front house, whose offset rear ell appears to be original or very early. Anderson, a ship carpenter, still owned only half the house, apparently sharing ownership of the $1000 house with Annis Sterrett, a woman ten years his senior living in his household. Sterrett's wife Ann, their carpenter son Charles, and their daughter Catherine shared their house with joiner John and Jane Pettigrew.

Yeaton sold the next lot north in 1845 to joiner Thomas L. Pickering, who sold it with a house to Andrew Lynn the next years. 48 Winter Street demonstrates the persistence of the L-house form into the 19th century and exhibits a fine glazed winter doorway across its recessed entry. Valued at $600 in 1850 the house was long the home of Andrew and Eliza Lynn and their five children; Lynn was a machinist at the Portsmouth Steam Factory.

By 1846 Yeaton had already constructed buildings on the next lot north and sold them to gardener and laborer Hunking S. Marden. In 1848 Marden bought a second lot from Yeaton, this one on the corner of State Street. By 1850 he owned two houses and the next year sold the first to carpenter William Hazlett. This is 62 Winter Street, another version of the gable front house with offset rear ell, boasting a glazed screen across the top of its recessed entry. Marden's other house, 70 Winter Street at the corner of State Street, provides an example of the smaller gable front houses; it has been expanded to the rear and along its south side. Marden and his wife Winifred were joined by their son and three men in their twenties, one of whom reported his occupation as joiner. Perhaps Sylvester Ham had built Marden's second house.

CWD

STATE STREET BEYOND SUMMER

The majority of the buildings along State Street west of Summer Street date to the next decade of the 1850s. The building forms chosen for this area had much in common with those on the easterly block. Large double houses were built on the corner lots next to Summer Street, including the large house at 664 State Street, and the smaller one opposite at 663. Ell houses remained popular as examples at 649, 692, and 728 State Street attest. Two large duplexes were added at 718-20 and 767-69 State Street, and two gable front houses were built side by side at 698 and 708. While Greek Revival ornament remained popular, the new Italianate fashion was used on twice as many houses. In Portsmouth this style most often employs many of the earlier features of ornament, including entablature treatments to edges, and pilasters at corners. Those pilasters are commonly panelled, the cornice bracketed, and at the entry a narrow hood is supported by large bold consoles, or an entry porch. At least one of the houses added during the 1850s was replaced by a fashion conscious builder, apparently within twenty years of constructing his first house.

R.H. Beacham moved his existing building, turning it into a "house on wheels" in 1874 and moving it further west on State Street, and on the lot constructed the large Second Empire double house that now serves as the Farrell Funeral Home (684 State St.).

Ichabod Goodwin's large parcel on the north side of the street opposite Winter Street remained open and was made a city park in 1887 and was briefly in the 1890s known as the Common. Beyond Goodwin Park on State Street at the corner of Cabot is a row of three houses known as a "Cottage Block" when erected by another local carpenter, William F. Currier, in 1850. The two western units were sold to widows Elizabeth Varrell and Amy Bean, while the eastern unit was sold to laborer Joseph W. Gordon. Gordon and Bean appear here in the 1851 city directory, but a tailor John J. Marston then occupied the corner unit. Currier, who then lived on Cabot Street, bought land to build a house for himself on State St. in 1851. Directly across State Street on the corner, a new Cabot Street School was erected in 1860. Its door originally faced State Street, in the first bay of the long wall. It has been used by The People's Church, the Greek Orthodox, and other faiths throughout the 20th century. Here additions rather than losses have altered the landscape, with the construction a small handful of houses at the turn of the 20th century when the rear portions of large lots facing Islington Street were subdivided.

CWD

The Joseph G. Sise House

Built 1852
698 State Street

This section of State Street, on the south side, was subdivided by heirs of Mathew S. Marsh, Esq. and platted by surveyor Benjamin Akerman. This lot, number five, measured 46 feet across State Street and runs 101 feet back to Chatham Street, and was sold in 1850 to Oren Bragdon, a Portsmouth cordwainer. The sale included a restriction that "no other buildings are to be erected or set up on said lot except one dwelling house and necessary outbuildings for the term of ten years . . . and that neither the dwelling house nor other buildings shall ever be placed nearer than eight feet to State Street." In 1853 Bragdon sold the "dwelling house lately erected by me" to the Market Street tea merchant Joseph G. Sise.

Joseph G. Sise House.

The house provided a useful alternative to the simple gable front, side/corner passage plan. Although the front pile of the house retains the 3-bay façade, a set back entry bay along the east wall provides a secondary door and a wider room behind the stairs and entry hall. Thus, the plan includes three ample rooms in the front block rather than the more common two large and one small room. The house next to this one (708 State St.) constructed by Sylvester Ham used this common plan [*see J.W. Hutchinson House*]. After Sise died, the house was sold in 1874 to lawyer Calvin Page, who was one of Frank Jones's closest associates and administrator of his estate. Page served as police marshall, Democratic state senator, and judge in the early years of the 20th century.

RMC & CWD

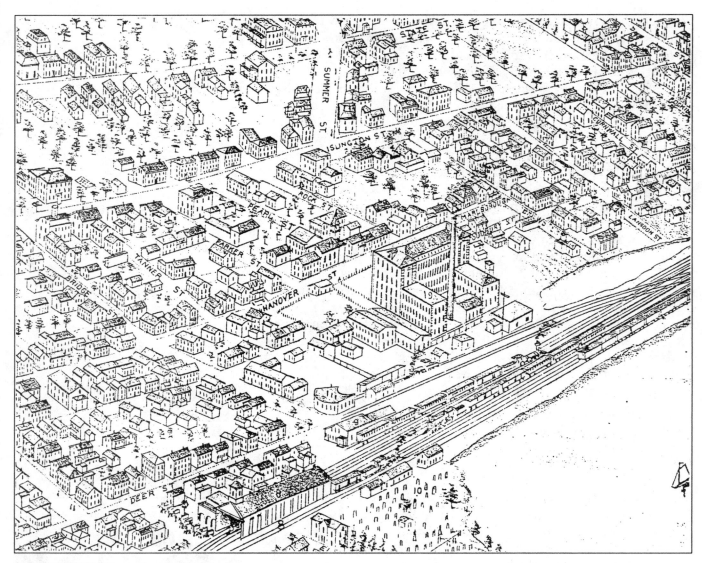

Detail, 1877 bird's eye view, looking south.

INDUSTRIAL PORTSMOUTH
ISLINGTON STREET

While much altered by the automobile culture of the twentieth century, Islington Street became a major thoroughfare in the 1790s. Several large Federal houses built for merchants and sea captains were fully equivalent to those on Haymarket Square and Middle Street. All of those have been vastly altered or destroyed; what remains include smaller early 19th-century homes and several large double houses. Many were built after factories dominated the Rock Pasture behind Islington Street Federal mansions of merchants like Ichabod Goodwin, a director of the Eastern RR and the first president of the steam factory, who invested in the new industries. Ornamented duplexes were intermingled with substantial single-family homes like those on State and Middle Streets. An 1873 writer noted "how westward the star of improvement" was "beautifying... Islington, as well as Middle and other Streets."

Warner–Buckminster House

Built ca. 1730 for Daniel Warner
7 Islington Street, corner of Bridge St.

It is unknown when Daniel Warner built the house, but he did leave a good room listing in his 1778 inventory. He also owned a Negro man named Chester and had 30 pounds of Spruce Yellow and a bucket. Was this the exterior color? No mention is made of the staircase to the cupola in the garret, but it is clearly 18th century. Inheriting in 1778, Daniel's son Jonathan Warner *[see MacPhaedris house]* tried to settle Daniel Warner's intestate estates debts. But 1784 executions gave Sarah Marsh "the westerly half of the house and the northern most kitchen"; the Eastern half was taken to satisfy debts due George Atkinson, Esq. The two owners shared "the fore Entry," staircase, yard and well in common; deeds record two kitchens, suggesting the appearance of a rear ell by the mid-1780s. Both halves were tenanted by Eliphalet Ladd, an Exeter-born merchant, who bought the whole house in 1793. His 1806 inventory suggests additions to the rear ell by that date. Widow Abigail Hill Ladd occupied the house with her second husband, the Rev. Joseph Buckminster of the North Church, remaining in the house until her death in 1838.

Abigail Ladd Buckminster's heirs leased the house to widow Anna Maria Thompson as a boarding house. The 1840 census shows Anna Mari as head of household. One of the four women in their twenties was her daughter Eliza, and the only girl under ten was her daughter Ann. A girl under five is unknown, perhaps a daughter of one of the three unidentified women in their twenties. Only the youngest male, her son George (age 9), was directly related; two teenage boys, four men in their twenties and one ten years older boarded here. They were a physician, a dry goods merchant, a teacher at a private school and Joseph Haven Thacher, a druggist who later married Mrs. Thompson's daughter.

In 1853, the last of Eliphalet Ladd's sons, Alexander Ladd *[see Moffatt-Ladd house]* sold the property to the Portsmouth Steam Factory. The company acquired it for a building lot in the garden to the west. Here the factory agent, Col. William A. Stearns, soon built a new house that was later improved with bays and oriels. The factory resold the "Buckminster Mansion House" back to George Tompson and his brother-in-law Joseph Thacher in 1856. Four Thompsons in two generations and the Thachers (husband, wife and 5 year old daughter) shared the property in 1860 with boarders and two domestics. By 1880, George Thompson had found his own home and the Thacher family occupy the whole house with Joseph's sister-in-law Eliza A. Thompson and two female servants. Remodeling of the central hall and staircase as well as several marble fireplace surrounds were a product of Thompson-Thacher ownership. In 1906 the property reverted to a boarding house again and in 1919 undertaker J. Verne Wood combined his business with room rentals here. The side entry facing Islington Street was apparently added at this period.

RMC

18th century stair to cupola, attic, Warner-Buckminster House.

Room Names in 1778		
Ground Floor	**Second Floor**	**Attic**
NW Lower Room	NW Chamber	NW Garret
SW Lower Room	SW Chamber	
Lower Entry		
SE Lower Room	SE Chamber	SE Garret
Kitchen	Kitchen Chamber	NE Garret

Research by Rita Conant, Carolyn Eastman, Richard Candee.

NORTH OF ISLINGTON STREET
TO HANOVER, SUDBURY, AND MCDONOUGH

Courtesy Portsmouth Athenæum

Free Will Baptist Church, 1851.

Thomas Bailey Aldrich, who grew up in Portsmouth during the 1840s and used those memories to sustain his literary career, later blamed the arrival of the railroad, "freighted with so many hopes," for killing Portsmouth's "LOCAL CHARACTER" (his caps). This image was a perceptive metaphor for the old town's changing physical and social organization. Between a huge steam cotton mill on the former Adams estate and the small hosiery factory at the west end of the mill pond, new foundries, machine shops, a cotton spinning mill, and a gas works sprang up. Just as railroad stations (on the site of earlier ropewalks) pulled commercial development westward from the old core, new and expanded working neighborhoods emerged around these industrial sites. The location of the Free Will Baptist church (1851) directly opposite the Portsmouth Steam Factory, with the Adventist congregation to the east on Hancock Street, the enlargement of the Middle Street Baptist Church in 1852, and the construction of the new Roman Catholic church on Mason's Hill all reflect the rapid redevelopment of the West End at this period.

Industrialization profoundly altered existing patterns of landscape, demography and architecture in Portsmouth and dramatically changed the social and material complexion of the "old town by the sea." Nowhere is this more evident then in the corridor bounded by Islington Street and the North Mill Pond, an area known as the Rock Pasture in the early years of the 19th century. The development of an industrial neighborhood in the Rock Pasture in the mid-19th century pulled the city inland, away from the waterfront, and fueled the growth of suburban Portsmouth. A survey of 1815 subdivided the Rock Pasture into numerous small parcels, but the many vacant lots remained. Several 18th century houses in and east of the Rock Pasture [see map p. 2.] were joined by a number of modest federal structures, but their numbers fell far short of the wishful plan of the real estate speculators. Far greater schemes were being hatched, however, for on July 12, 1823 a Portsmouth Steam Factory was incorporated. It would be some twenty years before ground was broken on this endeavor and debate over the proposed mill would reach fever pitch before the first brick was laid. The Eastern Railroad arrived in 1840 and subsequent lines followed this path by filling part of the cove for rails, roundhouses, and freight yards. This location of the railroad tracks along this mill pond, rather than into the densely built south end as originally projected, determined the future industrial character of the West End.

"RAISE THE STEAM!" shouted the editorial for the *Portsmouth Journal* on October 28, 1843. Decidedly pro-industry the paper catalogued the city's surplus housing. "A Company need not erect any boarding houses: if enough are not already to be had, the owners of real-estate are ready to proceed to erect more, and would be glad of the opportunity." This echoed many promoters of steam factories in aging urban ports, assumed that the mill operatives would be integrated into existing housing, but failed to take into account the determining role played by the mill's eventual location along the southern edge of the North Mill Pond. While solicitations appeared in the newspapers for lots of land "on the river side" for a factory, the relatively open space of the Rock Pasture presented the most promising site for a steam-powered textile mill. The few buildings that were in the way of the proposed five-story factory were quickly moved across the landscape, "like the men on a checker board," according to the newspaper. There was a certain logic, beyond the mere availability of land, for situating the Steam Factory in a part of town already identified as a location of textile production. One water-powered hosiery producing concern, the Portsmouth Manufacturing Company, was ensconced at the head of the North Mill Pond and its predominantly foreign-born operatives lived in a fairly homogenous ethnic enclave on the outskirts of the city. The introduction of the Steam Factory and later the Sagamore Mill created an industrial corridor running from Bridge Street along the railroad tracks past the end of the mill pond.

Originally intended to put native-born mechanics to work, the large textile-producing company and the smaller spinning-mill quickly attracted large numbers of English and Scottish operatives. Because the factory was planned for expansion on either side of its central core, older houses to the east and west were included in its land holdings. Over the next thirty years speculative tenements and boarding houses were constructed by many local investors on surrounding streets. Census records clearly identify the large boarding houses that were home to immigrant families and individual women in the 1850s. While Irish immigrants in the older sections of the city were largely laborers and domestics, the textile factory worker of the North and West End neighborhoods was typically an English immigrant. Half of all male textile workers were English or born of English parents elsewhere in the British Isles; only a quarter were New Hampshire natives. In the older hand-powered hosiery industry, proportions were even more disparate. Two-thirds were English "weavers"

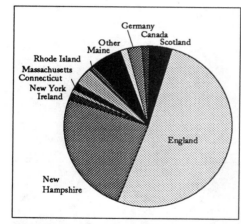

Place of birth, Portsmouth male textile workers (310 identified from 1850 U.S. Census).

Eliza McClennen, cartographer

Textile mill workers from 1850 U.S. Census with country of origin.

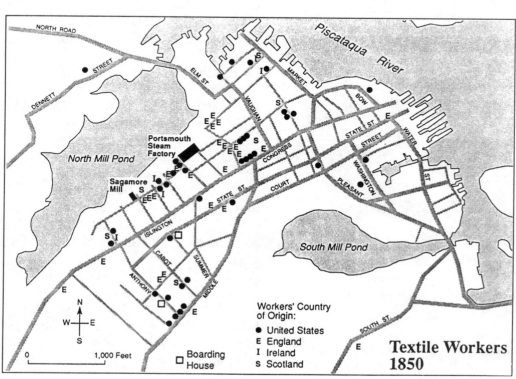

Textile Workers 1850

Workers' Country of Origin:
● United States
E England
I Ireland
S Scotland

☐ Boarding House

0   1,000 Feet

and only slightly more than 16% were New Hampshire natives with 5% from Germany and smaller numbers from nearby states and the Canadian maritimes. It was these new workers, families and single boarders, who increased the city's population by being absorbed into the single, double and multi-family houses built throughout the West End. By the time of the Civil War hosiery production was a comparatively small part of the city's manufacturing activity, although it continued until the turn of the century. The Steam Factory was reorganized several times between 1850 and 1880 but never made the huge profits for its owners that some anticipated. The loss of the factory to fire in 1880 and its conversion to a foundry followed the shift to brewing as the main product of local manufacturing.

RMC & TD

Portsmouth Steam Factory

Built 1845–46
361 Hanover Street opposite Pearl Street
engineering by Charles T. James
architecture attributed to Jeremiah S. Young, agent

In 1843 there was widespread recognition that the city needed "something to give a stir to the business of Portsmouth," and a committee of local men proposed a $10,000 factory toward which each pledged $1000. The next day, "some of our capitalists, among them...William Jones & Co., who seeing so much interest taken in the matter by middling interest men, proposed something on a larger scale." In a few weeks "more than $200,000 were subscribed in this city and in Boston for the Portsmouth Steam Factory." Charles T. James of Newburyport, who built several steam mills in that and other coastal cities, spoke to a public meeting in favor of steam powered textile production and may have engineered the factory. The design of the building may have been placed in the hands of the company agent, Jeremiah S. Young, a former minister turned manufacturer. "Mr. Young superintended the laying out of the grounds in good taste and the building of the Factory in a symmetrical and substantial manner and completed plans for more than doubling its front extension." Stock shares and other woodcuts all illustrate the factory as envisioned, with long wings to either side of the six-story 204'-long central block that was the only part actually built. It was only this projected expansion that allowed local boosters to describe the mill as the largest of its day.

Six stories tall, including one story in the attic beneath a sky-lit roof, the 200' x 70' main block of the brick factory rested on an arcaded ground story. Entrances at each front corner were articulated in granite and the walls quoined at their edges. Two 100' x 30' rear ells and a low connector joined the steam plant to the mill and provided additional manufacturing space. In 1847, its first full year of operation, the building was hit by a tornado that carried away its original roof. It was immediately rebuilt and in 1849 made "the finer class of cotton fabrics, as jaconets, plain and figured muslins and lawns." Its 21,250 spindles

Courtesy Strawbery Banke Museum
Proposed design for the Portsmouth Steam Factory, 1845.

The mill is located in a central part of the town, on the bank of the north mill pond, has spacious grounds around it, and the Boston and Portland and the Portsmouth and Concord Railroads pass immediately in the rear. For location, and architectural character of the mill without, as well as for general arrangement and appearance of the rooms and machinery within, this is one of the most attractive manufacturing establishments in the country.

Hayward's *Gazetteer of New Hampshire*
(1849): 119.

Courtesy Portsmouth Athenæum
Portsmouth Steam Factory as built.

Sources:

Portsmouth Journal, 28 Oct. 1843; 18 Nov. 1843; 9 Oct. 1847; 1 June 1850; 6 Dec. 1880.

and 420 looms were driven by a high pressure steam engine of 200 horse power, and some 400 hands were employed.

For all its beauty it was never successful. It was reorganized in 1866 as the Kearsarge Mills and largely controlled by new Boston investors. In December 1880 the mill suffered a disastrous fire that cracked the granite quoins and left only the three lowest stories standing. The owners decided not to rebuild and the empty ruin was sold. During the 1890s the Portsmouth Machine Company occupied the remaining part of the mill after converted it to a foundry. The company manufactured, among other things, some of the cast-iron store fronts on Market Square. After a second fire while later occupied by an automobile dealership, the building was further reduced to its present size. It is occupied today by JSA Architects and an educational publishing firm.

RMC

From *Leading Manufacturers . . . 1887*
Portsmouth Machine Co. (after 1880 fire).

Portsmouth's Two- and Three-Deckers

Built ca. 1910-16
317- 351 Hanover Street

A regionally distinctive late 19th- and early 20th-century New England building form, the three-decker (now sometimes mislabeled as triple-decker) contains flats designed to house one family on each floor. The façade is defined by the entry bays and the flanking porch and window bays. Their are characterized by a stack of porches which typically clings to the rear of the building. Many also have front porches, although these may be smaller and often only two stories high. Between 1870 and 1930 tens of thousands of these multi-family houses were built throughout the region, yet their origin remains obscure. They have been linked to the side-entry row house *[see 80-92 McDonough St.]* and in form to both tenements and mansard-roofed flats.

Three-deckers were built in many styles for both the middle and working classes. Like other apartment houses, they combined affordable rent with ease of one-floor living. But three-deckers were closer in scale and appearance to the independent suburban residence with light and air on all four sides than larger apartment buildings. They provided an economical option for home-owner-ship which might otherwise have remained out of reach for many families. Yet many architects and housing experts after the turn of the century decried wooden three-deckers as nothing more than insidious tenements and severe fire hazards. The collapse of the building industry in the 1930s brought an end to their construction.

One of the handful of three-deckers in Portsmouth is #349-351 Hanover Street. This and its neighboring "two-deckers" were all built between 1910 and 1916. Most of the early tenants were skilled workers, foremen, and clerks who worked in walking distance from their homes. By the Depression, the mostly Irish names had changed to a mix that included Italians, Greeks, and French-Canadians. The "two-deckers" are unusual in that they resemble three-deckers with the top story removed.

Drawing by Amy Amidon, measured by R. Candee, Claire Dempsey, and Diane Rodolitz
Second floor plan, 327 Hanover Street.

The floor-plan belongs to the second story apartment of #327 Hanover Street. The building has two separate entrances so that the stair to the second floor is private and opens immediately into the apartment. The plan of these buildings is a bit unusual in that the front room is not a parlor, but a bedroom. More typical is that the dining room/ sitting room is grouped with the pantry and kitchen, and the toilet room and pantry are adjacent and stacked to minimize plumbing. The kitchen is next to the rear service stair and rear porch, which was used for clothes drying and other domestic chores. While the spread and ornament of three-deckers have been studied by cultural and historical geographers, the variety of their interior planning has not been as well defined.

DR

The Sagamore Mill (destroyed)

Built 1846
Formerly on McDonough Street between Rockingham and Cabot Streets

Construction of a large textile mill encouraged others to participate in smaller textile production. Founded by local investors (including lumber dealer Thomas Call) in 1846, the mill backed up to the railroad tracks below the mill pond. By 1849 the Sagamore Mill contained only 3,400 spindles making fine twists or double warps used in stuff goods and cheap wollenetts. Some fifty hands were employed, and the mill was driven by a steam engine. By the 1850 looms had been added to its capability and unmarried women weavers were living in the rowhouses across McDonough Street east of the mill. In 1863 the mill was doubled in capacity under new owners from Boston. In 1872 the Came Brothers, carriage makers, nearly commenced operations in new quarters at "the Sagamore and Rockingham Mills," when the old hosiery factory was destroyed by fire. The Sagamore mill has since been replaced by a large brick industrial structure on McDonough Street between Rockingham and Cabot Streets.

RMC

Courtesy Strawbery Banke Museum
Sagamore Mills before 1863.

80-92 McDonough Street

Built 1847

The row houses nearly opposite the site of the Sagamore Mills beyond Rockingham Street, demonstrate a revived interest in multi-family housing, the first since the experiment on Sheafe Street. In both its location and early occupants, these rows were a direct response to the new textile factories. Once three four-unit rows were located along this part of McDonough Street, 80-92 was originally owned by two partners. When separated into two separate properties in 1849, the east end unit (80) became individually owned. As it is a foot wider with a solid party wall between it and the other three units, perhaps the partners planned on this division of property before construction. The remaining houses remained

Courtesy Portsmouth Athenæum
Rowhouses, McDonough Street.

in the ownership of Jeremiah Mathes, a middling Bow Street grocer, for the next thirty years. The only four-unit building on this street in the 1850 U.S. census, its male occupants were all English-born textile workers at the Portsmouth Steam Factory or Sagamore Mills living with their wives and children; only two men were boarders. By 1857, however, four individually listed female weavers at the Sagamore Mills are listed at the same address in the city directory; perhaps one unit then functioned as a boarding house.

Only three of the four units in the row beyond, first appeared in 1850 and were owned by another downtown grocer as investment properties. Acquiring the corner house in 1876, by 1892 all eight units between Cornwall and Rockingham streets were part of the widespread real estate holdings of local contractor B.F. Webster. On Islington Street near the hosiery factory and Jones Brewery a similar block of five houses with "each tenement entirely separate" was credited to architect-builder Jacob Haddock in 1871.

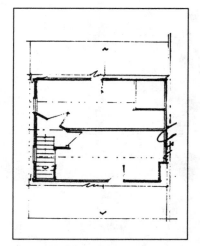

Third floor – left.

RMC

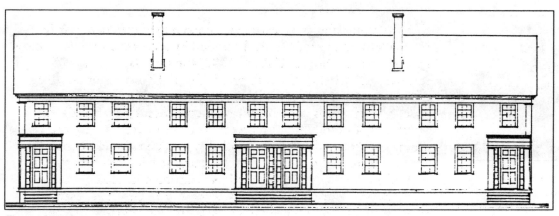

Front elevation.

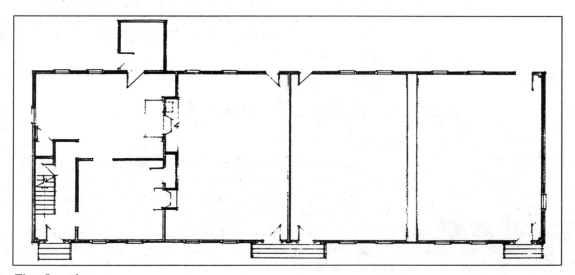

First floor plan.

Drawings by Steven McHenry, Interface Architects
80 McDonough St.

Courtesy Portsmouth Athenæum

Morley Button Factory, 1891.

From *Leading Manufacturers . . . 1887*

Portsmouth Shoe Company.

INDUSTRIAL DEVELOPMENT OF ISLINGTON STREET

At the western end of the North Mill Pond was an 18th century village around the sawmill known as Islington. In the 1860s it became the city's industrial center with the development of breweries and shoe factories near the junction of Islington Street and Creek (later Bartlett St.). English-born John Swindell, whose 1856 malt house located at the end of Jewell's Court (where so many English stocking weavers lived), produced some 10 barrels of ale a day. Swindell was heavily mortgaged and lost the plant in 1859 to his young partner, Frank Jones. From 1871 through the 1880s, the Frank Jones Brewery (see p. 4) expanded south of Islington Street behind the Jones Cass Street home. Nearby, the Eldredge Brewing Company also began making ale on the site of the old Portsmouth Stocking Factory building on Creek Street in 1858; the smaller Portsmouth Brewing Company was located on Bow Street where another stocking factory formerly operated. The Jones brewery was the largest, producing 250,000 barrels in 1896 or five times that of the Eldredge brewery.

Also on Islington Street was the brick factory of Portsmouth Shoe Company, incorporated in 1886, and by 1896 employed 1200 workers. Like so many Portsmouth businesses, it was financed by Frank Jones and after his death it failed in 1904. Its successor, the Gale Shoe Co., reduced the workforce by half. Related to the shoe industry is the Morley Button Company, begun in 1891 by Frank Jones's son-in-law Charles Sinclair (also a Portsmouth Shoe Co. investor), to manufacture paper-maché buttons for shoes and clothing. Its power house generated electricity for the factory as well as for the new electric street railway that ran its trolly lines throughout Portsmouth's expanding neighborhoods.

These economic engines were the major source of employment in Portsmouth after the 1880 destruction of the Portsmouth Steam Factory and before the establishment of Prohibition in 1918. The city's small but steady growth in population from 1880 to 1910, followed by a surge of 2300 new residents by 1920, is reflected in the large number of homes built about the turn of the century at the western edge of the city.

RMC

Courtesy Strawbery Banke Museum
Eldredge Brewing Company.

Sources

Ray Brighton, *Frank Jones, King of the Ale Makers* C.S. Gurney, Portsmouth Historic and Picturesque

Leading Manufacturers and Merchants of New Hampshire, NY: International Publishing Co., 1887: 41.

Portsmouth Journal, Dec. 9, 1880

"Button Making...At the Morley Factory," *Portsmouth Herald*, Feb. 1, 1906, p.5.

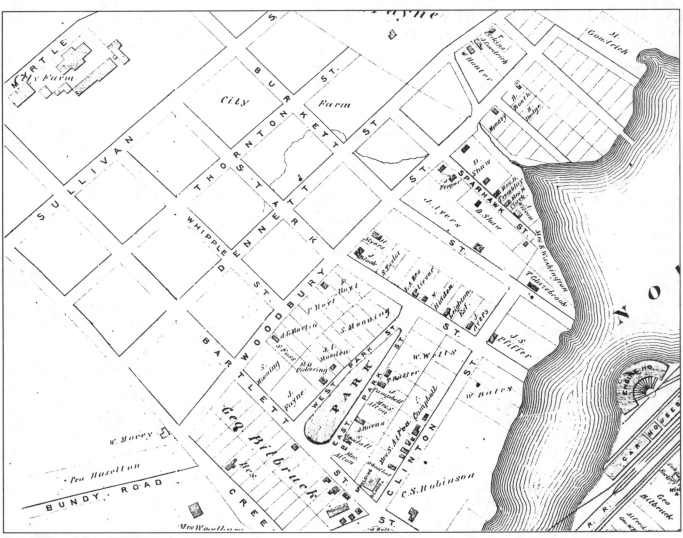

Detail, Beers Map of Portsmouth, 1876.

THE CREEK

The northern edge of the North Mill Pond was farmland well into the 19th century. As early as 1812 John Miller, one of the town's leading joiners, tried to develop 50 houselots south of Dennett Street along Sparhawk and Langdon (later Burket) streets on land acquired from Henry Langdon. [see map p. 112] Miller's proposed neighborhood was to be connected to the Rock Pasture across the mill pond by a bridge whose timbers were gathered on the shore at his death in 1813. Although his own house and barn were located here, few others built homes here until later in the century.

At the far end of the Creek, Capt. Samuel Ham erected a 3-story federal mansion in 1809, which became the home of Levi Woodbury in 1819. governor, U.S. Senator, Secretary of the Treasury, and Justice of the U.S. Supreme Court, Woodbury was a leading contender to the Democratic nomination for president at his death in 1851. His heirs retained the estate as a summer home and sold it to Frank Jones in 1899. Jones proposed to restore the house "to its old time glory," but died in 1902 before improving the house.

North of Dennett Street is the 165 acre farm of Thomas Sheafe that was purchased in 1833 for a new City Farm. A brick almshouse and institutional farm complex was erected here on Myrtle Street in 1833-34 and served as the poor house for 50 years. By the 1870s nearly half the land was laid out into city blocks. In 1887 the City Farm complex was sold off to the builder-developer Benjamin F. Webster, who then sold the remaining 80 acres to Frank Jones. (Democratic Councilmen Mahoney and Casey, who opposed the sale, found themselves out of a job at the Jones Brewery and Shoe Company.) By the 1890s a number of new houses had been built on either side of Dennett Street.

Courtesy Portsmouth Athenæum
City Farm/Almshouse, built 1834.

Worker housing appeared at the Creek in the 1860s in the form of Morning Street stocking weavers cottages next to the factory. To the east, subdivided farmlands remained largely undeveloped through much of the century. Those few houses built in the 1870s were often 1-story with a central peaked gable in the front of the roof to light the attic story room. Others were gable fronted like those throughout the west end. The area became sufficiently populated to require a new school, and in 1870 the city advertised for bids to erect a wooden school at the corner of Bartlett and Clinton streets. Between 1890 and 1910 many empty lots were filled and the population of the Creek, especially west of Burket Street, became increasingly Irish. In 1902 the city employed William A. Ashe to remodel the Spaulding school.

RMC

Spaulding School, built 1870, remodeled 1902.

Sources

Ray Brighton, *Frank Jones, King of the Ale Makers*

"The Alms House & Town Farm," *Portsmouth Journal*, March 28, 1846

Sagamore Fire Company and Ward Hall

Built 1899, enlarged 1905-6
Bartlett Street at Pine St. Park
architect: William A. Ashe

Architect William Ashe was paid $100 in 1899 for plans for a new brick engine house 28' wide and 32' deep at the end of the park on Bartlett Street which was described at year end as unfinished but nearly complete. Herbert A. Marden acted as contractor, using local suppliers and day laborers. The fire chief recommended a hose company of ten men to operate the old Sagamore Steam Engine placed there on reserve. By 1901 the fire company's membership reflected the neighborhood's Irish character. In 1905 Ashe and Marden, with brickmason Guy Smart, were credited with the design and building of a 25'x 23' brick annex to the Bartlett Fire House for a Ward Hall that became the community center of this neighborhood and the Creek Athletic Club.

RMC

Sources

William A. Ashe memorandum book, Portsmouth Athenæum

City Reports, 1898-1906

Portsmouth Herald, Jan. 1, 1902

<u>Source</u>

Julian Ursyn Niemcewicz, *Under the Vine and Fig Tree: Travels through America in 1797-99, 1805 with some further account of life in New Jersey.* Metchie J. E. Budka, trans. and ed. Elizabeth, NJ: Grassman Publishing for NJ Historical Soc., 1965.

BEYOND THE CREEK AND CHRISTIAN SHORE

Woodbury Avenue continued beyond the Ham-Woodbury estate through northern farms and converged with North Road, now Maplewood Avenue. From the 1790s, the road led to a toll bridge over the Piscataqua at Newington six miles away. This bridge, an early engineering landmark, was one of Portsmouth's first internal improvements and quickly became the place where Portsmouth's elite gathered in the summer. In 1798 one foreign visitor noted:

> *It is the fashion to ride there for tea. On the deck of the bridge there is a windowed opening which when lifted reveals a stairway to a hall or bower built directly under the arch of the bridge and over the stream. It is an interesting sight to see the crowd of Portsmouth elegants hung, as if in a cage, over the water near the bridge, with the cabriolets running over their heads. This is a remarkably cool place.*

Maplewood Farm

Built ca. 1860, remodeled 1880 (Jesse Edwards, designer/builder)
1094 Maplewood Ave.

At the junction of Woodbury and Maplewood avenues stands the remains of Frank Jones rural residence, Maplewood Farm. The 35-year old Jones acquired Sparhawk and Myers farms in 1867 and added to the estate over the years. Here he soon began building a large stable for his horses and carriages. The barn for prize cattle and oxen, like the house itself, were already on the Myers property.

In 1879, when he purchased and began enlarging the Wentworth Hotel in New Castle, he also enlarged and remodeled

courtesy Portsmouth Athenæum

Maplewood Farm before (above) and after (below) 1880 improvements.

from Hurd, Rockingham County History, 1882

Maplewood Farm. Jesse B. Edwards, a Salem house mover for the Boston & Maine RR, was described in 1896 as having been the "architect" of the Wentworth 1879-80 remodeling and responsible for "building the residence and reconstructing the brewery of Hon. Frank Jones." The Jones' added a large addition with a new entrance, a tower (capped by a Mansard roof like the hotel's) and a piazza 147 feet long. Old outbuildings were moved back 150 feet from the road behind a new lawn and elaborate Victorian flower beds. Woodbury Avenue was lined with 100 maple trees and the estate's landscaping was given over to Jones's German-trained gardener, W. S. Patterson and his son, for whom Jones had already built five greenhouses. The 1880 renovation added more greenhouses as well as summer houses, statuary, a grapery and forcing house for both the plantings of the Wentworth Hotel as well as those of Maplewood Farm. Trustees of Jones' estate sold Maplewood Farm and from 1909 through the 1920s the house was the psychiatric sanatorium of Dr. Boris Sidis. After his widow moved to Boston in 1930, the extensive gardens and formal estate landscape of the Sidis Institute was broken up for new houses and smaller gardens.

RMC

Courtesy Portsmouth Athenæum
Interior Maplewood Farms after 1880.

Sources

Ray Brighton, *Frank Jones, King of the Alemakers*

Portsmouth Daily Chronicle, Feb. 15, 1896.

Maplewood Acres

Built 1941–47
Lucien O. Geoffrion, architect for Hampton Development Corp.

Maplewood Acres was created on two tracts of the Jones farm by the Hampton Development Corporation in 1940. One tract, 19 acres west of Woodbury Avenue, between Woodlawn Drive and Echo Avenue, contained Jones's former house and grounds. A second, named the Terrace Park Division, was an irregular 6 acre wedge at the junction of Maplewood and Woodbury avenues.

A June 1941 ad illustrated 1238 Maplewood, a "Garrison colonial" described as "THE home for a single, appreciative family...the ONLY home of its type in Maplewood Acres" stating, "every detail is studied, authentic, just as true to type as its Pilgrim forebears." Its amenities included log-burning fireplaces in the living room and knotty-pine panelled basement game room, modern air-conditioned heat, electric range and refrigerator, "snap-out" aluminum windows, and linoleum floors. The promotion also capitalized on its location overlooking "a tranquil artificial pool," (opposite) with exotic trees planted by Frank Jones including a Japanese ginko on the front lawn. All this for a mortgage of "only 52.98" a month!

Eleven houses fronting on Maplewood and Woodbury avenues were built or nearly finished by June 1941. Five more on either side of the Jones mansion were finished by at least 1947. All were designed by the corporation's architect, Lucien O. Geoffrion (1908 —), who learned his trade at the Boston Architectural Club while working as a draftsman for a Boston architectural firm. Geoffrion describes the style of Maplewood Acres as "eclectic colonial" and recalls drawing details from professional periodicals. Common to each house is a massive chimney, centered front door,

1238 Maplewood Ave.

999 Woodbury Ave.

1050 Woodbury Ave.

a symmetrically arranged façade, small-paned windows, and a connected 1-story garage. Three houses are 1 ½ story colonial capes, one with brick ends; the others are 2-stories, with 3- or 5-bay façades. Individuality comes from varying features from different regions and periods of the colonial era. Four houses have pyramidal hip roofs, the others have gable roofs. Two have "garrison" second story overhangs. One of these overhangs boasts large pendant drops and sits above a brick-faced first story that has one large multi-paned window on either side of the front door. Plain or fluted pilasters, and in one case columns, decorate the entrances; 2-story pilasters divide the façade of two homes. Heavy Georgian-style broken pediments with urns appear over the front doors of two houses; simpler arched and triangular pediments are used over doors and windows of others. One house has a wall dormer, another has low second-story windows after the Greek Revival homes of New York state. Most were clapboarded, others shingled; many were later sided and most have added a second story above the garage.

The booming defense industry for WW II must have helped sales. Many war-time occupants worked at the Portsmouth Naval Shipyard, one worked for New England Tool Company, and another supervised vocational training for war production work. In the late 1940s smaller 1-story colonial capes were built on the east side of Fairview Drive, a curving street off Maplewood Avenue. A plat for the larger tract west of Woodbury Avenue projected 60 houses on several paper streets, but only Hillcrest Drive was actually built. Home building here and on the east side of Echo Drive at the northwestern edge of the subdivision was fitful, using a variety of post-war architectural styles.

JP

Sources

Portsmouth Herald, June 21, 1941.

Telephone interview with Lucien Geoffrion, June 10, 1992.

1240 Maplewood Ave.

BUILDING VICTORIAN PORTSMOUTH

Thomas E. Call, lumber merchant

As early as 1845 the city had a sash and door manufactory and the first of several steam powered planing mills associated with lumber yards along the docks and railroads at the North End. Thomas E. Call was just one of several such lumber dealers who supplied both the shipbuilding and housing industries with pine, spruce and hemlock from Maine and New Brunswick. His own half of a two-family house built in 1862, formerly located at the corner of Court and Pleasant streets, exemplifies the application of machine manufacture to a wide range of wooden and other building parts for domestic construction before the Civil War. Planed lumber for floors, flush boarding, or the rusticated treatment of Call's own façade, were all made possible or less expensive by the new building technologies. Turned brackets of diverse shapes and sizes, such as various moldings, window caps, and details of the porch, were all made commercially available through building suppliers.

RMC

Courtesy Portsmouth Athenæum

T.E. Call & Son lumber yard, Green and Market Streets, photograph ca.1880.

Courtesy Portsmouth Athenæum

T.E. Call house (left), Pleasant and Court streets.

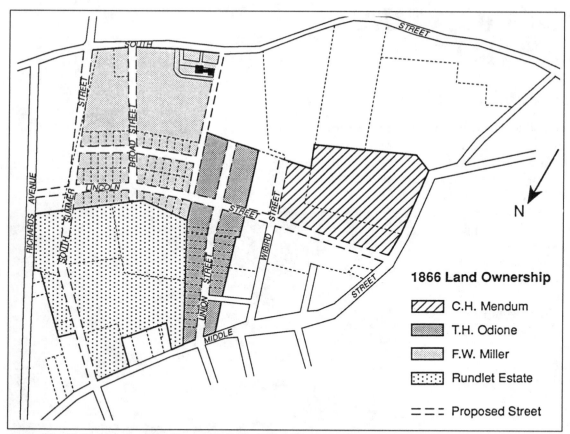

map by Eliza McClennen after Hoyt, Portsmouth Public Library

1866 plan of proposed streets and lots showing major landholders.

1866 Land Ownership

- C.H. Mendum
- T.H. Odione
- F.W. Miller
- Rundlet Estate
- = = = Proposed Street

Detail, 1877 bird's eye view, looking south, Middle to South Street.

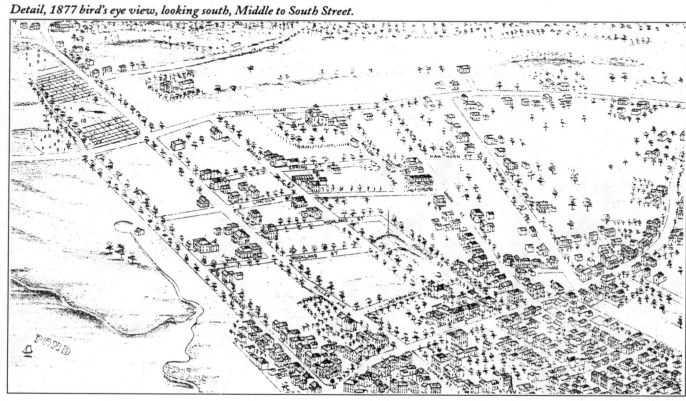

THE VICTORIAN DISTRICT
BETWEEN MIDDLE STREET
AND SOUTH ROAD: 1870–1892

Most homes in Portsmouth were built during spurts of population, such as that of the federal period rebuilding and expansion or the growth that accompanied the introduction of steam powered industry in the decades before the Civil War. Yet, while the total population [see chart p. 4] and the number of dwellings remained almost static — about 1670 homes for slightly more than 2000 families — from 1850 to 1890, Portsmouth also created its first large, middle class, Victorian suburb. Between South Road and Middle Street west of Richards Avenue a dozen new streets were laid out and nearly a hundred new houses built from the end of the Civil War to the turn of the century. The city's growth to the south and west became home to many downtown service professionals and merchants, a diverse group of artisans and tradesmen, as well as those who invested in the brewing, shoe, and other industries along the North Mill Pond.

Lincoln Hill

Suburban development began after 1865 when the old Packer Pasture, a 30-acre tract off South Road and the highest part of the city, was acquired from John Elwyn and renamed Lincoln Hill by newspaperman Frank W. Miller. In 1866 Miller and his neighbors proposed several new streets, especially Lincoln Avenue running from Richards Avenue (described in 1870 as "one of the meanest streets in the city") to Middle Street. It crossed an extended Union Street, controlled by T. H. Odion, C. C. Whittemore, C. M. Sides, and J.C. Carr, and was laid out beyond Wibird Street abutting land of C. H. Mendum.

The city accepted Union Street and Lincoln Avenue as public streets in 1867. Miller's plan, by local surveyor Alfred M. Hoyt, also proposed an extension of Summer Street to the south through extensive lands controlled by the heirs of James Rundlet. The heirs refused to cooperate. Instead, Miller tried to buy the rights to an earlier street opposite Summer Street that Rundlet had been permitted to close when Langley Boardman developed Joshua Street. Nevertheless, Miller Avenue (first called South Summer Street) would not be developed for several years, and real estate development initially occurred along Union Street, South Road, and Lincoln Avenue.

Miller retired from the city's first daily paper when he purchased Lincoln Hill and immediately erected a large French "cottage" with a semicircular drive between the house and elaborate beds of flowers. Miller was active in the 1873 "Return of the Sons" to attract former natives back to Portsmouth, perhaps as a promotional devise for his development, and was elected as mayor in 1874. Retiring from politics he mortgaged some of his undeveloped land and began the *Portsmouth Weekly*, but died in 1880. In 1871 a

Photograph by Noel Clews
F.W. Miller

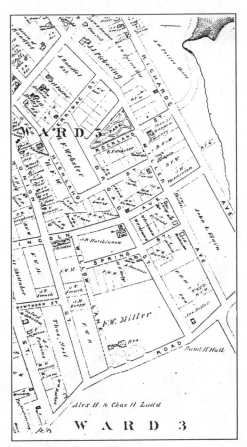

Courtesy of Library of Congress
Detail, Beers' 1876 map of Portsmouth.

161

Courtesy SPNEA
F.W. Miller House, Lincoln Hill.

J.H. Hutchinson House.

Sources

"Reminiscences of Portsmouth," Portsmouth Journal, Sept. 30, 1871, p.2.

N.B. Sides 4 family rowhouse, 448–462 Lincoln Ave.

returning son who had recently visited Portsmouth found "new and tasteful homes that give grace and animation to a locality so long uninhabited."

> *A most attractive feature in the way of public improvements is also the new and fast growing neighborhood of South Portsmouth... Apart from its healthful position, the new suburb has views to present... and from the price paid recently, for some of the choice building sites on South street, very evident it is that such an advantage was not lost sight of by the purchaser, whether desiring the ground for improvement or as a good investment. There yet remain positions for building not less desirable, to say the least, than that of Mr. Miller of Lincoln Hill. They would not long remain unoccupied in this vicinity.*

Local jeweller J.H. Hutchinson built a towered center-entry house (374 Lincoln Ave.) in 1875 near the corner of Broad Street that was surrounded by greenhouses (soon run by his wife as a florist) on the entire block to Spring and Willow streets. Amos Pearson, was another florist who in 1872-73 established his home (208 Broad St.) and hot houses immediately across Spring Street. In 1880 the small gable-front house was also home to portrait painters Mary E. Miller (Mrs. Pearson's sister) and Ulysses D. Tenney who boarded here; nine year old Helen Pearson would follow in their path and become an artist. These greenhouse parcels extended the pattern of single homes on large landscaped lots that Miller established with his own nearby estate.

Only along Union Street, parts of Lincoln Avenue, and near South Road did individuals build homes on the narrow lots originally laid out. Houses like those already common in the West End, gabled or small Mansard cottages, were built here by neighborhood carpenters. It is, perhaps, a reflection of its artisan character that the local newspaper saw Union Street as "a good location for a chapel of the colored people." Although Union and Wibird streets continued through to South Road, many lots south of Lincoln Avenue were held by investors and most houses were not built until later. Among Miller's large speculative investors was the prominent local builder Benjamin Franklin Webster, who in 1867 took the entire block between Miller and Lincoln avenues, and Spring and Broad streets and bought other lots after Miller's death. Webster developed three houses at 484, 492, and 500 Union Street by 1892. Local architect Henry S. Paul provided plans, apparently drawn from Palliser's mail order catalog [see p. 17], for three individuals at the southern end of Wibird Street (244, 280, and 307) in 1889.

One of the most interesting of Miller's individual sales was that in 1874 to Nathaniel B. Sides on the corner of Lincoln and Union streets. The newspaper soon noted that foundations were being laid for a double house, but by 1875 Sides was taxed for "4 tenements" still "unfinished" that became a two-story, Mansard-roofed row of four units (448-462 Lincoln Ave.) that long remained income properties.

RMC

Langdon Park

Portsmouth's suburban development was accompanied by significant relandscaping of the city. Mrs. Edward Cutts bequeathed funds for improving Richards Avenue, South Cemetery was laid out as a landscaped park, and the Hon. John Langdon offered land below the South Mill Pond if the city would build a bridge for direct access from downtown to South Street. As early as 1852 local artist Thomas P. Moses drew a fancy sketch showing a Portsmouth "Common" in the Elywn field across the South Pond "and the display of forrest trees which appear, shading inviting avenues, render the idea of a Common very popular." Two alternative plans to lay out the access and grounds leased in 1867 to trustees for these "public grounds" are known. One of 1876 proposed a bridge placed behind the courthouse that gave its name to Court Street and leading to a park of Victorian landscaped beds. Another, platted in 1875, followed Elwyn's preferred route and the one most like that eventually adopted. In it the bridge (later filled as Junkins Ave.) crossed the water

Sources:
Brighton, *They Came to Fish*: II: 233
Morning Chronicle, 26 Mar. 1867; 12 Feb. 1869
Portsmouth Times, 19 June 1852
Rockingham Deeds, 418:118-119

Courtesy Portsmouth Athenæum
Langdon Park ca. 1880.

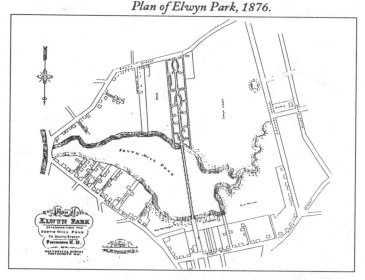

WPA after Hoyt, Portsmouth Public Library
Plan of Elwyn Park, 1876.

Plan, road bordering the South Mill Pond, 1875.

B.F. Webster.

B.F. Webster House, 292 Austin St., 1851.

Oracle House, 2 Court St., before being moved in 1937.

just off Pleasant Street, a marginal road ran along the north edge of the pond, and new streets were to be built east of Richards Avenue. Frank W. Miller supervised the planting of 600 donated trees after Langdon Park opened in May 1876.

RMC

Benjamin F. Webster, Builder: 1847–1867

Although many participated in this neighborhood's creation, no one was more responsible than Benjamin Franklin Webster (1824-1916) for "improving the city by building new houses, improving old ones, and making pleasant the waste places." Apprenticed to Austinborough joiner Benjamin Norton at age 17, Webster's career overlaps and contrasts sharply with that of Oliver Manson. The older carpenter entered the trade during the nadir of domestic building and while he worked enough to build his modest home on Union Street [see p. 133], most of his work was building clipper ships. Webster, too, took advantage of the boom in shipbuilding in the 1850s. Unlike Manson, however, he invested his profits in real estate and soon became a building contractor. In 1847 he bought a small tract of land at the corner of Madison and Austin streets and the next year acquired another at the western corner of Middle and Park streets. He subdivided the Park Street parcel, sold undeveloped house lots, built a small house at 26 Park Street, and erected another on Middle Street (since removed) over the next three years. In 1849 he married Sarah Senter and the next year purchased a Cabot Street house and carpenters shop behind Benjamin Norton's. In 1851 he built their first new home (292 Austin St.), a board and batten cottage derived from published designs [see p. 16], near the corner of Madison Street. In 1855, the Websters moved from Austinborough to the Oracle house [see p. 46] at the corner of Haymarket Square at 2 Court Street, a small gambrel with additions occupied as a two-family dwelling. Here he lived until 1881 while he followed his trade, joined St. John's Masonic Lodge (becoming Worshipful Master in 1864-65 and its treasurer for 29 years), was admitted to the Mechanics Fire Society (1866) where he served as president 1874-75 and 1903-04, and became a proprietor of the Portsmouth Athenæum (1868).

In the late 1850s, his real estate holdings grew: an empty lot nearby on Court Street, half a house on Middle Street, lots on McDonough and Salem streets, and a wharf and store on Bow Street. In 1860 he repurchased his little gothic cottage for rental and resale, added a tenant house and his own carpentry workshop to his holdings along Bow Street, and built more houses along McDonough Street. After the Civil War Webster acquired houses along State Street behind his own home where in 1872 he erected a large $5000 Mansard-roofed house (438 State St.) opposite the Rockingham which he advertised for sale.

He also worked for others, renovating three local churches, including the joiners work for the 1858 interior redecoration of the Universalist church *[see Pleasant Street]* and building the Cabot Street School (1860). In 1862 he sold his extra Court Street lot to the Christian Society *[see Central Baptist Church]* with a single story meeting house built in 1860 for the Brodhead Methodist Episcopal Society. (Enlarged in 1875 it achieved its two story and towered appearance from the 1889 designs of local architect Henry S. Paul in 1891.) By 1865 Webster also held shares in several different ships and soon supervised construction of two major commercial blocks on Congress Street, the Kearsarge Hotel and the now-destroyed Congress Block, in which he was part-owner with Frank Jones and other investors.

RMC

Sources

Charles A. Hazlett, *History of Rockingham County* (Chicago: 1915): 898

Rockingham Deeds, 394:330

Central Baptist Church records, Portsmouth Athenæum

research by R. Candee and Martha F. Clark

B.F. WEBSTER'S NEIGHBORHOOD
MILLER AND LINCOLN AVENUE, HIGHLAND, MERRIMAC AND BROAD STREETS

Webster's 1867 purchase of Millers lots at Lincoln Hill was followed in 1870 by the relocation of his workshop to the foot of Rogers Street along the South Mill Pond. Here he erected a large (75'x 25') 2-story building with doors at each end, those facing the pond to permit floating timbers into the shop. Having established his business nearby, in January 1872 he bought most of the remaining Rundlet estate, agreed to share road building costs along the property line and "if I should build any houses adjacent... I will put the fronts of them toward the road." This $17,000 purchase, partly mortgaged to Caroline Rundlet, also allowed Miller Avenue and Broad Street to be extended and crossed by a grid of new streets. When a local paper noted in 1874 that more new houses had been built in Portsmouth "than for many previous years" and that home ownership "is coming to be popular again," it stated most of these new homes were in "the west end extension of the city between Middle and South streets, Miller Avenue and Wibird Street.

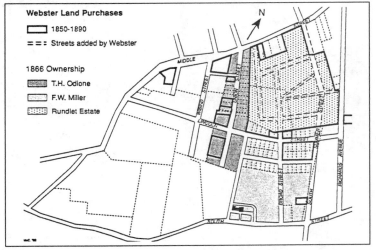

Eliza McClennen after Hoyt, Portsmouth Public Library

B.F. Webster land purchases south of Middle Street, 1850 - 1890.

   The houses first built on Webster's lands, like those of other streets in this new suburb, were of two basic types. One group was of small usually gable fronted houses that were constructed by a number of builders on southern Union Street and Lincoln Avenue. The 1875 home of carpenter George E. Stackpole (196 Miller Ave.) was nearly identical, except for the addition of bay windows in his own home, to one he built two years earlier and sold to former mayor J.B. Adams (312 Lincoln Ave.). The homes of bookseller Samuel Badger (1873), later sold to A.W. Parsons, at the corner of Lincoln and Broad, and of Timothy A. Tucker (1877) at Highland and Broad streets are of this common west end type.

   The homes built by Webster himself, usually on double lots, were of entirely different forms. All are square or rectangular with

Adams–Fernald House, 312 Lincoln Ave. George Stackpole, builder, 1875.

Courtesy SPNEA
Arabella Morgan School.

Courtesy Portsmouth Athenæum
J.J. Pickering House ca. 1862

Courtesy Portsmouth Athenæum
Miller Ave. and Highland St. ca. 1890

a central front door on the long façade facing the street. The largest of these are four-square houses of two stories and attic. Some are covered by Mansard roofs to create a third attic story and others by a low hip roof with façade gable in the center bay. Most of these houses in the 1880 census had live-in servants, presumably occupying the attic rooms.

The first building in this development was the Mansard roofed boarding school that Webster planned and built for Miss Arabella Morgan. Built in 1874 on the corner of Miller Avenue at 234 Rockland Street, it was soon enlarged to the east with a smaller mansard addition. Its severe façade is divided into three wide sections with a bay window on either side of its front porch. Like the 1875 Nowell house on the corner of Highland Street at 212 Miller Avenue, only two windows at each story on each side light the interior. A similar but more elaborate house for lumber merchant and active Republican political leader John H. Broughton was built in 1874 at 586 Middle Street at the corner of Cass Street at a reported cost of $8000.

Webster's hip roof three-bay houses usually have a projecting central bay, capped by a gable with a circular window in its middle above the broken cornice line. These features all follow the local model established by J.J. Pickering, Esq. at the terraced lot on corner of Miller Avenue and Middle Street, whose 1862 house was described as the architectural "chef d'oeuvre of the year in building." This elaborate home had the same tri-part division and fenestration of the façade, projecting central pavilion, and a hip roof capped by an octagonal cupola. It was far more elaborate than its followers, with rusticated or "block finish on the outside ... coated with sand" to imitate light granite. Examples of the same type built on Webster's land include houses for the photographer Charles Davis (1876-77) at 183 Miller Avenue, milliner J.M. Tebbetts at 186 Miller Avenue (remodeled 1891 by local architect William Ashe), and 284 Richards Avenue built for sparmaker Charles Young. Land title was often vested in women; Young's widowed daughter is named in this deed just as Lydia Nowell owned the land on which her husband's home was built.

Another example of this large house type is that at 439 Middle Street at the corner of Highland Street built by H. F. Gerrish in between 1867-69 in direct imitation of the J. J. Pickering house. Webster acquired it from Gerrish's estate after 1886 and owned it as a rental. About 1894 it was sold to True L. Norris, editor of the *Portsmouth Times*, member of the Governor's Council, and after 1893 Collector of Customs. Described in 1895 as "one of the stately, old-time mansions" of the city, it suggests how deceptively well these hip roofed houses of the 1860s and 1870s conformed to the traditional plan and scale of Portsmouth's earlier federal mansions.

A larger variation of this form is the house at 81 Merrimac Street built in 1876 by Webster and sold in 1877 to customs inspector John Pender. It has an angled corner tower that originally continued into a third story above the wide bracketed cornice that defined the roofline of all these houses. A smaller variation of this house is the 1875 house erected for city clerk D. J. Vaughan at 70 Highland Street. This continues the older L-house plan but with a central pavilion that continued into a full tower partly hidden by a 1-story porch across the front. Neither house has a projecting central bay.

Two houses on Highland Street reflect a less expensive and simpler version of the same form adopted by middle class families without live-in servants. For machinist J.M. Jarvis (112 Highland Street) in 1878 Webster built a gable-roof house with a central façade gable. The gable is also flush with the front wall and marked by a break in the front bracketed cornice. Two gable windows on each end light attic rooms and an arched window provides light from the front gable, just like the 1882 house for photographer Lewis G. Davis (208 Highland St.) at the corner of Broad Street. One and two story bays in various locations and front porches of various lengths provide sufficient variations to create a degree of diversity within a limited range of large house forms.

RMC

Charles Davis House, 183 Miller St., 1876.

John Pender House, 81 Merrimac St., 1876.

Sources:

Portsmouth Journal, 15 Nov. 1862; 1 Oct. 1870; 1 Nov. 1873; 2 May, 11 June, 12 Sept., 31 Oct. 1874

Agreements, Jan. 1872, Rundlet Collection, SPNEA Archives

1880 U.S. Census

James A. Wood, *New Hampshire Homes* (Concord, NH: 1895) I: 87-88

research by Martha F. Clark and R. Candee

Courtesy Portsmouth Athenæum
Highland St. ca. 1890 looking north.

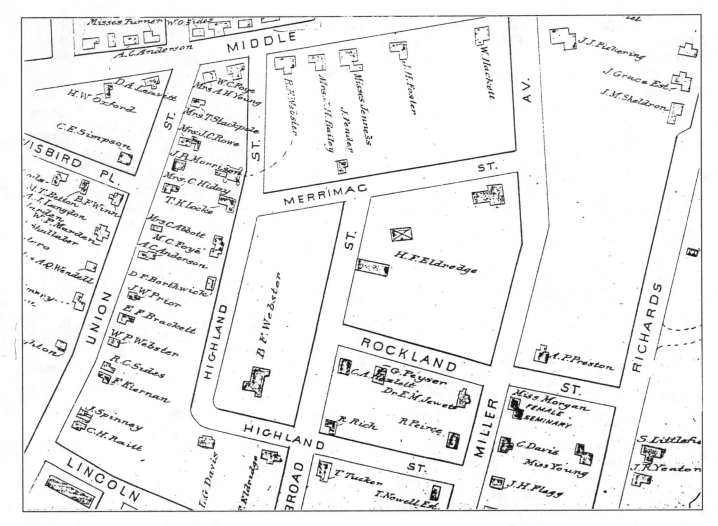

Detail 1892 map of Portsmouth.

Benjamin F. Webster House

now Buckminster Chapel

Built 1878-1880
84 Broad Street
architect: Albert C. Fernald

It is impossible to see this mansion, "one of the largest, handsomest, and best-built in the city," as anything but the product of Webster's desire to demonstrate his ability and his success. The house rivaled in size Frank Jones' similar suburban home then being remodeled *[see Maplewood Farm]*, but was a far more unified architectural design. Located atop Rundlet's Mountain on a 600' by 200' lot encompassing all the land between Highland, Broad, and Merrimac streets, the building's 72'x 54' main block is organized around a four story central tower. The Renaissance revival style employed many decorative wooden details found on Italianate buildings throughout the city since the 1850s. Quoins mark the corners, paired and single brackets support wide cornices and eaves, and round arched windows light the attic gables. Inside the front door, a broad central stair hall provides access to front and rear

B.F. Webster House, 84 Broad St.,
1878-80.

168

parlors and a stair to corresponding bedrooms in the north ell above. To the south of the stair hall are the dining room and related service rooms on the ground floor and bedrooms above.

In 1878 the local papers noted when Webster began excavating a cellar for a "large and costly" house for his own use. After blasting the ledge and digging a cellar, Webster turned to Albert C. Fernald to provide in January 1879 a set of architectural drawings for this new home. A. C. Fernald, the 25 year old son of lumber dealer A.A. Fernald, advertised himself as an "architect" working out of his father's home at 312 Lincoln Avenue, where he boarded from 1877 until 1883. After 1880 he is also listed in Boston city directories and must have tried to keep some Portsmouth work until in 1883 he found work as a draftsman in the large architectural office of William Gibbons Preston, who practiced in urban and suburban Boston as well as Savannah, Georgia. Beginning in 1890 Fernald worked as a draftsman in the Boston city architect's office, although most of his known drawings and commissions are also from the late 1890s and 1900s. The straightforward lines of his first known drawings show alternate floor plans and indicate that the front porch was a late addition to the design. What is most noteworthy about Fernald's early Portsmouth career, however, is the fact that the young man was perhaps the first local draftsmen to advertise himself as an "architect" without a prior or simultaneous career as a builder. In supplying design services to a builder like Webster, he played a new role that many professionally trained Boston architects promoted as essential to the creation of "artistic" homes.

The Webster family was not yet occupying the mansion in March 1880 when a flight of 17 marble steps up the terraces to the front porch were ordered, nor when the 1880 US Census was taken. Later use, as the Buckminster Chapel, has preserved its elaborate interior decoration of fine walnut, mahogany, and gum wood with very little alteration. After selling much of the Rundlet land by 1889, as the local mercantile agent for the R.G. Dun Company noted, Webster no longer did much building for others but "is principally looking out for his large [real estate] investments." While Webster probably continued to erect houses on lots near his home and in other parts of the city, those built after the 1880s were usually designed as rental properties. At 94-96 Highland Street he built a double tenement occupied by merchants Morris Foye and D.F. Borthwick. While the house may have been owned by Foye until after he built a house on the corner of Middle Street [see Morris C. Foye house], it was back in Webster's hands by 1896 when he gave Borthwick a ten year lease on the whole duplex for $325 a year.

RMC & MFC

Courtesy J. Verne Wood Funeral Home
Front elevation B.F. Webster House, A.C. Fernald architect, 1879.

Sources

R.G. Dun Collection, Baker Library Archives, Harvard Business School, 16: 209.

Morning Chronicle, 28 Sept. 1878; 1 August, 6 Nov 1879; 29 March 1880.

Jean Ames Follett-Thompson, *The Business of Architecture: William Gibbons Preston and Architectural Professionalism in Boston During the Second Half of the Nineteenth Century*, Ph.D. diss, Boston University, 1985.

1880 U.S. Census.

Research by Martha Fuller Clark, Roger Reed, and Richard Candee

HOMES BY ANDERSON & JUNKINS, BUILDING CONTRACTORS, 1877-92

In addition to houses known or attributed to Webster himself, several other architects and builders began to affect the visual character of the neighborhood in the 1880s. Among the most important new contracting firms was that of Anderson and Junkins, a partnership of two local builders organized in 1877 with a shop and warehouse on Penhallow Street. Albert C. Anderson had previously been in business five years on his own and, like Albert R. Junkins, was active in local politics, fraternal organizations, and the Mechanics Fire Society. Within a decade their crew of "twelve to eighteen skilled workmen" completed more than "fifty of the finest residences in Portsmouth" including the large Stick Style home of John Sise (1881), now the Sise Inn at 40 Court Street off Haymarket Square, the Charles E. Walker house (1883-86) at 659 Middle Street near the junction of Middle and Lafayette roads, the house at 461 Middle Street (1891) [see Morris C. Foye house], and Junkin's own home at 659 Middle Street (ca. 1880).

Three large homes on double corner lots along Miller Avenue can also be definitely assigned to this firm. One, at the corner of Lincoln Avenue opposite the Laighton house, is the house that Anderson and Junkins built for small beer and soda water manufacturer Charles E. Boynton between 1886 and 1887. So similar is it to the C.E. Walker house and the large dwellings previously erected by Webster, that this may have been one of the buildings for which the contractors drew plans from the local vernacular tradition and common building practice. The large 2-story rectangle has a plain pitched roof and its front wall is enlivened by an especially decorative front porch.

RMC

Charles M. Laighton House
now Pearl's Colonial Apartments

Built 1878-79
229 Miller Ave., corner of Lincoln Avenue
architect: William A. Ashe, contractors: Anderson & Junkins

The earliest home yet identified with Anderson and Junkins as builders is the handsome Second Empire style structure erected for grocer Charles M. Laighton on land at the corner of Lincoln and Miller Avenues. Its owner, the younger partner of Charles E. Laighton & Son, acquired the site from J.H. Hutchinson by taking the remaining term of a 25 year land lease from surveyor Alfred Hoyt, who had surveyed and platted the lands for Miller and other real estate developers. The lease was apparently designed for eventual purchase, but also permitted removal of any buildings erected on the site during the leasehold. In December 1878 the *Portsmouth Weekly* noted that "William E. Ash" [actually William A. Ashe] was the architect of both the Portsmouth Music Hall and Laighton's new home. A draftsman at the Navy Yard, Ashe rented a nearby house on Union Street near Lincoln Avenue and

Sources

Leading Manufacturers and Merchants of New Hampshire (NY: International Publishing Co., 1887): 49

Mechanics Fire Society, *Biographical Roster* (Portsmouth, 1966): 62-3.

Charles E. Laighton, 229 Miller Ave.

witnessed Webster's 1874 deed to a neighbor on Highland Street. In 1874 Ashe also prepared "a beautiful design" of the front elevation of a new church proposed (but never built) for the Court Street Christian Society, which "it is rumored they intend erecting near the new Seminary on Miller Ave."

RMC

Sources

Leading Manufacturers and Merchants of New Hampshire (NY: International Publishing Co., 1887): 49

Portsmouth Weekly, 7 Dec. 1878

Portsmouth Journal, 1 Aug. 1874

Montgomery–Eldredge House

Built 1880, with additions 1887, 1899–1902
3 Merrimac Street, corner of Miller Avenue
landscape architect: Charles Eliot; contractor: Anderson & Junkins

Two other residences later credited to contractors Anderson and Junkins, the homes of D.H. Montgomery and Herman F. Eldredge, are, in fact, the same building. This is the large hip roofed dwelling at the corner of Miller Avenue at 3 Merrimack Street. The house was built on land Webster originally sold to Capt. W.W. Low of the US Navy in 1872. Whether Low intended to build or simply hold it as an investment is unknown, but his heirs sold the empty lot to music and piano store owner D.H. Montgomery in 1880. He immediately began building the house that was described in a deed for additional land adjoining along Miller Avenue, purchased from B.F. Webster later that year, as Montgomery's "newly erected dwelling". By 1886, after Montgomery's death, H. Fisher Eldredge of the Eldredge Brewery bought the property and began improving it. A. C. Anderson designed a new adjoining stable also built in 1886 (it was remodeled in 1947 by architect Lucien H. Geoffrion for a rehabilitation center). Eldredge also purchased from Webster more undeveloped land in the remaining part of the block and replaced Webster's triangular garden projected along Rockland Street by constructing tennis courts, a shelter (built by Joshua Stackpole), and an "ornamental pond...spanned by a bridge."

These improvements were part of 1888-90 designs by "Charles Eliot, ... landscape artist" of Boston. After this noted landscape architect planned the estate, Eldredge added a porte cochere to the house and between 1899 and 1902 constructed a large 2-story semicircular bay west of the main entry. The pond was filled in 1926 to build the Portsmouth Apartments, designed by Boston architect Henry A. Mears.

RMC

Courtesy SPNEA
Montgomery-Eldredge Estate, after 1890.

courtesy Portsmouth Athenæum
Montgomery-Eldredge Estate looking north, ca. 1886.

Sources

Leading Manufacturers and Merchants of New Hampshire (NY: International Publishing Co., 1887): 49

C.A. Gurbey, *Portsmouth, Historic and Picturesque* (1902)

Morning Chronicle, 19 July, 24 Oct. 1889

Portsmouth Herald, 3 April 1897, 15 April 1899, 25 Oct. 1900, 14 Jan. 1947

Rockingham Deeds, 406: 437,449: 353, 485:143

James E. Wood, *New Hampshire Homes* (Concord, 1895) I: 84

research by Richard Candee and Jane Porter

Clara and J.S. Rand House

Built 1889-90
209 Miller Ave.
building contractor: George A. Jackson

One of the most interesting Queen Anne style suburban cottages along Miller Avenue is that built on land B.F. Webster sold to Clara M. Rand in April 1888. She was first taxed for a house here in 1890, the same year James A. Rand appears in the directories at 5 Miller Avenue. Perhaps they were siblings for there was a 45 year old Clara M. Watts in the 1880 census on Miller Avenue at the corner of Spring Street, living with her children and her 73 year old mother Harriet H. Rand. Until moving to this address, James lived nearby but was little taxed.

Construction of this house is attributed to building contractor George A. Jackson on the unusual basis of his architectural advertisement in the 1897-1901 city directories. Unlike most builders who used interchangeable cuts of houses, the drawing of the Rand house was only used by Jackson. The house is, in fact, Design No. 490 from *Shoppell's Modern Homes*, a quarterly series of mail-order plans published in 1886-89. The plans were provided by the Co-operative Building Plan Association of New York, a staff of fifty architects working for publisher Robert W. Shoppell. For this $4000 "artistic' home, either Jackson or his client paid $40 for a complete set of plans and specifications – about a quarter of the price for an architect's custom design. In developing suburban areas, mail-order plans such as this found a ready audience among local builders during the 1880s and 1890s.

The attic story, supported by three curved brackets, projects over the second story and the gable eaves are supported by two large brackets with an even deeper projection over paired attic windows. This set of features is a distant and vastly simplified vernacular echo of the west front of the Watts Sherman house in Newport, R.I. designed by H.H. Richardson in 1876, one of the earliest Queen Anne summer homes in America. Below, a porch wraps around the first story and joins the projecting façade to the square main block. At the rear is a two story bay terminating in a hip roof that intersects with the nearly pyramidal main roof. Old photographs show that the angled dormer above the staircase has been removed, but the Rand's house still has the same lattice decoration in the front porch gable, clapboard and shingled walls, and window placement specified in Shoppell's plans.

RMC

Rand House, 209 Miller Ave.

Illustrations: Portsmouth City Directory 1897
Advertisement for George A. Jackson, contractor.

Shoppell's Design 490.

Sources

Rockingham Deed, 511: 365

Shoppell's Modern Homes, vol. 5 (1886-89): design 490.

James Garvin, "Mail-Order House Plans and American Victorian Architecture." *Winterthur Portfolio* 16 (Winter 1981): 309-334.

Jeffrey K. Ochsner and Thomas C. Hubka, "H.H. Richardson: The design of the William Watts Sherman House," *Journal of the Society of Architectural Historians* (June 1992): 121-145.

Wallace Hackett House

now a Masonic Temple

Built 1891-92
351 Middle Street
architects: Ball & Dabney

The last major lot sold by the Rundlet heirs, at the corner of Middle Street and Miller Avenue, was purchased by lawyer Wallace Hackett in 1889. Described as one of the "most desireable locations in the city" it was expected to "be occupied by an elegant and commodius residence in the near future." Rather than turn to a local architect, Hackett gave the commission to Henry Ball. The former Portsmouth native provided his client with a yellow brick version of the Boston double bow-front elaborated with colonial revival detailing in the front porch, dormers, and porte cochere. The plans were admired by the local press as early as December 1890, and construction continued through the next year. This commission followed from the architects' 1889 design for the new Cottage Hospital on Junkins Avenue and may have led to a number of subsequent ones *[see Portsmouth Athenæum, Morris C. Foye House]*, including the extremely large 1897 home for National Bank president Edward Kimball, 644 Union Street at the corner of 889 South Road that was designed by the successor firm Dabney & Hayward.

RMC

Courtesy Strawbery Banke Museum
Wallace Hackett House, 1891-2.

Sources
Morning Chronicle, 13 July 1889
James E. Woods, *New Hampshire Homes*, I: 85

Morris C. Foye House

Built 1891
461 Middle Street
architects: Dabney & Ball; contractors: Anderson & Junkins

Morris C. Foye was a successful dry goods merchant, a director of the NH National Bank, member of the Mechanics Fire Society and several fraternal organizations, and elected state representative. He and his wife first lived in 94-96 Highland Street and in 1888 purchased the lot at the corner of Highland and Middle streets. Surviving accounts for the land purchase and construction of the house they built there show that he repaid his $2500 mortgage to Webster in irregular monthly payments of principal (with interest figured every six months) from Jan. 1888 through August 1890. In 1891 he began to construct his new home. Besides the land and mortgage Webster's name appears only for providing a team and man to help excavate the cellar. Architectural plans were provided by Ball & Dabney of Boston *[see Wallace Hackett and Portsmouth Athenæum]* for which they were paid $225. The mason was Everett W. Trefethen, and Anderson & Junkins were the builders. The total construction cost for the house, exclusive of the $2663 for land and interest, was $5115.

The Foye House is among the first in-town examples of the Shingle Style that combined the region's traditional wall shingles with other allusions to "colonial" architecture such as Palladian windows to create new domestic building forms. Such homes became common in the early 1880s as the preferred style of professional architects respond-ing to the interest in vernacular buildings as a source for an American architectural vocabulary; the style was first used for clients in coastal summer resorts *[see Hall House]*. Ball's partner, William Dabney, participated in this new movement by designing summer homes and a church at York Harbor, Maine, in this mode.

RMC

Sources
Building Accounts 1888-1891, Foye collec-tion, Portsmouth Athenæum

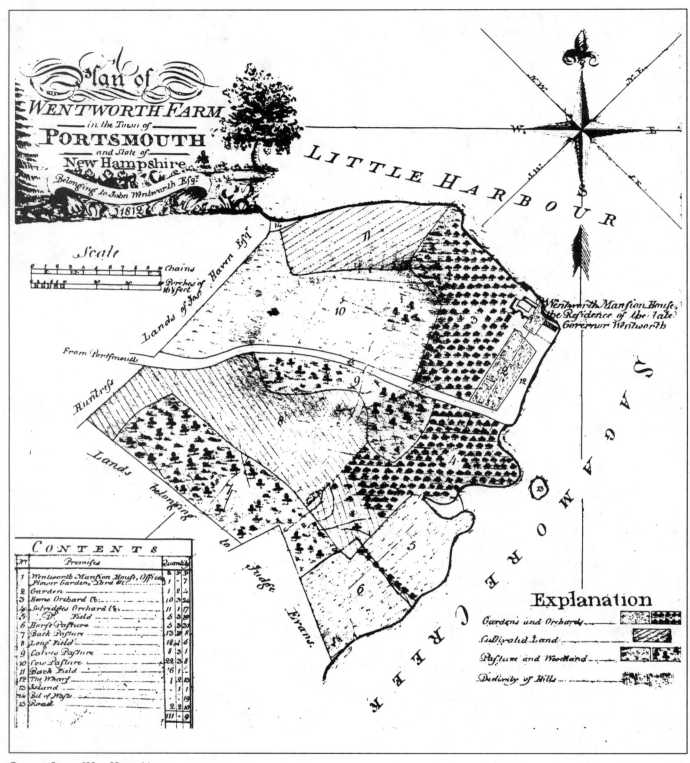

Courtesy State of New Hampshire

J.G. Hales, plan of Wentworth Farm, Little Harbor, 1812.

LITTLE HARBOR

Little Harbor is the body of water that wraps around the south and west sides of New Castle and in part, the town of Rye. On this edge of Portsmouth in the 1880s, there grew up a summer colony populated mainly by socially prominent people from Boston and, to some extent, New York. The nucleus had been classmates at Harvard College in the 1870s. The social and visual landscape of the Little Harbor summer colony in the late 19th and early 20th centuries was thus defined by this close-knit group of Harvard-trained artists and their friends. Their aesthetic appropriation of the past played out in new summer homes, especially around the remodeled Wentworth mansion at Little Harbor, demonstrates the impact of 19th-century tourism on Portsmouth's periphery.

The Wentworth-Coolidge Mansion

Built 1750-1760
Little Harbor Road
owner: State of New Hampshire

Benning Wentworth (1696-1770) served as Royal Governor of New Hampshire from 1741 to 1767. He rented a wooden house on Daniel Street in Portsmouth from 1728 until his appointment. Between 1741 and 1759 he occupied the impressive brick mansion across the street that he also rented from his sister, the widow of Archibald MacPheadris. *[See MacPhaedris-Warner House]* Wentworth built his own mansion – one of the few existing colonial Governor's mansions in America – on an old family farm at Little Harbor about 1750. The first concrete evidence of his permanent move there appears in 1753. Unable to persuade the General Assembly to buy or extensively repair the MacPheadris House, Wentworth sent the legislature a message on April 26, 1753:

> *This being the most advantageous season to make Provisions for a Provincial House, I am hoping you will Embrace it, that neither myself or the Government may be put to any further inconvenience on that account. For this end, I have Provided a house to remove my furniture into, that the workmen may have no interruption from me if the Brick House should be thought most convenient.*

Thereafter, Benning apparently stayed at Little Harbor for the remainder of his life, creating an 18th century country gentleman's farm with gardens, orchards, fields, and pastures, eventually covering more than 100 acres. What buildings he inherited on the site remain a mystery. Architecturally, it is an assemblage of at least four, and possibly five, pre-existing buildings, linked with awkward passages and transitions and appended with small, seemingly useless rooms. None of the structures appear to predate the early 18th century, one of the earliest perhaps being the two-story kitchen area. The heavy framing and flooring of this unit and the fact that it originally lacked any

Courtesy Coolidge family
Wentworth-Coolidge Mansion, ca. 1886.

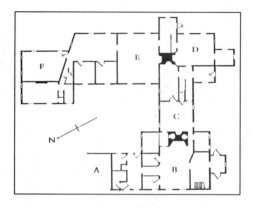

From *American Architect and Building News,* 1877

Robert S. Peabody, west side Wentworth Mansion.

fireplace indicate that this portion of the house may have once been a warehouse or shop.

Exactly when each of these sections was originally constructed has not been clearly established, but all the various parts seem to have been brought together by June of 1760 when the first known depiction of the "Governour's House" appeared. The same year Benning married his twenty-three year old maidservant, Martha Hilton (his first wife having died five years previously) and had his full-length portrait painted by Joseph Blackburn. Wentworth hired a joiner named Neal from 1759-1765 and the so-called "Council Wing," constructed from another pre-existing building, was probably added at this time to serve as a ballroom with its parlor and dressing rooms.

Writing about the chimneypiece in the Council Room, the English writer John Cornforth has noted:

> *Rightly it has been recognized as being derived from the one in the Stone Hall at Houghton engraved by Kent in his Designs of Inigo Jones....But surely what is even more interesting is to find the Royal Governor so consciously imitating the famous British Prime Minister: is it not a statement about his political position?"*

Not only did Benning Wentworth identify with the Prime Minister's politics, but with his expectations about the rewards of royal service represented in the construction of Houghton Hall, Norfolk (1722-32). Mark Girouard notes that "Walpole built the most sumptuous house of its day out of the proceeds of public service." Walpole used that country house to entertain colleagues in government and the local gentry who assembled there twice yearly "to drink, hunt, eat and indulge in bawdy, gossip, sight-seeing and politics" in the "informality of the rustic." The source of the Council Room chimneypiece does suggest that Wentworth, the center of a New Hampshire's political oligarchy and major benefi-ciary of its vast holdings in western lands, may have thought of his estate in a similar provincial way.

The Wentworth mansion at Little Harbor became an icon of the earliest phases of the colonial revival movement. The house was first open to visitors as early as the 1840s. Interest in the mansion was reinforced by Henry Wadsworth Longfellow's retell-ing of the marriage of the older governor to his maid (1863) and demonstrated in the 1870s by commercial stereopticon cards of the building's interior. Next came the artists and architects who promoted New England's buildings as an image at the heart of a new colonial revival architectural style. Robert Swain Peabody's plea that the architectural profession stop copying English Queen Anne forms but look for inspiration in native Georgian architecture was published in 1877 with his sketch of the Wentworth mansion. The next year, Arthur Little, a draftsman in the offices of Peabody and Stearns, placed the mansion on the title page of *Early New England Interiors.*

One artist of the summer elite was John Templeman Coolidge III of Boston, who graduated from Harvard in 1879 and soon married Katherine Parkman, daughter of the historian Francis Parkman. Templeman was probably introduced to Portsmouth by a fellow student from New York, Barrett Wendell (Harvard Class of 1877), whose family originated here. Barrett's parents, Jacob and Mary Wendell, spent summers at the Appledore Hotel, on the nearby Isles of Shoals, and the Jacob Wendell house on Pleasant Street in Portsmouth had been in the family since 1815. Templeman bought and restored the Wentworth mansion and its grounds, converting an existing poultry barn to a guest house. The Hennery, as the remodeled structure became known, was almost certainly redesigned by his Harvard classmate, Alexander Wadsworth ("Waddy") Longfellow, Jr., the poet's nephew and a successor to H.H. Richardson's Boston architectural practice, who changed its pitched roof to a gambrel and added a long ell on one side.

The mansion presented Templeman Coolidge with a major restoration project; gradually the rambling house was repaired and some formal elements were added to the grounds, although the Coolidges, like most of the Little Harbor settlers, lived a notably informal life in the summer. Gregory Wiggins, a sculptor from Pomfret, Connecticut, carved wood sculptures for the Wendells and the grounds around the mansion were also decorated with two French 18th century garden figures of cast concrete, brought back by Templeman in the 1880s.

NM, RMC, WO

Council Chamber Wentworth Coolidge Mansion.

Sources:

John Cornforth, "Decorations of Georgian Dynasties: The Houses of Portsmouth, New Hampshire," *Country Life*, Ap. 26, 1979; 1271.

Mark Girouard, *Life in the English Country House.* New Haven and London: Yale University Press, 1978: 3, 162.

Sarah L. Giffen and Kevin D. Murphy, eds., *"A Noble and Dignified Stream,"* The Piscataqua Region in the Colonial Revival, 1860 - 1930.

Arthur Little, *Early New England Interiors... Salem, Marblehead, Portsmouth, Kittery.* Boston: A. Williams & Co., 1878.

[Robert Swain Peabody.] "Georgian Houses of New England," *American Architect and Building News* (Oct. 20, 1877): pp. 95, 338-339.

Woodard D. Openo, *The Summer Colony at Little Harbor in Portsmouth, NH and its Relationship to the Colonial Revival Movement.*

Courtesy Coolidge family
"The Hennery," with Rogé McKim, ca. 1890.

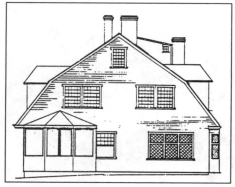

End elevation.

Front elevation.

The Hall House

Built ca. 1890
Little Harbor Road

Architect "Waddy" Longfellow also designed a house about 1890 for a Coolidge sister, Elise, and her husband, Dr. Richard Hall. This house follows the arrangement of large summer homes of the time, like Arthur Astor Carey's nearby "Creek Farm," in having a clearly-defined servants' wing. Set on rock ledge behind the Wentworth-Coolidge mansion, the Hall house is essentially symmetrical on the façade, unlike the functional back, which faces the water. It has been little changed by subsequent owners, except for lightening most of the woodwork (except in the dining room), enlarging the kitchen to take in the pantry, and adding a bay window to that room in place of a double window.

WO

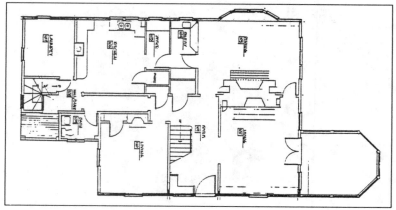

First floor plan.

Sources

Woodard D. Openo, *The Summer Colony at Little Harbor in Portsmouth, NH and its Relationship to the Colonial Revival Movement.*

20TH CENTURY SUBURBAN HOMES

From 1890-1920 the city grew rapidly through immigration and war work; since WW II the city's population double in size. As its historic core aged and declined, a ring of suburban development followed the advent of the automobile. As in the past century, farmlands surrounding the city center provided new sites for garden suburbs that leapfrogged beyond the edge of urban building.

Selected examples of neighborhood development and changing construction practices in this century must serve to represent a far more complex story. Shingled and clapboarded colonial revival styles vied with new bungalows along Mendum Avenue and other western streets. Atlantic Heights and Pannaway Manor reflect the special character of worker neighborhoods built for the area's wartime shipyards. While most homes continued to be built by carpenters and other building tradesmen working on site from original designs of an architect or mail-order plans, some were constructed of home-made materials such as concrete block; others came direct from a factory. Examples of factory-made homes suggest that many more are yet to be identified, while a local producer of modular and panelized houses, New England Homes, brings the story of Portsmouth builders and changing building technologies into the present.

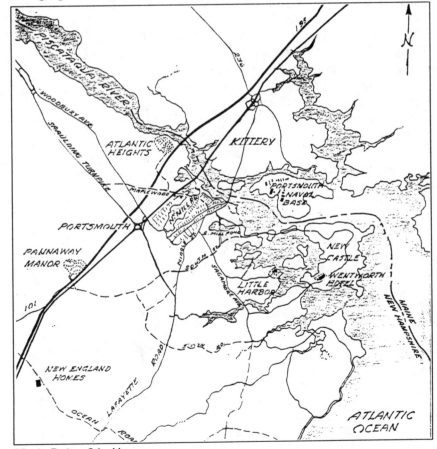

Map by Barbara Schmidt

Collection of Charles Leary

Concrete block house, 9 Middle Road, corner Lawrence Street.

One of many bungalows on Mendum Ave.

Front elevation, C.E. Jackson House.

First floor plan.

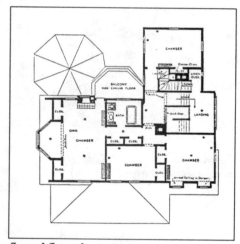

Second floor plan.

Sources

"New Buildings," *Portsmouth Herald*, 2 Jan. 1904

"Work of Portsmouth's Builders for the Past Twelve Months," *Portsmouth Herald*, 6 Jan. 1905

"A Shingled House at Portsmouth, N.H.," *Carpentry and Building* (Nov 1907):343-5

Suburban Homes with Constructive Details, 2nd. ed. (NY: David Williams, 1912): design no. 8

TURN OF THE CENTURY SHINGLED HOUSES

By the early 1890s, shingle-style or "colonial" shingled houses were being built on empty lots along many streets of Portsmouth's western neighborhoods and by the turn of the century had become a staple of local architects and builders for less elite, middle class, and suburban clients. At 99 Broad Street on the corner of Highland Street, a clerk at the Portsmouth Naval Shipyard named Robert E. Rich built a shingled home ca. 1890-91. [see p. 166] Another large shingle house at 33 Islington Street on the corner of Tanner Street was designed and built in 1903-4 by the local architect-builder W.W. Ireland as a home for saloon-owner True W. Priest. Many similar homes drew upon designs in popular plan books and trade magazines, but only one Portsmouth home was published in this manner as a source for others.

Cyril E. Jackson House

Built 1902-3
640 Middle Street
architect: Fred. Crowell Watson, mason: Joseph H. Holmes, builder: D.P. Pendexter

Fred. Crowell Watson was an architect from Bar Harbor who designed several summer homes in the area as a draftsman for York, Maine, builder E.B. Blaisdel from 1899 to 1901. In November 1907 he published plans and specifications for "A Shingled House at Portsmouth, N.H." in *Carpentry and Building* magazine that were later reprinted in *Suburban Homes with Constructive Details* (1912). The house was built for stockbroker Cyril E. Jackson in 1902-03. It has a large open hallway with formal rooms to either side and a rear off-set stair to the second floor bedrooms. A service stair in the kitchen ell serves as access to the third floor "servant's room and bath." Watson's design "was somewhat modified in the process of erection," the kitchen ell was originally intended as 2 ½ stories "instead of one and one-half, as finally built." The hall mantel is specified as of molded brick, while others throughout the house were "of colonial design." Interior walls in the parlor, hall and "nooks" were to be painted white, "Master's section" was stained cypress with painted trim, the dining room a weathered oak stain covered in varnish, the kitchen and pantry were simply varnished matched boarding. The architect recommended the wall shingles be stained a bronze green with a darker shade for the roof.

RMC

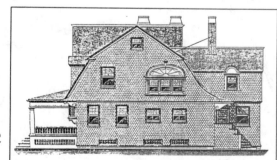

Side elevation.

WILLIAM A. ASHE, ARCHITECT OF THE STREETCAR SUBURBS

William Allyn Ashe's career as an architect followed the development of Portsmouth housing as it moved west from the city's center. Ashe probably came to the area from Boston in 1866 to survey the newly-acquired Seavey's Island for the Portsmouth Naval Shipyard. He returned two years later, at the age of 25, taking up residence in Portsmouth. Ashe worked for the Navy Yard as a draftsman, a position he held for the next 25 years until establishing his own full-time practice.

Ashe quickly settled into his new home. In July, 1870 he married Delta Spinney, five years his junior. Their first child, William Huntress Ashe, was born in 1872 while boarding at D.H. Spinney's on Spinney Road. There may have been a daughter who died before a second son, Leon, was born. By 1875 the Ashes moved to the newly developing end of Union Street After Leon's birth in 1883 the family moved the end building of row housing on State Street. They would continue to rent this property for more than 20 years. Ashe was a social man who joined numerous Portsmouth clubs including the Masons, Knights of Templar, the Elks, and the Warwick Club. Ashe continued to design buildings until his death in 1918. His oldest son, William, had died tragically young of pneumonia in 1872; his wife, Delta, proceeded him to the grave by a year.

The record of Ashe's work from 1868 to 1890 — during his employment at the Navy Yard — is still incomplete [see Music Hall and Charles Laighton House]. We do know that, like others, he moonlighted while holding a full-time job at the Navy Yard. But at 47 years of age, in 1890, Ashe opened his own architecture office at 7 Market Square. He continued to keep an office until at least 1905. His account book, which begins with 1890 and continues into 1902, chronicles the activities of an architect in a small urban community. Ashe's commercial projects included everything from the addition of a counter in the post office to the design for the enormous Peirce Block on Ladd Street, from altering the old Academy Building for use as the Public Library to the design of the new county jail and jailer's residence on Penhallow Street.

Courtesy Strawbery Banke Museum
County Jail and jailer's residence, 1891.

The houses Ashe constructed also reflected the range of his clients' needs. He designed a modest house for clerk Richard Call at 320 South Street in 1901. Ashe planned investment properties such as a double house on Tanner Street and another on Cabot Street. And he designed comfortable homes for the emerging middle class who settled between Middle and South streets, and at the end of the trolley line around Middle and Lafayette roads, at the turn of the century.

The 1894 house of the widow Mary Billings (63 Union St.), as well as those of neighbors plumber Fred Wood and postal carrier

William Sides (1896), and a very large house for tailor/merchant Charles Wood at 438 South Street (1901) are good examples of Ashe's style. He favored angled bays, triangular dormers, porticos with triangular pediments or balconies, and stained glass or leaded, multi-paned windows for ornamentation. Many of Ashe's houses utilized multiple shingle styles to give the building visual interest and texture.

Ashe built two houses on Wibird Street (216 and 137), one in 1895 for insurance cashier Wallace D. Smith and another in 1902, across the street, for Robert Kirkpatrick, an insurance and real estate vice-president. Both were in the $10,000 range to build. These comfortable houses displayed many of Ashe's favorite design elements. The Kirkpatrick house was thoroughly modern with electric wiring, gas, and hot water.

Wallace D. Smith House (left), Wibird St. before 1902.

Source:

William A. Ashe, Memorandum Book, Portsmouth Athenæum.

Ashe designed a large group of houses in the Lafayette and Middle Road area, on the western edge of the city, at the end of the trolley line. In 1898 he built a substantial home for grocer George Joy at 921 Middle Street at the intersection of Lafayette Road. Two rounded bays, 1-story and 2-story in height, characterize this $12,000 building. The widow Lillie Philbrick's home, across the street on the corner of Lawrence Road at 35 Middle Road, had an $8000 budget that precluded elaborate bays and dormers.

Just two blocks further at 199 Middle Road Ashe designed a house for the machinist John Hayes. This building provides an unusually detailed example of Ashe's work for two reasons: unlike many of Ashe's buildings it has not been covered with siding, and the ten-page typed construction specifications are extant. Ashe's instructions include shingles for the roof and dormer windows, clapboards elsewhere. The piazza, as Ashe called it, was to have "moulded rails, fancy turned balusters, and turned posts of the Doric order." An iron finial would grace the crest of the circular roof. And, like other Ashe buildings, a skylight would illuminate the stairs. The interior detailing was no less precise. Lathing was to receive "one good coat of well haired mortar, of lime and beach sand . . . All the plastering to be finished with a skim coat of lime and Plum Island sand, well troweled down to a smooth and even surface." The specifications called for the owner to supply "any mantels required" as well as "locks, knobs, escutcheon plates and butts for all large doors, window posts, sash lifts, and drawer pulls."

Ashe built a number of large homes. In 1891, at the edge of Goodwin Park (115 State St.), an Ashe-designed house and stable were constructed for Horace E. Frye at a cost of $25,000. An imposing building, it featured a 2-story projecting bay terminating in an open porch and a 1 ½ story hip roof surmounted by a balcony. Two other houses, built on opposite corner lots at the intersection of Lafayette and South streets, also emerge as extraordinary

Horace E. Frye House, 115 State St., 1891

Ashe buildings. In 1897, Charles Trafton, an insurance agent, built a $27,000 house and stable at 169 Lafayette Road to accommodate his young family. Ashe's account book records estimates for "painting & finishing, wallpapering, and enameling." The Thomas A. Ward house (demolished 1968), perhaps even grander than its neighbor, was constructed in 1898-99. Ward, a partner in the family business of distributing liquors and distilling rum, erected an impressive house. It had a rounded bay and separate tower, a projecting covered porch with a balconied roof, and a stable/garage.

Courtesy Strawbery Banke Museum
The Charles Trafton House (right above), Thomas A. Ward House (below).

EF

Lafayette School

Built 1914-1915
Lafayette Road at South and Middle streets
architect: Clarence P. Hoyt, Boston, MA; builders: Lord and Perkins, Berwick, ME

With a significant increase in population Portsmouth faced serious space shortages in several neighborhood primary schools. The old Farragut School, constructed to hold 220 children, had 305 in 1911; the Whipple School with a capacity of 280 held 341. Suburban residential building along the electric railway or trolley lines also increased the number of students living in the western edge of the city and the Board of Instruction spent several years trying to convince the City Council to build a new primary school. They were already attempting to purchase the land on which Lafayette School was eventually built, when Thomas A. Ward offered the lot across from his home as a gift. Because the offer was restricted that the city agree to build no other buildings on the site, the City Council rejected Ward's gift. However, they negotiated to purchase the land without restriction at a price below their tax valuation and voted $20,000 to build a new school there. The red brick of the new Lafayette School was part of its "colonial design," a form that was strictly guided by modern ideas of educational architecture.

RMC

Sources:
Ray Brighton, *They Came to Fish*, I: 253-4.
Portsmouth City Reports, 1911-15.

Courtesy of Portsmouth Athenæum
C.P. Hoyt rendering Lafayette School, 1914.

U.S. Shipping Board, Emergency Fleet Corp., *Types of Housing for Shipbuilders.*
Aerial View, Atlantic Heights as originally designed, 1918-19.

ATLANTIC HEIGHTS

Built 1918-19 for Atlantic Corporation
architects and planners: Kilham & Hopkins, Boston

Atlantic Heights is a garden suburb built during World War I for
shipyard workers at the adjoining Atlantic Corporation. This
private shipyard, like the Shattuck Shipyard in Newington, was
created to revive America's shipbuilding industry prior to World
War I. The Atlantic Corporation occupied a defunct paper mill,
established after 1902 at Freeman's Point, and remodeled it as a
steel ship building facility in 1917 and 1918. When the United
States entered the First World War the federal government created
the quasi-public Emergency Fleet Corporation to fund the massive
ship building program and emergency housing needed to sustain
those yards. The Atlantic Corporation took advantage of this
government funding to both renovate the shipyard and build
Atlantic Heights. Under this war emergency program, the design
and construction was approved and monitored by the Emergency
Fleet Corporation's staff of progressive reformers and designers.

The key figure in Atlantic Heights's unified design was
Boston architect Walter H. Kilham (1868-1948). An 1889 gradu-
ate of M.I.T., Kilham became as deeply involved with the study of
historic architecture as he was with reforming house design for
working people. In partnership with James C. Hopkins after 1901,
the firm of Kilham and Hopkins became well-known for the
design of schools, town halls, suburban homes, and workers housing. In this work the firm was engaged in what Greer Hardwicke
has called the "culture of recall," an ideology that sought to restructure the landscape using architectural symbols of community and
civic values often drawn from colonial sources. On the basis of the
firm's earlier reform housing efforts in Massachusetts, Kilham was
invited in April 1918 to design and plan a million-dollar residential
development for the Atlantic shipyard in Portsmouth. In only ten
days the village plan was created and several house designs were
submitted to the government agency for approval. Construction
began that May and, despite the need for design approval for all
stages and building materials shortages due to the war, the project
was substantially completed within the year.

Located along the Piscataqua River, a mile beyond the city
core, Atlantic Heights contained 278 family houses in 150 permanent individual structures, eight dormitories, a store, cafeteria, and
school laid out as a self-contained "village" according to ideals
promoted by the English Garden City movement. Streets conformed to topography, winding around trees and rocks and were
all named for famous Portsmouth-built ships. No curbing was used
for the road, nor any garages originally planned, as it was assumed
no worker would have an automobile; transportation was provided
by buses into Portsmouth. Homes were clustered informally to
recreate a sense of community and conformed to eight different
plans recombined in various ways.

Kilham had sketched Portsmouth's historic buildings as a
student and wrote about the city's important colonial and federal

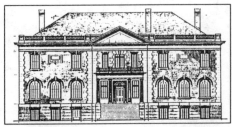

Measured drawing by Philip H. Kendrick, architect
*White Mountain Paper Co. Office, (later
National Gypsum Co.), Freeman's Point,
built 1902, moved 1918, destroyed 1984.*

Journal of the AIA, September, 1918
*Architect's drawing showing mature
planting and proposed sidewalks (not built).*

The American Architect, October 16, 1918
*View on Raleigh Way, Kilham & Hopkins
drawing showing incorporation of ledges
into siting of houses.*

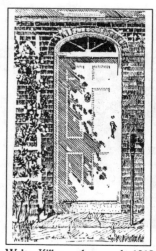

Walter Kilham, photograph, 1918
Folsom-Kingsbury doorway.

American Architect, Oct. 1918
Atlantic Heights doorway.

period brick homes in 1902. His first step in planning this new addition to the port city was to photograph old buildings whose form or details might be adapted to the houses his firm had already built elsewhere. Gambrel roofs, simple federal-style fanlights set in brick arches, and triangular georgian pediments over doorways of the city's old homes provided particular models. One reporter concluded that the architects had followed as far as possible the colonial lines of the city, "many of the houses having reproduction[s] on a smaller scale of some of the best of the colonial doorways." Using these different ornamental doorway details, brick bonding patterns, or occasional clapboard wall on seven different basic house plans not only provided variety but evoked symbolic association with local and regional building tradition. Public buildings, set around what was conceived as a New England town common at the head of the only road into the project, included a proposed village recreational hall with connected shops "of old-fashioned type" to be built in "colonial red brick with white trimming" to look not unlike a miniature Independence Hall. Such architectural symbols were designed, literally, to instill civic pride and harmony through its colonial style.

This shipbuilders' housing program was the first use of federal funds for housing. In an era and a region suspicious of government intervention in the private market, reformers tried to win acceptance of this radical idea by wrapping the two dozen American war housing projects in colonial garb. The architects and planners wanted to demonstrate that improved housing could be competitive with speculative forms of worker housing. They argued that such projects might also improve the nation's social order and that such stylistic associations could help avoid labor strife by inculcating American values among ethnic workers.

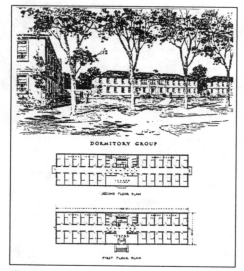

Dormitories.

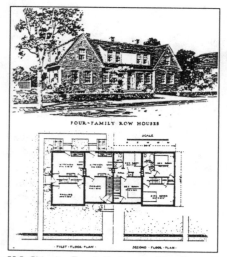

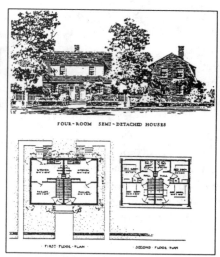

U.S. Shipping Board, Emergency Fleet Corp., *Types of Housing for Shipbuilders*, 1919.

Four-Family Row House.   *Two-Family House.*   *Single-Family House.*

Nevertheless, Congress canceled the program immediately after the war, and the government sold all of the housing it had financed during the war. The houses at Atlantic Heights were sold to private owners in 1925 after the Justice Department won a suit against the Atlantic Shipyard over its ship building contracts. The town added a school, designed by Robert Coit of Boston in 1924, one dormitory became a church, and several new homes have since been added to those originally built. When the I-95 bridge was erected, the remaining dormitories and a few homes were removed from the eastern edge of the village.

RMC

Sources:

Greer Hardwicke, *Town Houses and the Culture of Recall: Public Buildings and Civic Values and the Architectural Firm of Kilham, Hopkins & Greeley, 1900 - 1930*, Ph. D. diss., Boston College, 1986.

Richard M. Candee and Greer Hardwicke, "Early Twentieth-Century Reform Housing by Kilham and Hopkins, Architects of Boston," *Winterthur Portfolio* 22 (Spring 1987): 47-80

Richard M. Candee, *Atlantic Heights: A World War I Shipbuilders' Community* . Portsmouth: Portsmouth Marine Society, 1985.

U.S. Shipping Board, Emergency Fleet Corp., *Types of Housing for Shipbuilders.* [Philadelphia: 1919].

Courtesy Portsmouth Public Library
Auction Broadside, 1925. Stores (above) Atlantic Heights School (in oval).

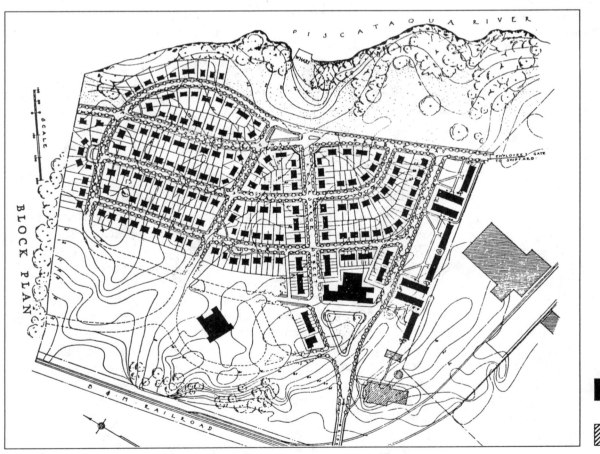

Atlantic Heights

Atlantic Shipyard

Kilham & Hopkins Plan, 1918.

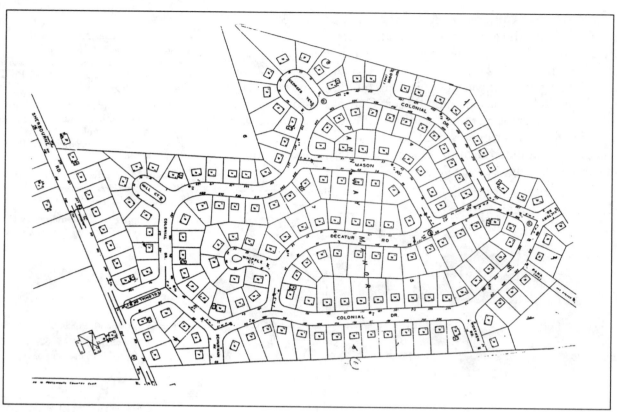

Sanborn Insurance Company Map
Plan, Pannaway Manor 1944.

PANNAWAY MANOR

Built 1941 by Defense Homes Corp.

In the opening years of World War II, the Portsmouth Naval Shipyard expanded its submarine construction to employ 11,000 workers, about twice as many as during World War I. Nationwide, more than 9 million Americans relocated to work in the defense industry, and government help was needed to provide workers two million new housing units. Defense workers "answered the call of their country to help win the battle of production," and their new homes were "built to cope with the greatest voluntary migration of free men and women in the history of the world." The country responded with faith in the sanctity of the single family home as "the second line of defense." *American Home* magazine proclaimed that the "Strength of its workers stems from the homes they live in" and "even as we arm for war, we are building for peace." Although the federal government financed about one-third of all defense housing projects, they would be sold to private owners after the war emergency to relieve the federal government of landlord responsibilities.

Pannaway Manor, a neighborhood of 159 single-family homes built by Defense Homes Corp., was one of three large-scale defense housing projects built in the Portsmouth area. Defense Homes was one of many federal agencies involved with worker housing during World War II, and Pannaway Manor was one of the first permanent construction projects completed as the contractors used new on-site small power tools. In March 1941, the 37 acres of farmland along Sherburne Road was sold to Defense Homes and ground was broken in April. Initial plans for 122 homes quickly grew to 159. By May, 106 defense workers applied to rent at Pannaway, by October 360 were on the waiting list, and the first residents moved in by Christmas 1941. Rents ranged from $40 to $55 a month. Pannaway Manor benefited from its construction early in the war. Later defense projects, including the small Holly Lane neighborhood built just north of Pannaway, were affected by construction material shortages and time constraints. In the projects that followed, houses often were built on concrete slabs and made greater use of prefabrication and new synthetic materials such as plywood and wall board.

The design of Pannaway homes relied on small house designs and philosophies codified by the architectural profession and the Federal Housing Administration in the 1930s. FHA economic policies to stimulate building during the Depression widely popularized the "small house" – homes less than 1000 square feet in size. Small houses were most often designed in the colonial revival style, called capes or neo-colonials, but were just as easily given an international style exterior. In 1936 and 1937, the editors of *Architectural Forum* published two books of small house designs; Royal Barry Wills published *Homes for Good Living* in 1940 and *Better Homes for Budgeteers* in 1941. These houses were most often one story, with an expandable second floor, four to six rooms and direct circulation between rooms. The designers of Pannaway Manor borrowed heavily from such models. Three floor plans were used; the exteriors differed by the use of clapboarding or cedar shingles and a gable or hip roof. Exterior colonial revival details included shutters, contrasting trim, pilasters and a small pediment framing the entry and a plain cornice. Inside, plaster walls were painted with textured paint and oak flooring was laid. Panelled doors and 6/6 window sash throughout the house and dark woodwork and hard-wood cabinets in the kitchen completed the picture. Electric refrigerators and stoves and porcelain sinks were installed in the kitchens. The baths were tiled, with a boxed-in tub and shower. The units had full cement basements and were insulated and heated with oil furnaces. Second floors were left unfinished.

The smallest unit, about 640 square feet, contained 4 rooms: a living room, kitchen, bath and two bedrooms. The center entry was flanked by a single window on either side. These four-room homes were concentrated on Colonial Drive, the street that circles the perimeter of Pannaway. The next largest unit, approximately 680 square feet, had 4 ½ an additional dining alcove was separated from the kitchen by swinging, half-length double doors. The block containing the two bedrooms was set back from the façade by about two feet, and a one-car garage was attached to the house by a breezeway. Only 13 of these homes were built, all but two on corner lots. The remaining units were 5 ½ room homes, containing a living room, dining alcove, three bedrooms, bath and kitchen.

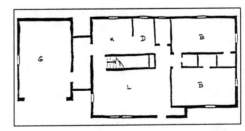

Drawings by Elizabeth Hostutler
First floor plan, 4-room type.

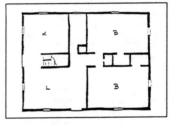

First floor plan, 4 ½-room type.

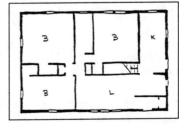

First floor plan, 5-room type.

The entry was located to the left or right of a group windows, and square footage measured just more than 700 feet.

In the fifty years since their construction, many Pannaway houses have been remodeled into ranch-style floor plans. As built, only the 4 ½ room floor plans in Pannaway divide neatly into the three zones of the typical ranch house – sleeping, living, and garage or work space. The 4- and 5 ½ room floor plans did not incorporate a garage or work space, and a bedroom intruded into the living space. A vast majority of owners have added a garage, attached by a breezeway or additional room, usually an enlarged kitchen or den. In most 5-room room units, the third bedroom, next to the kitchen, is now used as a dining room, with a doorway cut between the two rooms. The sense of closure between the kitchen, eating and living spaces often is opened up by the removal of doors between these areas. With the addition of garages, driveways and more access from the kitchen to the rest of the house, the importance of the front entry has shifted to the side door into the kitchen.

The exteriors have likewise changed. Most of the houses are now sided with vinyl or aluminum siding, which covers the original colonial trim. Many small-paned windows have been replaced with double-insulated two-light windows or bowed picture windows and shed dormers increase second floor living space.

The 159 homes in Pannaway Manor line winding streets, a design by the Federal Housing Administration, Land Planning Division. The government's twenty-year protective deed convenants, which excluded "persons of color" from occupying the units, also mandated minimum lots sizes and a set back of 25 feet from the street. The rhythm of the street layout has not changed, the streets have not been widened, and all 159 original units remain. Cut off by the later construction of Interstate 95 to its east and Pease Air Force Base to its north and west, no through roads have interrupted the original pattern of the neighborhood.

EH

Sources:

The Architectural Forum, *The Book of Small Houses*. NY: Simon and Schuster, Inc., 1936 and 1937.

John DeCourcey, "World War II History of Pannaway Manor," mss at Portsmouth Public Library, nd.

Federal Housing Administration, *Planning Neighborhoods for Small Houses*, Technical Bulletin, Washington: U.S. Government Printing Office, 1936.

National Housing Agency, *Third Annual Report*. Washington: U.S. Government Printing Office, 1945.

National Housing Agency, *War Housing in the U.S.* Washington: U.S. Government Printing Office, 1946.

Portsmouth Planning Board, First Annual Report, 1941, Portsmouth City Hall.

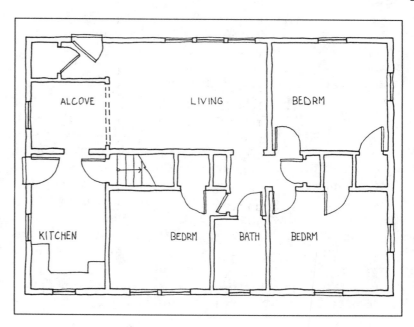

Measured drawing by Elizabeth Hostutler
First floor plan, 5 1/2 room type, 116 Decatur Road.

PREFABRICATION IN PORTSMOUTH

There is a long tradition in the Piscataqua of framing buildings to be shipped and erected elsewhere. More than 100 timber house frames, including "12 frames for Negro hutts," shipped from Portsmouth to the West Indies are listed in custom records between 1770 and 1775. Most were probably venture cargo, but one 1772 pre-fabricated building frame was ordered from a Portsmouth merchant for erection on Grenada in the West Indies. The client specified a "pavillion" roof and a gallery across the front of three rooms *en suit*. During the California Gold Rush, moreover, the local newspaper reported:

> Several houses have been built in this town to be shipped to California and more contracted for. They are about 15 x 25 feet in size, one story with an attic. They have five windows and two doors. The roofs of some are of wood, others sheet iron. They are put together with screws, painted, marked, and then taken apart for shipping. Thomas Norton [of Union and Austin streets] is the builder...The houses made here which cost but little over $100 probably will sell readily there for a thousand.

The pre-cut house saw its beginnings at the end of the 19th century. Aladdin Company of Bay City, Michigan and Sears, Roebuck of Newark, NJ were early entries into this type of prefabricated housing. Assembly lines for milling, grading and cutting the lumber enabled the company to engage in the large-scale purchasing and processing of lumber. Hence, the pre-cut home's price was easily fixed.

Until World War II, prefabricated designs — often promoted by well-known architects — accounted for less than 1% of all housing built in the United States. By 1942, however, prefabs supplied 16% of the single-family housing market. The US Federal Housing Authority added 116,000 prefab units during the war, while other federal and private endeavors built an additional 80,000. During these years substandard materials, dictated by material shortages during the war, gave manufactured housing a reputation for shoddy construction. Thus, local building codes were difficult to meet, and consumers had difficulty financing a prefabricated house. Still, at the end of the war, there were more than 75 manufacturers hoping to market prefabricated houses to provide the nation with desperately needed post-war housing. In 1946, the Veterans Emergency Housing Program proposed the ambitious construction of 2.7 million housing units by 1947. Ultimately, however, only some 37,000 prefabricated units were produced in these years. Many companies, including General Panel and Lustron, lasted less than a decade after the war. Only one of three 1950 all-metal Lustron homes sold in Portsmouth, 150 Sherburne Road, has been indentified.

Other firms were more successful. By the early 1950s, National Homes Corporation, was selling more than 15,000 houses

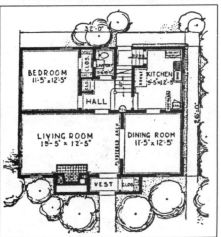

Courtesy Preservation Press
Sears, Roebuck, and Co., "The Dover".

Sources:

Alfred Bruce and Harold Sandbank. *A History of Prefabrication*. Raritan, NJ: John B. Pierce Foundation, Housing Research Division, 1945.

Gilbert Herbert, *The Dream of the Factory-Made Home*. Cambridge: MIT Press, 1984.

Burnham Kelly, *Design and Production of Houses*. New York: McGraw-Hill, 1959.

_____. *The Prefabrication of Houses*. Cambridge: Technology Press/Wiley, 1951.

Charles E. Peterson, "Early American Prefabrication." *Gazette des Beaux-Arts*. 6 (1948): 33.

"Portsmouth Prefabs, 1772 and 1849," *Journal of the Society of Architectural Historians*, 23:1 (March 1964): 43-4.

Red Book of Housing Manufacturers 1989. F.W. Dodge/LSI, National Information Services, 1989.

Watkins, A.M. *The Complete Guide to Factory-Made Houses*. 2nd ed. Piermont, NY: The Building Institute, 1980.

per year and became the nation's largest manufacturer of factory-built housing. Founded in 1954, Cardinal Industries, Inc. of Columbus, Ohio, is currently the nation's leader in the production of modular homes and the second largest residential builder in the United States.

Operation Breakthrough, initiated in 1968 and headed by a former auto industry executive named George Romney, was the next large government involvement in prefabrication in the building industry. This federal program advocated the industrialization of housing production and encouraged corporate interest in the field. Funded by HUD, Operation Breakthrough set a goal of 26 million housing units by 1978 and subsidized the research and construction of prefabricated housing until 1973. Although never completed, the project was a catalyst for the building industry; it developed new labor agreements, promoted uniform coding for the industry, and introduced advancements in transportation.

SA & RMC

Sears Homes

628 Broad Street, "The Hazelton"
127 Middle Road, "The Westly"
73 Sagamore Road, "The Dover"

20th century factory-made housing in Portsmouth begins with Sears, Roebuck's "mail-order" houses pre-cut dwellings. Sears homes used balloon-frame techniques common to many stick-built houses at that time, but the components were all milled, cut and numbered off-site at a factory, and delivered by rail to the building site for assembly. Nearly everything except the plumbing and masonry was provided by the manufacturer, including interior woodwork, paint and nails.

Sears houses were marketed through mail-order catalogues, the first of which was the Modern Homes Catalogue of 1908,

"The handsomest residence in this vicinity, and there are many."

C. L. DeWitta (Owner),
Bay Shore, N. Y.

Courtesy Preservation Press

Sears, Roebuck and Company, "The Hazelton."

192

featuring 22 styles ranging in price from $650 to $2,500 including the plans and materials. Three levels of housing were offered: the basic Simplex Sectional cottages, the moderate Standard Built home, and the best-quality Honor Bilt houses. Houses were sometimes depicted in the catalogues with fully furnished interiors, enticing the customer to purchase more than the house from Sears. Initially the customer provided the local labor to erect the house and this allowed for changes in design and materials. Later, Sears even provided for construction crews to build the houses it sold. The houses proved to be good quality products that were easy to assemble and available at a reasonable price. Between 1911 and 1935, the manufacturer also provided financing for the homeowner. Although by 1930 nearly 50,000 houses had been sold through Sears, and in 1938 sales were over $2 million, by 1940 Sears was no longer manufacturing or selling pre-cut houses. It is estimated that a total of nearly 100,000 houses were sold by Sears in its 32 years in the housing business.

SA

Sources:

Kay Halpin, "Sears, Roebuck's Best Kept-Secret." *Historic Preservation.* Fall 1981.

David M. Schwartz, "When Home Sweet Home Was Just a Mailbox Away." *Smithsonian.* November 1985.

Robert Schweitzer and Michael W.R. Davis. *America's Favorite Homes: Mail-Order Catalogues as a Guide to Popular Early 20th Century Houses.* Detroit: Wayne State University, 1990.

Katherine Cole Stevenson and H. Ward Jandl. *Houses By Mail: A Guide to Houses from Sears, Roebuck and Company.* Washington, DC: Preservation Press, 1986.

Courtesy Preservation Press
Sears, Roebuck, and Co., "The Westly."

Photograph, John Nanian
*New England Homes, 3-decker,
Dorchester, MA.*

Courtesy New England Homes
Perspective and plan.

Sources:

Interviews with Robert P. Killkelly and Mike Donahue, New England Homes.

Red Book of Housing Manufacturers 1989.
F.W. Dodge/LSI, National Information Services, 1989.

A.M. Watkins, *The Complete Guide to Factory-Made Houses.* 2nd ed. Piermont, NY: The Building Institute, 1980.

"Where the Action Is!" US: Manufactured Housing Trends: Sales and Production Data By State 1981-1987. Crofton, MD: F.W. Dodge, 1988.

New England Homes

at 270 Ocean Road, Greenland

New England Homes was founded in 1961 as a manufacturer of panelized houses and in 1968 became the first producer of modular homes in New England. Its products help define a significant part of the region's contemporary landscape. The business is carried out on a wholesale basis within the six-state New England region; a subsidiary company at its manufacturing facility provides retail sales to individual homebuyers from the seacoast area. Most New England Homes customers are established building dealers who will resell the completed homes to individual buyers.

New England Homes has manufactured more than 10,000 domestic and commercial buildings in the last thirty years. A third of these structures have been assembled on sites within a 50 mile radius of Portsmouth. Indeed, 98% of the company's modular housing is shipped to and assembled on sites within 300 miles of the factory, although some New England Homes can now be found as far away as Pennsylvania and Israel. Rural areas traditionally offer fertile ground for the sale and distribution of manufactured homes; high urban land values often preclude even moderately priced housing. But New England Homes is not limited to rural New Hampshire, Maine, or suburban Massachusetts; new three-deckers in Dorchester, Massachusetts have also been built for urban infill.

Using computer-aided design, New England Homes provides two essential services to the client. The company offers nine "section" designs which can be combined and altered to suit particular needs. Almost every New England Home produced ultimately includes changes to the basic designs offered by the company. The changes range from altering the location of a window to modifying or customizing other designs for the customer. The computer design system enables New England Homes to build to the building codes of each state in the region.

Factory tours are available by appointment at their headquarters on the Portsmouth - Greenland line. Here, houses are constructed in sections, year round, in the company's new 2-acre factory. Production of houses peaks in the spring, when as many as thirteen houses (usually 26 sections) can move through the factory, and a whole house can be completed in merely eight days. In a banner year New England Homes produces nearly 500 structures. During slow times of the year, approximately 20 workers are employed. Each worker remains at one station, while the building section makes its way from station to station on rollers or by overhead cranes. Initially, the deck (floor) is framed and electrical attachments are made. Alongside, walls are framed and run along tracks to conveniently meet up with the deck unit upon each section's completion. Meanwhile, above this work area, the roof has been constructed using trusses purchased from an outside vendor. The deck unit is then rolled to the next work station, where plywood or OSB board is glued and nailed to form the floor. The walls are then attached to the floor unit. The roof is lifted with an overhead crane and attached to the walls with spikes. The interior of the house is almost completely finished with plumbing, doors, windows floor coverings and painting as well as kitchen cabinets appliances installed in the factory. The front and rear elevations of the house are finished off and the roof is shingled; gable ends of the house are left unsided until the sections of the house are attached at the building site.

Construction of each section allows for its subsequent journey between the factory and the building site. Comparable on-site construction generally consists of three girders to support the bearing walls; New England Homes builds with four girders and uses state-of-the-art adhesives more extensively than conventional construction. The completed sections are delivered to the building site on flat-bed trucks and placed on the foundation with a crane. Lolly columns are set and house sections are toenailed to the sill. The house is then sided on the gable ends to obscure the area of attachment. The bottom 2 or 3 courses of siding on the front and back elevations are generally finished on-site for the same reason. A crew of four (plus the crane operator) make up not only the trucking crew but also the on-site assembly crew. In less than a day, the structure arrives in sections and is set on the foundation; the sections are attached, with all utility and plumbing connections made as well.

SA

Courtesy New England Homes
On-site construction of modular units.

POST-WAR COMMERCIAL STRIP

Changes to Portsmouth's ever-evolving landscape are too numerous and many too recent to fully assess. New residential suburbs, Pease Air Force Base, and the commercial development along U.S. Route 1, the Portsmouth Circle and Route 4 are all products of America's post-WW II automobile culture. One architectural symbol of that interaction of commerce, tourism and the automobile — the development of The Strip — may represent a larger group of less well-known local examples of this modern vernacular phenomenon.

Yoken's Thar She Blows Restaurant

Built 1947 with many alterations and additions
U.S. Route 1

In 1947 Harry and Clarice Yoken opened Yoken's Restaurant selling 99¢ dinners at a counter with 20 stools in a new streamlined building along U.S. Route 1. At the cash register they also offered English bone china teacups and saucers as souvenirs. Two years later, the Thar She Blows Restaurant sign, manufactured by C. I. Brink of Boston at a cost of $20,000, was added to the growing eatery and its Whale Gift Shop. After Mr. Yoken's brother-in-law, Harry MacLeod, Sr., took over in 1958, the building continued to grow and change. In the 1950s, when Pease Air Force Base brought economic benefits of the Cold War to Portsmouth, the façade echoed the commercial image of Mount Vernon. The present exterior, enveloping the older sections of the restaurant and an expanded gift shop, was begun some 14 years ago and extended to the north three years ago for a new conference center. The restaurant serves one million meals a year, seating up to 750 people at once, and employs 130 workers year round. The gift shop occupies 20,000 square feet, and claims to be one of the largest in New England.

RMC

Armsden Collection, Portsmouth Athenæum
Yoken's Restaurant, 1951.

SELECTED BIBLIOGRAPHY

General History, Portsmouth, NH and the Piscataqua:

John P. Adams. *Drowned Valley: The Piscataqua River Basin.* Hanover, NH: University Press of New England, 1976.

Nathaniel Adams. *Annals of Portsmouth.* Portsmouth, NH: 1825, reprint ed. 1971.

Charles Brewster. *Rambles About Portsmouth.* 2 vols. Portsmouth, NH: 1859-1869.

Raymond A. Brighton. *They Came to Fish.* 2 vols. Portsmouth, NH: Portsmouth 350 Inc., 1973.

_____. *Frank Jones, King of the Alemakers.* Portsmouth, NH: Peter E. Randall, 1976.

_____. *The Prescott Story.* Portsmouth, NH: Portsmouth Marine Society, 1982.

Charles E. Clark. *The Eastern Frontier, The Settlement of Northern New England, 1610-1763.* N.Y.: Alfred A. Knopf, 1970.

Gurney, C. S. *Portsmouth Historic and Picturesque.* Portsmouth, NH: 1902, reprint ed. 1981.

D. Hamilton Hurd. *History of Rockingham County.* Philadelphia: J.W. Lewis & Co., 1882.

Gertrude M. Pickett. *Portsmouth's Heyday in Shipbuilding.* Portsmouth: Joseph G. Sawtelle, 1979.

Architecture of Portsmouth and the Piscataqua:

Richard M. Candee, Wooden Buildings in Early Maine and New Hampshire, A Technological and Cultural History, 1600-1720. PhD. diss., University of Pennsylvania, 1976. University Microfilms # 76-22,664.

_____. *Atlantic Heights: A World War I Shipbuilders' Community.* Portsmouth, NH: Portsmouth Marine Society, 1985.

_____. "Boundry Surveys of William and John Godsoe, Kittery, Maine, 1679-1769" in The Proceedings of the Dublin Seminar, 1980, *New England Prospect.* Boston: Boston University, 1982.

_____. "First-Period Architecture in Maine and New Hampshire: The Evidence of Probate Inventories," in *Early American Probate Inventories.* The Dublin Seminar for New England Folklife Annual Proceedings 1987: Boston University, 1989.

_____ and Greer Hardwicke, "Early 20th century Reform Housing by Kilham & Hopkins, Architects of Boston," *Winterthur Portfolio* 22 (Spring 1987): 47-80.

James L. Garvin. Academic Architecture and the Building Trades in the Piscataqua Region of New Hampshire and Maine. Ph.D. diss., Boston University, 1983. University Microfilms #83-19977.

_____. "Ebenezer Clifford, Architect and Inventor," *Old-Time New England* 65 (Winter-Spring): 23-37.

_____. _Historic Portsmouth, Early Photographs from the Collections of Strawbery Banke, Inc._ Somersworth, NH: New Hampshire Publishing Co., 1976.

_____. "Mail-Order House Plans and American Victorian Architecture." _Winterthur Portfolio_ 16 (Winter 1981): 309-334.

_____. "Portsmouth and the Piscataqua: Social History and Material Culture," _Historical New Hampshire._ 26:2 (Summer 1971):3-48.

_____. "That Little World, Portsmouth," in _Portsmouth Furniture._ Brock Jobe, ed. Hanover: SPNEA & Univ. Press of New England, 1992.

Jane C. Giffen. "Moffatt-Ladd House in Portsmouth, NH" _Connoisser,_ 175 (1970): 113-22, 201-7.

Sarah L. Giffen and Kevin D. Murphy, eds., _"A Noble and Dignified Stream": The Piscataqua Region in the Colonial Revival, 1860-1930._ York: Old York Historical Society, 1992.

Faith Harrington. "The Emergent Elite in Early 18th Century Portsmouth Society: The Archaeology of the Joseph Sherburne Houselot." _Historical Archaeology,_ 23:1 (1989): 2-18.

John Mead Howells. _The Architectural Heritage of the Piscataqua._ Baltimore: Architectural Book Co., 1937 (reprint ed. 1965).

Michael Hugo-Brunt. "Portsmouth: Prototype of Canadian Settlement," _Plan._ Journal of the Town Planning Institute of Canada. 1:3 (Nov. 1960): 145-70.

Brock Jobe and Johanna McBrien, "The Craft of Portsmouth Hands," in _Portsmouth Furniture._ Brock Jobe, ed. Hanover: SPNEA & University Press of New England, 1992.

Anne Mankin Masury. "Landscape and Gardens," Strawbery Banke Museum issue, _Antiques_ (July 1992): 116-121.

Woodard Dorr Openo. The Summer Colony at Little Harbor in Portsmouth, NH and its Relationship to the Colonial Revival Movement. Ph.D. diss., University of Michigan, 1989.

Steven R. Pendery. "Urban Process in Portsmouth, New Hampshire: an Archeological Perspective," in _New England Historical Archeology._ Dublin Seminar for New England Folklife Annual Proceedings 1977: Boston University, [1978]. _The Portsmouth Book,_ Boston: George Ellis [1899].

Elizabeth Adams Rhoades. "The Furnishing of Portsmouth Houses, 1750-1775," _Historical New Hampshire._ 28 (Spring 1973): 1-20.

Bryant E. Tolles, Jr. _New Hampshire Architecture: An Illustrated Guide._ Hanover, N.H.: University Press of New England, 1979.

Gerald W.R. Ward. "Furnished Houses," Strawbery Banke Museum issue, _Antiques_ (July 1992): 76-89.

_____ & John Schnitzler,."The Buildings," _Antiques_ (July 1992): 66-75.

Philip Zimmerman. Ecclesiastical Architecture in the Reformed Tradition in Rockingham County, New Hampshire, 1790-1860. Ph.D. diss., Boston University, 1985. Ann Arbor, MI: University Microfilms, # 8418796.

INDEX

House name

Numbered Houses

Other building types

Builders craftsmen and designers